Bloom's Modern Critical Views

GEOFFREY CHAUCER
Updated Edition

Edited and with an introduction by
Harold Bloom
Sterling Professor of the Humanities
Yale University

BLOOM'S
LITERARY CRITICISM
An imprint of Infobase Publishing

Bloom's Modern Critical Views: Geoffrey Chaucer—Updated Edition

Copyright ©2007 Infobase Publishing

Introduction © 2007 by Harold Bloom

Bloom's Literary Criticism
An imprint of Infobase Publishing
132 West 31st Street
New York, NY 10001

Library of Congress Cataloging-in-Publication Data
Geoffrey Chaucer / [edited by] Harold Bloom. — Updated ed.
     p. cm. — (Bloom's modern critical views)
  Includes bibliographical references and index.
  ISBN-13: 978-0-7910-9438-9
  ISBN-10: 0-7910-9438-3
  1. Chaucer, Geoffrey, d. 1400—Criticism and interpretation. 2. Civilization, Medieval, in literature. I. Bloom, Harold.

  PR1924.G35 2007
  821'.1—dc22   2007010198

Bloom's Literary Criticism books are available at special discounts when purchased in bulk quantities for businesses, associations, institutions, or sales promotions. Please call our Special Sales Department in New York at (212) 967-8800 or (800) 322-8755.

You can find Bloom's Literary Criticism on the World Wide Web at http://www.chelseahouse.com

Contributing Editor: Janyce Marson

Cover designed by Takeshi Takahashi

Cover photo: The Granger Collection, New York

Printed in the United States of America.

Bang EJB 10 9 8 7 6 5 4 3 2 1

This book is printed on acid-free paper.

All links and web addresses were checked and verified to be correct at the time of publication. Because of the dynamic nature of the web, some addresses and links may have changed since publication and may no longer be valid.

Contents

Editor's Note

My Introduction celebrates Chaucer's powers of characterization, surpassed only by Shakespeare's, which they influenced.

The most eminent scholar-critic of Chaucer, E. Talbot Donaldson, superbly summarizes the complexities of how *Troilus and Criseyde* concludes.

Robert Worth Frank, Jr., meditates upon the function and aesthetic freshness of the "Prologue" to *The Legend of Good Women*, after which Richard Neuse contrasts Chaucer and his precursor Dante, with the Knight and the Miller of *The Canterbury Tales* set against one another, and both seen also in the ultimate context of *The Divine Comedy*'s "epic theater."

The Wife of Bath is interpreted by Manuel Aguirre as a precursor of Katherine in Shakespeare's *The Taming of the Shrew*, while Michael A. Calabrese sees the Wife as "an ageless Ovid" continuing to teach the arts of love.

The Second Nun's Tale is studied by Eileen S. Jankowski as Chaucer's equivocal response to Christian apocalypse, while Barrie Ruth Straus uncovers Oedipal reversals in three of the *Tales*.

Boccaccio, Chaucer's prime (and unacknowledged) precursor, is established by John Finlayson as a source of the English poet's free spirit in amatory matters.

Chaucer's rhetoric of temporality, with its dialectic of good and ill, is the subject of Martin's Camargo's essay, after which *Troilus and Cryseida*, perhaps his masterpiece, is considered with respect to Chaucer's aesthetic by John M. Hill.

HAROLD BLOOM

Introduction

Chaucer—as Donald Howard eloquently showed us—led almost too interesting an outer life: fighting in two wars, endless travels in Europe, personal dealings with the kings and leading nobles of his time, and literary relations with most writers of note. Shakespeare, the only English writer who surpassed Chaucer, fought no wars, was never out of England, and for the most part confined his relations with people of power carefully to the theatrical sphere. It is not that Shakespeare's world was void of violence, but Shakespeare evaded angry events as best he could. We have comprehensive legal records concerning him, and they are virtually all commercial. There is nothing like the somewhat sensational document in which one Cecily Champain released Chaucer from legal actions concerning her rape: Chaucer doubtless had disbursed a large cash settlement.

In the 1380s, when Chaucer was in his prime, Richard II struggled desperately for power, and England was in turmoil. During the decade 1389-99, Richard gradually lost ascendancy, while Chaucer remained his faithful servant. Though the deposing of Richard by Henry IV possibly cost Chaucer nothing in patronage, it must have saddened him. In any case, a year later the great poet died.

There is a curious difference, almost a gap, between what we know of Chaucer's life and era, and his poetry. The age was violent, but Chaucer

was an ironist of genius, and *The Canterbury Tales* and *Troilus and Criseyde*
transcend their historical context. G. K. Chesterton remarked that Chaucer's
irony was so large that sometimes we have trouble even seeing it. Chaucer is
sublimely sly, whether in expressing his own pathos, or in acknowledging his
authentic literary precursors, Dante and Boccaccio. Boccaccio particularly
made Chaucer possible, in some of the same ways that Chaucer enabled
Shakespeare to people a world. Chaucer's tales are *about* tale-telling, because
Boccaccio had perfected the kind of fiction that is aware of itself as fiction.
Stories rhetorically conscious that they *are* rhetoric behave very differently
from stories that mask such consciousness. Clearly, Chaucer's heightened
sense of story has some relation, however evasive, to the *Decameron*.

Chaucer likes to cite imaginary authorities, while avoiding any mention
of Boccaccio, but that returns us to Chaucerian irony. Unlike Boccaccio,
Chaucer will not admit to his own passional misadventures, except as jests, or
as self-parodies. We are made confidants by Dante, Petrarch, and Boccaccio:
Chaucer's anguish stays well within him. Part of Chaucer's genius emerges
as self-distancing and comic perspectivism, anticipations of Shakespearean
irony. What is extraordinary in Chaucer's own invention is his sense of
personality, which allows the Wife of Bath, the Pardoner, even the Prioress
(whom I just do not like!) each to speak in her or his own voice. The miracle
of mature Shakespeare, which is the individualization of voice in Falstaff,
Hamlet, Iago, Cleopatra and their peers, relies upon Chaucer's provocation
to Shakespeare's developing genius. Sir John Falstaff is the Wife of Bath's
son, as it were, and Iago's superb nihilism is anticipated by the Pardoner's joy
in his own power of manipulation.

E. Talbot Donaldson, shrewdest of modern Chaucerians, illuminated
Chaucer's two principal *personae*, Chaucer the Pilgrim in *The Canterbury Tales*
and the narrator of *Troilus and Criseyde*. Chaucer the Pilgrim is everyone's
favorite: friendly, more than tolerant, exuberantly receptive to every colorful
scoundrel with whom he travels, but also always prepared to admire authentic
goodness. The speaker of *Troilus and Criseyde*, presented as a would-be but
unlucky lover, falls so intensely in love with Criseyde that most of us (men
anyway) come to love her as Chaucer evidently does. Chaucer the Pilgrim is
the greater ironist; the narrator of *Troilus and Criseyde* is finally so heartbroken
that he transcends his own ironies.

II

Chaucer is one of those great writers who defeat almost all criticism, an
attribute he shares with Shakespeare, Cervantes, and Tolstoy. There are writers
of similar magnitude—Dante, Milton, Wordsworth, Proust—who provoke

inspired commentary (amidst much more that is humdrum) but Chaucer, like his few peers, has such mimetic force that the critic is disarmed, and so is left either with nothing or with everything still to do. Much criticism devoted to Chaucer is merely historical, or even theological, as though Chaucer ought to be read as a supreme version of medieval Christianity. But I myself am not a Chaucer scholar, and so I write this only as a general critic of literature and as a common reader of Chaucer.

Together with Shakespeare and a handful of the greater novelists in English, Chaucer carries the language further into unthinkable triumphs of the representation of reality than ought to be possible. The Pardoner and the Wife of Bath, like Hamlet and Falstaff, call into question nearly every mode of criticism that is now fashionable. What sense does it make to speak of the Pardoner or the Wife of Bath as being only a structure of tropes, or to say that any tale they tell has suspended its referential aspect almost entirely? The most Chaucerian and best of all Chaucer critics, E. Talbot Donaldson, remarks of the General Prologue to *The Canterbury Tales* that:

> The extraordinary quality of the portraits is their vitality, the illusion that each gives the reader that the character being described is not a fiction but a person, so that it seems as if the poet has not created but merely recorded.

As a critical remark, this is the indispensable starting-point for reading Chaucer, but contemporary modes of interpretation deny that such an illusion of vitality has any value.

I once walked through a park in Frankfurt, West Germany, with a good friend who is a leading French theorist of interpretation. I had been in Frankfurt to lecture on Freud; my friend had just arrived to give a talk on Joyce's *Ulysses*. As we walked, I remarked that Joyce's Leopold Bloom seemed to me the most sympathetic and affectionate person I had encountered in any fiction. My friend, annoyed and perplexed, replied that Poldy was *not* a person and that my statement therefore was devoid of sense. Though not agreeing, I reflected silently that the difference between my friend and myself could not be reconciled by anything I could say. To him, *Ulysses* was not even persuasive rhetoric, but was a system of tropes. To me, it was above all else the personality of Poldy. My friend's deconstructionism, I again realized, was only another formalism, a very tough-minded and skeptical formalism. But all critical formalism reaches its limits rather quickly when fictions are strong enough. L. C. Knights famously insisted that Lady Macbeth's children were as meaningless a critical issue as the girlhood of Shakespeare's heroines, a view in which Knights followed E. E. Stoll who, whether he knew it or not, followed

E. A. Poe. To Knights, Falstaff "is not a man, but a choric commentary."
The paradox, though, is that this "choric commentary" is more vital than
we are, which teaches us that Falstaff is neither trope nor commentary, but
a representation of what a human being *might* be, if that person were even
wittier than Oscar Wilde, and even more turbulently high-spirited than Zero
Mostel. Falstaff, Poldy, the Wife of Bath: these are what Shelley called "forms
more real than living man."

Immensely original authors (and they are not many) seem to have no
precursors, and so seem to be children without parents. Shakespeare is the
overwhelming instance, since he swallowed up his immediate precursor
Christopher Marlowe, whereas Chaucer charmingly claims fictive authorities
while being immensely indebted to actual French and Italian writers and to
Boccaccio in particular. Yet it may be that Chaucer is as much Shakespeare's
great original as he was Spenser's. What is virtually without precedent in
Shakespeare is that his characters *change themselves by pondering upon what they
themselves say*. In Homer and the Bible and Dante, we do not find sea-changes
in particular persons brought about by those persons' own language, that is,
by the differences that individual diction and tone make as speech produces
further speech. But the Pardoner and the Wife of Bath are well along the
mimetic way that leads to Hamlet and Falstaff. What they say to others, and
to themselves, partly reflects what they already are, but partly engenders also
what they will be. And perhaps even more subtly and forcefully, Chaucer
suggests ineluctable transformations going on in the Pardoner and the Wife
of Bath through the effect of the language of the tales they choose to tell.

Something of this shared power in Chaucer and Shakespeare accounts
for the failures of criticism to apprehend them, particularly when criticism is
formalist, or too given over to the study of codes, conventions, and what is
now called "language" but might more aptly be called applied linguistics, or
even psycholinguistics. A critic addicted to what is now called the "priority
of language over meaning" will not be much given to searching for meaning
in persons, real or imagined. But persons, at once real *and* imagined, are
the fundamental basis of the experiential art of Chaucer and Shakespeare.
Chaucer and Shakespeare know, beyond knowing, the labyrinthine ways in
which the individual self is always a picnic of selves. "The poets were there
before me," Freud remarked, and perhaps Nietzsche ought to have remarked
the same.

III

Talbot Donaldson rightly insists, against the patristic exegetes, that
Chaucer was primarily a comic writer. This need never be qualified, if we also

judge the Shakespeare of the two parts of *Henry IV* to be an essentially comic writer, as well as Fielding, Dickens, and Joyce. "Comic writer" here means something very comprehensive, with the kind of "comedy" involved being more in the mode, say, of Balzac than that of Dante, deeply as Chaucer was indebted to Dante notwithstanding. If the Pardoner is fundamentally a comic figure, why, then, so is Vautrin? Balzac's hallucinatory "realism," a cosmos in which every janitor is a genius, as Baudelaire remarked, has its affinities with the charged vitalism of Chaucer's fictive world. The most illuminating exegete of the General Prologue to *The Canterbury Tales* remains William Blake, whose affinities with Chaucer were profound. This is the Blake classed by Yeats, in *A Vision*, with Rabelais and Aretino; Blake as an heroic vitalist whose motto was "Exuberance is Beauty," which is an apt Chaucerian slogan also. I will grant that the Pardoner's is a negative exuberance, and yet Blake's remarks show us that the Wife of Bath's exuberance has its negative aspects also.

Comic writing so large and so profound hardly seems to admit a rule for literary criticism. Confronted by the Wife of Bath or Falstaff or the suprahumane Poldy, how shall the critic conceive her or his enterprise? What is there left to be done? I grimace to think of the Wife of Bath and Falstaff deconstructed, or of having their life-augmenting contradictions subjected to a Marxist critique. The Wife of Bath and difference (or even "differance")? Falstaff and surplus value? Poldy and the dogma that there is nothing outside the text? Hamlet and Lacan's Mirror Phase? The heroic, the vitalizing pathos of a fully human vision, brought about through a supermimesis not of essential nature, but of human possibility, demands a criticism more commensurate with its scope and its color. It is a matter of aesthetic tact, certainly, but as Oscar Wilde taught us, that makes it truly a moral matter as well. What devitalizes the Wife of Bath, or Falstaff, or Poldy, tends at last to reduce us also.

IV

That a tradition of major poetry goes from Chaucer to Spenser and Milton and on through them to Blake and Wordsworth, Shelley and Keats, Browning and Tennyson and Whitman, Yeats and Stevens, D. H. Lawrence and Hart Crane, is now widely accepted as a critical truth. The myth of a Metaphysical counter-tradition, from Donne and Marvell through Dryden, Pope, and Byron on to Hopkins, Eliot, and Pound, has been dispelled and seen as the Eliotic invention it truly was. Shakespeare is too large for any tradition, and so is Chaucer. One can wonder if even the greatest novelists in the language—Richardson, Austen, George Eliot, Dickens, Henry James, and the Mark Twain of *Huckleberry Finn* (the one true rival of *Moby-Dick* and *Leaves of Grass* as *the* American book or Bible), or Conrad, Lawrence, and Faulkner in this century—can approach Shakespeare and Chaucer in the astonishing art of somehow creating fictions that are more human than we generally are. Criticism, perhaps permanently ruined by Aristotle's formalism, has had little hope of even accurately describing this art. Aristophanes, Plato, and Longinus are apter models for a criticism more adequate to Chaucer and to Shakespeare.

Attacking Euripides, Aristophanes, as it were, attacks Chaucer and Shakespeare in a true prolepsis, and Plato's war against Homer, his attack upon mimesis, prophesies an unwaged war upon Chaucer and Shakespeare. Homer and Euripides, after all, simply are not the mimetic scandal that is constituted by Chaucer and Shakespeare; the *inwardness* of the Pardoner and Hamlet is of a different order from that of Achilles and Medea. Freud himself does not catch up to Chaucer and Shakespeare; he gets as far as Montaigne and Rousseau, which indeed is a long journey into the interior. But the Pardoner is the interior and even Iago, even Goneril and Regan, Cornwall and Edmund, do not give us a fiercer sense of intolerable resonance on the way down and out. Donaldson subtly observes that "it is the Pardoner's particular tragedy that, except in church, every one can see through him at a glance." The profound phrase here is "except in church." What happens to, or better yet, *within* the Pardoner when he preaches in church? Is that not parallel to asking what happens within the dying Edmund when he murmurs, "Yet Edmund was beloved," and thus somehow is moved to make his belated, futile attempt to save Cordelia and Lear? Are there any critical codes or methods that could possibly help us to sort out the Pardoner's more-than-Dostoevskian intermixture of supernatural faith and preternatural chicanery? Will semiotics or even Lacanian psycholinguistics anatomize Edmund for us, let alone Regan?

Either we become experiential critics when we read Chaucer and Shakespeare, or in too clear a sense we never read them at all. "Experiential" here necessarily means humane observation both of others and of ourselves, which leads to testing such observations in every context that indisputably is relevant. Longinus is the ancestor of such experiential criticism, but its masters are Samuel Johnson, Hazlitt and Emerson, Ruskin, Pater, and Wilde. A century gone mad on method has given us no critics to match these, nor are they likely to come again soon, though we still have Northrop Frye and Kenneth Burke, their last legitimate descendants.

V

Mad on method, we have turned to rhetoric, and so much so that the best of us, the late Paul de Man, all but urged us to identify literature with rhetoric, so that criticism perhaps would become again the rhetoric of rhetoric, rather than a Burkean rhetoric of motives or a Fryean rhetoric of desires. Expounding the Nun's Priest's Tale, Talbot Donaldson points to "the enormous rhetorical elaboration of the telling" and is moved to a powerful insight into experiential criticism:

> Rhetoric here is regarded as the inadequate defense that mankind erects against an inscrutable reality; rhetoric enables man at best to regard himself as a being of heroic proportions—like Achilles, or like Chauntecleer—and at worst to maintain the last sad vestiges of his dignity (as a rooster Chauntecleer is carried in the fox's mouth, but as a hero he rides on his back), rhetoric enables man to find significance both in his desires and in his fate, and to pretend to himself that the universe takes him seriously. And rhetoric has a habit, too, of collapsing in the presence of simple common sense.

Yet rhetoric, as Donaldson implies, if it is Chaucer's rhetoric in particular, can be a life-enhancing as well as a life-protecting defense. Here is the heroic pathos of the Wife of Bath, enlarging existence even as she sums up its costs in one of those famous Chaucerian passages that herald Shakespearean exuberances to come:

> But Lord Crist, whan that it remembreth me
> Upon my youthe and on my jolitee,
> It tikleth me aboute myn herte roote—
> Unto this day it dooth myn herte boote
> That I have had my world as in my time.
> But age, allas, that al wol envenime,
> Hath me biraft my beautee and my pith—
> Lat go, farewel, the devel go therwith!
> The flour is goon, ther is namore to telle:
> The bren as I best can now moste I selle;
> But yit to be right merye wol I fonde.
> (*WBP*, 1.475; E. T. Donaldson, 2d ed.)

The defense against time, so celebrated as a defiance of time's revenges, is the Wife's fierce assertion also of the will to live at whatever expense. Rhetorically, the center of the passage is in the famously immense reverberation of her great cry of exultation and loss, "That I have had my world as in my time," where the double "my" is decisive, yet the "have had" falls away in a further intimation of mortality. Like Falstaff, the Wife is a grand trope of pathos, of life defending itself against every convention that would throw us into death-in-life. Donaldson wisely warns us that "pathos, however, must not be allowed to carry the day," and points to the coarse vigor of the Wife's final benediction to the tale she has told:

> And Jesu Crist us sende
> Housbondes meeke, yonge, and fresshe abedde—
> And grace t'overbide hem that we wedde.
> And eek I praye Jesu shorte hir lives
> That nought wol be governed by hir wives,
> And olde and angry nigardes of dispence—
> God sende hem soone a verray pestilence!
>   (*WBT*, 1. 402)

Blake feared the Wife of Bath because he saw in her what he called the Female Will incarnate. By the Female Will, Blake meant the will of the natural woman or the natural man, a prolepsis perhaps of Schopenhauer's rapacious Will to Live or Freud's "frontier concept" of the drive. Chaucer, I think, would not have quarreled with such an interpretation, but he would have scorned Blake's dread of the natural will or Schopenhauer's horror of its rapacity. Despite every attempt to assimilate him to a poetry of belief, Chaucer actually surpasses even Shakespeare as a celebrant of the natural heart, while like Shakespeare being beyond illusions concerning the merely natural. No great poet was less of a dualist than Chaucer was, and nothing makes poetry more difficult for critics, because all criticism is necessarily dualistic.

The consolation for critics and readers is that Chaucer and Shakespeare, Cervantes and Tolstoy, persuade us finally that everything remains to be done in the development of a criticism dynamic and comprehensive enough to represent such absolute writers without reduction or distortion. No codes or methods will advance the reading of Chaucer. The critic is thrown back upon herself or himself, and upon the necessity to become a vitalizing interpreter in the service of an art whose burden is only to carry more life forward into a time without boundaries.

VI

The Knight's Tale is a chivalric romance, or purports to be; it is as much genial satire as romance, a triumph of Chaucer's comic rhetoric, monistic and life-enhancing. Talbot Donaldson charmingly sums up the poem's ethos as being rather more Stoic than Christian: "No matter how hard we look, we cannot hope to see why Providence behaves as it does; all we can do is our best, making a virtue of necessity, enjoying what is good, and remaining cheerful." Applied to most other authors, Donaldson's comments might seem banal. Chaucer's overwhelming representation of an immediate reality, in which we ride with the protagonists, enjoy what is good, and certainly become more cheerful, gives Donaldson's amiable observations their edge of precision. Since Chaucer the Pilgrim rides along with us, allowing his own narrative voice full scope, despite the authority of his storytellers, we hear more than the Knight's tonalities in the telling of his tale.

Donald R. Howard, admirably setting forth "the idea" of *The Canterbury Tales*, the totality of its vision, reminds us that Chaucer himself may be in a skeptical stance towards the Knight's Tale, if only because the voice of the Knight, as narrator, is so much at variance with Chaucer's larger idea or vision:

> And the work, because of this idea, discourages us from assenting to the tales, from giving them credence. Almost very tale is presented in circumstances which discredit it. Even the Knight's Tale, a high-minded story told by an ideal figure, gives us reason to approach it skeptically. In it ... Chaucer permits his own voice to intrude upon the Knight's. These ironic intrusions may discredit the tale itself, or the Knight, or the style and manner of its telling, or the cultural and literary tradition it represents. However explained, this ironic element raises questions in the reader's mind which the tale never settles. In other instances what we know about the pilgrim raises such questions. The Miller's Tale parodies the Knight's and holds some of its values up to ridicule; but the Miller does not get the last word and there is no reason to think Chaucer sided with him more than another—he is, we are told, a drunk and a churl. Besides, the Reeve's tale "quits" the Miller and his tale, discrediting both with another churlish viewpoint. Tales discredit each other, as with the Friar and Summoner. The Nun's Priest subtly discredits the Monk's tale and other tales which have preceded it. Whole groups of tales discredit one another by presenting various viewpoints in conflict—the sequence Knight-Miller-Reeve is an example, as is the "marriage group."

Talbot Donaldson places a particular emphasis upon one crucial couplet of the Knight's:

It is ful fair a man to bare him evene,
For alday meeteth men at unset stevene.

I remember walking once with the late and much mourned Donaldson, on an ordinary evening in New Haven, and hearing him quote that couplet, and then repeat his own superb paraphrase of it: "It is a good thing for a man to bear himself with equanimity, for one is constantly keeping appointments one never made." That certainly seems the Knight's ethos, and may have been Chaucer's, and doubtless does reflect *The Consolation of Philosophy* of Boethius. Yet Chaucer, as Donaldson helped teach us, is a very great comic writer— like Rabelais, Cervantes, Shakespeare. As a poet, Chaucer is larger than any formulation we can bring to bear upon him, and, again like Shakespeare, he tends to transcend genres also.

F. Anne Payne argues cogently that "the Knight's Tale, a philosophical parody with the *Consolation* and the romance as its models, belongs to the seriocomic tradition of Menippean satire." Less a genre than a grab bag, Menippean satire is essentially typified by Lucian, whose dialogues turn their mockery in several directions at once. Lucian is less a satirist than an extreme ironist, who exploits precisely that aspect of irony that the late Paul de Man termed "a permanent parabasis of meaning." The irony of irony, with its destruction of any fixed meaning, is the irony of the Knight's Tale, where nothing can be settled and much must be accepted. Donaldson. In his splendid final book, *The Swan at the Well: Shakespeare Reading Chaucer*, relates the irony of romantic love in *A Midsummer Night's Dream* to the irony of the Knight's Tale. Puck's "Lord, what fools these mortals be" falls short of the irony of Chaucer's Theseus: "who maie be a foole, but if he love?" The destruction of friendship by love, Chaucer's overt story, is itself Chaucer's metaphor for the dispersion of meaning by a love of philosophical disputation, which the Knight's Tale converts into a mockery. That must be why Shakespeare based his own Theseus more on Chaucer's Knight than on Chaucer's Theseus. The Knight is no philosopher but rather a chivalric skeptic, and so is Shakespeare's Theseus, who like the Knight will not go beyond his own experience.

Though the Knight's skepticism does not extend to his own tale-telling, there is always a remarkable gap between the complexity of his narrative and his own insistence that it is all a quite simple if rather sad matter. Donaldson compares this stance to that of the Nun's Priest, who blandly urges us to take the pith of his tale while ignoring its rhetorical reverberations, that alone give it power and universality. The Knight has tied up generations of Chaucerians with his famous red herring of a moral question:

You lovers axe I now this questioun:
Who hath the worse, Arcite or Palamoun?

As Donaldson remarks, the question is wrong because there is no authentic difference between the two love-crazed worthies. The Knight may be no Chaucerian ironist, but the gap between the Knight's experience of life and that of most among us necessarily and ironically defeats every attempt we could make to answer the question, unless indeed we qualify as experiential critics. No Formalist or method-based reading will be able to turn the Knight's question into its implied realization, which is that all of us must confront and absorb the possible worst, however unlooked-for and undeserved.

VII

Chaucer, writing at our American moment, would have written "The TV Evangelist's Tale," rather than "The Pardoner's Tale." Alas, we have no contemporary Chaucer to give us "The TV Evangelist's Prologue" and "The TV Evangelist's Epilogue," for which so much superb material has been provided in recent revelations. That is the context, aside from all historicisms, old and new, in which Chaucer's Pardoner should be seen. He is at once obscenely formidable and a laughable charlatan, thus arousing in us ambivalences akin to those provoked by certain eminent preachers on our home screens.

In the General Prologue to *The Canterbury Tales* we first encounter the Pardoner as the Summoner's lustful companion, boisterously singing the tavern air, "Come hither. Love, to me," and producing, with his Summoner friend, a sound surpassing the trumpet's cry. With his wax-like yellow hair, hanging like a lank of flax, thin and fine, and his piercing high voice, and his lack of beard, the Pardoner is the very type of the eunuch. We understand then why he hangs close to the authentically obscene Summoner, so as to pick up some sexual coloring, as it were. Beneath the overcompensation of lustful behavior, which fools nobody, the Pardoner is dangerously close to being an emblem of death, like the uncanny old man of his tale. The association of castration, blindness, and death, so crucial in Freud, is already a given in Chaucer, just as the strangely authentic power of the Pardoner's sermon, which transcends his overt tricksterism, testifies to the weird prolepsis of Dostoevsky in *The Canterbury Tales*. A professional hypocrite who yet can invoke the terror of eternity, truly despite himself, the Pardoner is the most powerful representation of depravity we can find in English before the creation of Shakespeare's Iago and Edmund. Even Talbot Donaldson underestimates, I think, the Pardoner's depth of self-destructiveness:

But the Pardoner's secret is, of course, a secret only to himself: at any rate Chaucer the pilgrim guessed it at once. But as long as the secret remains unspoken the Pardoner dwells securely in his own delusion, so that the secret remains valid for him. Yet at the end of his frightening story he wantonly imperils—and destroys—the fragile structure on which his self-confidence depends. Whatever his reasons—avarice, good-fellowship, humor—he concludes his sermon with an offer to sell his pardon to the pilgrims even after all he has told about his own fraudulence. Ironically he picks the worst possible victim, that rough, manly man who might be supposed to have a natural antipathy for the unmasculine Pardoner. The insult to the Host's intelligence is the first and last failure of the Pardoner's intelligence, for the Host's violently obscene reaction reveals the Pardoner's secret. Thereupon the man whose clever tongue has seemed to give him control of every situation is reduced to furious silence.

I do not think that "avarice, good-fellowship, humor" are the only reasons why the Pardoner so brazenly insults Harry Bailly, the most likely of all his listeners to give the brutal and inevitable riposte. Moved by the extraordinary intensity of his own tale-telling. The Pardoner achieves a kind of vertigo that mixes pride in his own swindling with something dangerously authentic out of the supernatural order of grace:

> O cursed sinne of alle cursednesse!
> O traitours homicide, a wikkednesse!
> O glotonye, luxure, and hasardrye!
> Thou blasphemour of Crist with vilainye
> And othes grete of usage and of pride!
> Allas, mankinde, how may it bitide
> That to thy Creatour which that thee wroughte,
> And with his precious herte blood thee boughte,
> Thou art so fals and so unkinde, allas?
> Now goode men, God foryive you youre trespas,
> And ware you fro the sinne of avarice:
> Myn holy pardon may you alle warice—
> So that ye offre nobles or sterlinges,
> Or elles silver brooches, spoones, ringes.
> Boweth your heed under this holy bulle!
> Cometh up, ye wives, offreth of youre wolle!
> Youre name I entre here in my rolle: anoon

Into the blisse of hevene shul ye goon.
I you assoile by myn heigh power—
Ye that wol offer—as clene and eek as cleer
As ye were born.—And lo, sires, thus I preche.
And Jesu Crist that is oure soules leeche
So graunte you his pardon to receive,
For that is best—I wol you nat deceive.
           (*PT*, II. 567-90)

A desperate good-fellowship and a kind of gallows humor certainly are present in those closing lines. What is also present is a sense that the Pardoner has been carried away, and by more than his tale's strength or his own rough eloquence as a preacher. A kind of madness or enthusiasm takes possession of him and drives him to the social suicide that Freud would have regarded as "moral masochism," the need for punishment due to an unconscious sense of guilt, perhaps even a retroactive self-recognition that might account for his emasculate condition. The drive for destruction again turns inward and rages against the self, so that in courting a kind of social death the Pardoner receives premonitions of the spiritual death he has earned. That perhaps explains the outrageousness of the Pardoner's address to his fellow-pilgrims:

It is an honour to everich that is heer
That ye mowe have a suffisant pardoner
T'assoile you in contrees as ye ride,
For aventures whiche that may bitide:
Paraventure ther may falle oon or two
Down of his hors and breke his nekke atwo;
Looke which a suretee is it to you alle
That I am in youre felaweshipe yfalle
That may assoile you, bothe more and lasse,
Whan that the soule shal fro the body passe.
           (*PT*, II. 603–12)

What can the Pardoner have expected as response to this outburst? The need for rebuke surely dominates the Pardoner's address to the Host, which asks for more than trouble:

I rede that oure Hoste shal biginne,
For he is most envoluped in sinne.
Com forth, sire Host, and offer first anoon,

And thou shalt kisse the relikes everichoon,
Ye, for a grote: unbokele anoon thy purs.
         (II. 613–17)

The Host's splendidly violent response, with its images of kissing the Pardoner's stained fundament and slicing off and carrying away his testicles, is precisely what the Pardoner was too shrewd not to expect. But the shrewdness here belongs to the Pardoner's unconscious death drive; the merely conscious ego of the wretch is stricken as silent as Iago was to be. Iago ends by saying that from this time forth he never will speak a word. His true precursor, the sublimely damned yet still comic Pardoner, also answered not a word: "So wroth he was no word ne wolde he saye."

E. TALBOT DONALDSON

The Ending of "Troilus"

One of Chaucer's familiar pretences is that he is a versifier utterly devoted to simplicity of meaning—for the reason that he considers himself, apparently, utterly incapable of complexity. He defines his poetic mission as the reporting of facts in tolerable verse, and he implies that that's hard enough to do. True poetry may, for all of him, do something much better but it is not clear to Chaucer exactly what it is or how it does it. He and *ars poetica* are, to be sure, on parallel roads, moving in the same direction; but the roads are a long way apart and are destined to meet, perhaps, not even in infinity. On the one hand, Chaucer, reciting his simple stories 'in swich Englissh as he can'; on the other, poetry, penetrating regions of complex significance far beyond the grasp of a simple straightforward versifier.

Chaucer's pretended inferiority complex on the subject of poetry must have stemmed from something real in his own life probably connected with his being a bourgeois writing for high-born members of the royal court. What interests me now however, is not the origin of the pose, but its literary value. For I think that Chaucer discovered in the medieval modesty convention a way of poetic life: that, by constantly assuring us, both through direct statement and through implication, of his inability to write anything but the simplest kind of verse, Chaucer creates just that poetry of complex significance that he disclaims striving for. In this paper I shall focus attention on the last stanzas

From *Speaking of Chaucer*: pp. 84–101. © 1970 by W. W. Norton.

15

of *Troilus*, where it seems to me that a kind of dramatization of his poetic ineptitude achieves for him a poetric success that not many poets in any language have attained. But I shall first consider briefly some characteristic Chaucerian "ineptitudes" in his other works.

Modesty is endemic both with Chaucer in his own first person—whoever that is—and with his dramatic creations: none of them can do much in the way of poetry. Like the Squire, they cannot climb over so high a stile, or, like his father, they set out to plough, God wot, a large field with weak oxen; or, if they are not ploughing a field, they're gleaning it, like the author of the Prologue to the *Legend of Good Women*, and are full glad of any kernel that their talented predecessors have missed. Or else, like the Prioress, they are so afflicted by infantilism that they speak no better than a child of twelvemonth old, or less. Like the Merchant and the Franklin, they are rude men, 'burel' men, they cannot gloss, they have no rhetoric, they call a spade a spade; they come after even such second-rate poets as that fellow Chaucer, bearing only *hawe bake*—pig food—and are reduced to prose, like the Man of Law in his Prologue. They can't even get the data down in the right order, like the Monk or like the narrator of the Prologue to *The Canterbury Tales*. Or, worst of all, as in the case of the pilgrim who recites the romance of Sir Thopas, their inability to frame a story of their own makes them resort to 'a rim I lerned a longe agoon', and when that is shot down in mid-flight, they have to take refuge in one of the most anaesthetic sermons that ever mortified a reader. If it is dramatically appropriate that they be capable rhetoricians, like the Clerk, they comply at once with a decree that declares high style to be inappropriate to their audience. In short, they seldom admit to more than a nodding acquaintance with the Muse.

The normal function of the modesty convention is, I suppose, to prepare a pleasant surprise for the reader when the poem turns out better than he has been led to expect, or, at worst, to save him disappointment when the implied warning is fulfilled. This latter alternative is perhaps valid in some of Chaucer's tales, notably the Monk's. But the really important function of the modesty convention in Chaucer is to prepare a soil in which complexity of meaning may grow most fruitfully. That is, the narrator's assertion, implicit or explicit, of his devotion to the principle of simplicity, his denial of regard for possible complexity, results, by a curious paradox, *in* complexity; for the harder he tries to simplify issues, the less amenable to simplification they become, and, in artistic terms, the more complex and suggestive the poem becomes. To epitomize, the typical Chaucerian narrator begins by assuring you, either by a modesty prologue or by the notable simplicity of his manner—sometimes by both—that in what you are about to hear there will be nothing but the most straightforward presentation of reality: the narrator's feet are firmly on the ground, but he is no poet, and his control of anything but fact is weak. Subsequently the poet Chaucer, working from behind the narrator, causes to arise from this hard ground a complex of possible meanings, endlessly dynamic and interactive, amplifying, qualifying, even denying the simple statement: these draw much of their vitality from the fact that they exist—or seem to exist—either unknown to or in spite of the narrator; indeed, the latter sometimes betrays an uneasy awareness that the poem has got out of hand and is saying something he doesn't approve of or at least didn't intend, and his resistance to this meaning may well become an important part of it. That is, the ultimate significance of the poem derives much from the tension between the narrator's simple statement and the complex of implications that have arisen to qualify it.

The Chaucer who tells of the pilgrimage to Canterbury provides an obvious example of this tension between the simple and the complex. At the very beginning of the Prologue he lets us know exactly what we may expect of his narrative—namely what he saw with his own two eyes, and not an adverb more. And, as I have tried to show elsewhere, his prospectus itself is a miracle of stylistic simplicity, its pedestrian matter-of-factness supporting by example the limited poetic ideal that it is expressing. Yet it is because he has succeeded in persuading the reader to expect no more than meets the eye that, when he comes to the portrait of the Prioress, the poet is able to reveal to us the profoundest depths of that rather shallow lady. The narrator, to be sure, describes her flatly as he saw her, and what he saw was attractive, and it attracted the warm fervour of his love; but what he did not see was that everything he did see amounted to a well-indexed catalogue of the Prioress's shortcomings, which seen coldly would produce a kind of travesty of a Prioress. But because of his love for the woman, he is unaware of the satirical potential of his portrait, so that this potential, while always imminent, is never actually realized. One feels that if any one had pointed it out to the narrator, he would have been horrified, as, indeed, the Prioress would have been horrified if any one had pointed it out to her—and as even today certain readers are horrified when one points it out to them. And quite rightly, too, because of the great love that permeates the simple description. But the effect achieved by means of a narrator who resists complexity is of a highly complex strife between love and satire, between wholehearted approval and heartless criticism. These are factors which in logic would cancel one another, as a negative cancels a positive; but in poetry they exist forever side by side—as they also do in reality wherever there are ladies at once so attractive and so fallible as the Prioress. Indeed, the two factors, love and satire, unite with one another to form a third meaning—one which both qualifies and enhances the Prioress's own motto, *amor vincit omnia*, by suggesting something of the complex way

in which love does conquer all. This occurs because the narrator, incapable
of complexity, adheres rigorously to the presentation of simple fact.

The ways in which Chaucerian narrators enhance the meaning of
their stories by missing the point of them are various. Occasionally, indeed,
a narrator will rise up in the pulpit sententiously to point *out* or at least to
point *to* what he takes to be his real meaning. The only trouble is that his
aim is likely to be poor: he will suggest a meaning which, while it bears some
logical relation to the ultimate significance, is at best no more than gross
oversimplification. For instance, the Nun's Priest, at the end of his remarkably
verbose epic of Chauntecleer, solemnly addresses his audience:

> Lo, swich it is for to be recchelees
> And necligent, and truste on flaterye.
> But ye that holden this tale a folye,
> As of a fox, or of a cok and hen,
> Taketh the moralitee, goode men.
>   (B²3736–40)

He then goes on to quote St. Paul in a way that suggests that doctrine is
produced every time a pen inscribes words on paper—a thought most
comforting to an author hard put to determine his own meaning. With
Pauline authority on his side, the Nun's Priest exhorts us:

> Taketh the fruit, and tat the chaf be stille.
>   (B²3443)

Now all this certainly bids us find a simple moral in the story; but, so far
as I know, no two critics have ever found the same moral: most agree only
in rejecting the Nun's Priest's stated moral about negligence and flattery.
The reason for this disagreement is, as I have tried to suggest elsewhere,
that the real moral of the Tale is in the chaff the rhetorical amplifications
which make of Chauntecleer a good representative of western man trying to
maintain his precarious dignity in the face of a universe and of a basic avian
(or human) nature which fail to co-operate with him. But the Nun's Priest,
characteristically, suggests this moral only by pointing towards another which
satisfies nobody.

Another Canterbury narrator, the Knight, similarly asks us to take
a simple view of a story which is really very complex. After describing the
languishing of Arcite in Theban exile and of Palamon in Athenian prison,
both of them quite out of the running in their race for Emily, the narrator
finishes off the first part of his poem with a *demande d'amour*:

You loveres axe I now this questioun:
Who hath the worse, Arcite or Palamoun?
    (A1347–8)

With this tidy rhetorical flourish the Knight suggests that his story is a simple one about a rivalry in love. The question invites the reader to take sides in this rivalry, to feel sorrier for one youth than the other, and hence to choose a favourite for the contest that is to come. He appeals, that is, to our sense of justice. Until recently, the majority of Chaucerian critics put their money on Palamon; and since at the end of the story Providence accords him Emily and lets him live happily ever after, while it buries Arcite, this majority have naturally felt that justice has operated in an exemplary manner, and nothing is pleasanter than to see justice behave itself. Yet there has always been a noisy group—with whom I deeply sympathize—who feel that Arcite is very badly treated by the story. This disagreement represents a kind of protracted response to the Knight's rhetorical question.

The lack of critical agreement, however, once again suggests that there is something wrong both about the question and about the debate. If intelligent readers cannot agree on which of the two young men is the more deserving, then there is probably not much difference between them. And indeed, the way the poem carefully balances their claims bears this out. On temperamental grounds you may prefer a man who mistakes his lady for Venus to a man who knows a woman when he sees one, or you may not; but such preference has no moral validity. The poem concerns something larger than the young men's relative deserts, though it is something closely related to that question. Recognition of their equality leads to the conclusion that the poem does not assert the simple triumph of justice when Palamon ends up with Emily, nor the triumph of a malignant anti-justice when Arcite ends up in his cold grave, alone. What it does suggest—and I think with every syllable of its being—is that Providence is not working justly, so far as we can see, when it kills Arcite, nor, so far as we can see, unjustly when it lets Palamon live happily ever after. For no matter how hard we look, we cannot hope to see why Providence behaves as it does; all we can do is our best, making a virtue of necessity, enjoying what is good, and remaining cheerful.

But to most of us this is an unpalatable moral, far less appealing than the one which will result if only we can promote Palamon into an unchallenged position of deserving; and it is a very stale bit of cold cabbage indeed unless it is as hard-won as the Knight's own battles. The experience by which the individual attains the Knight's tempered view of life is an important part of that view, and renders it, if not palatable, digestible and nourishing. This experience must include our questioning of relative values, our desire to discover that even-handed justice does prevail in the universe, and our resistance to the conclusion that justice, so far as we can see, operates at best with only one hand. The emotional history of the ultimate conclusion makes it valid; and the way the Knight's question is framed, pointing at what we should like to believe, and through that at what we shall have to believe, causes us to share in that experience—leads us through the simple to the complex.

It is at the end of *Troilus* that Chaucer, employing the kind of devices I have been discussing, achieves his most complex poetic effect. His narrator has worked hard, from the very beginning, to persuade us of his simplicity, though from the very beginning his simplicity has been compromised by the fact that, apparently unknown to himself, he wavers between two quite different—though equally simple—attitudes towards his story. It is the saddest story in the world, and it is the gladdest story in the world. This double attitude appears strongly in the opening stanzas, when he tells us that his motive for writing is, paradoxically, to bring honour to Love and gladden lovers with a love story so sad that his verses shed tears while he writes them and that Tisiphone is his only appropriate Muse. Yet though he starts out firmly resolved to relate the double sorrow of Troilus

> ... in loving of Criseide,
> And how that she forsook him er she deide.
>   (*TC* 1.55–6)

as the story progresses he seems to forget all about the second sorrow. The historical perspective, which sees before and after and knows the sad ending, gives way to the limited, immediate view of one who loves the actors in the story, and in his love pines for what is not so desperately that he almost brings it into being. The scholar's motive for telling a sad story simply because it is true finds itself at war with the sentimentalist's motive of telling a love story simply because it is happy and beautiful. The optimism that one acquires when one lives with people so attractive makes a gay future for all seem inevitable. Once launched upon the love story, the narrator refuses to look forward to a future that the scholar in him knows to be already sadly past; at moments when the memory of that sad future breaks in on him, he is likely to deny his own sources, and to suggest that, despite the historical evidence to the contrary, Criseide was, perhaps, not unfaithful at all—men have been lying about her.

For the greater part of the poem the intimately concerned, optimistic narrator is in full control of the story—or rather, the story is in full control of him, and persuades him that a world that has such people in it is not only the best of all possible worlds, but the most possible. When in the fifth book the facts of history force him back towards the historical perspective, which has always known that his happiness and that of the lovers were transitory, illusory, he does his best to resist the implications arising from his ruined story—tries to circumvent them, denies them, slides off them. Thus an extraordinary feeling of tension, even of dislocation, develops from the strife in the narrator's mind between what should be and what was—and hence what is. This tension is the emotional storm-centre which causes the narrator's various shifts and turns in his handling of the ending, and which also determines the great complexity of the poem's ultimate meaning.

So skillfully has Chaucer mirrored his narrator's internal warfare—a kind of nervous breakdown in poetry—that many a critic has concluded that Chaucer himself was bewildered by his poem. One, indeed, roundly condemns the whole fifth book, saying that it reads like "an earlier draft ... which its author lacked sufficient interest to revise." According to this critic, Chaucer "cannot bring himself to any real enthusiasm for a plot from which the bright lady of his own creation has vanished." And, elsewhere, "What had happened to the unhappy Criseyde and to her equally unhappy creator was that the story in which they were involved had betrayed them both." Now this is, in a rather sad way, the ultimate triumph of Chaucer's method. The critic responds with perfect sympathy to the narrator's bewilderment, even to the extent of seeming to suggest that the poet had written four-fifths of his story before he discovered how it came out. But in fact Chaucer's warmly sympathetic narrator has blinded the critic's eyes as effectively as he had blinded his own. It is not true that the bright lady of Chaucer's creation has vanished—Criseide is still very much present in book five. What has vanished is the bright dream of the enduring power of human love, and in a burst of creative power that it is not easy to match elsewhere.

For the *moralitee* of *Troilus and Criseide* (and by morality I do not mean "ultimate meaning") is simply this: that human love, and by a sorry corollary everything human, is unstable and illusory. I give the moral so flatly now because in the remainder of this paper I shall be following the narrator in his endeavour to avoid it, and indeed shall be eagerly abetting him in trying to avoid it, and even pushing him away when he finally accepts it. I hope in this way to suggest how Chaucer, by manipulating his narrator, achieves an objective image of the poem's significance that at once greatly qualifies and enhances this moral, and one that is, of course, far more profound and less absolute than my flat-footed statement. The meaning of the poem is not the moral, but a complex qualification of the moral.

Let us turn now to that part of the poem, containing the last eighteen stanzas, which is often referred to by modern scholars, though not by the manuscripts, as the Epilogue. I object to the term because it implies that this passage was tacked on to the poem after the poet had really finished his work, so that it is critically if not physically detachable from what has gone before. And while I must admit that the nature of this passage, its curious twists and turns, its occasional air of fecklessness, set it off from what has gone before, it also seems to me to be the head of the whole body of the poem.

The last intimately observed scene of the action is the final, anticlimactic interview between Troilus and Pandarus, wherein the latter is driven by the sad logic of his loyalty and of his pragmatism to express hatred of his niece, and to wish her dead. Pandarus's last words are, "I can namore saye," and it is now up to the narrator, who is as heart-broken as Troilus and Pandarus, to express the significance of his story. His first reaction is to take the epic high road; by means of the exalted style to reinvest Troilus with the human dignity that his unhappy love has taken from him. The narrator starts off boldly enough:

> Greet was the sorwe and plainte of Troilus;
> But forth hire cours Fortune ay gan to holde.
> Criseide loveth the sone of Tydeüs,
> And Troilus moot weepe in cares colde.
>   (*TC* v.1744–7)

But though the manner is epic, the subject is not: an Aeneas in Dido's pathetic plight is no fit subject for Virgilian style. And the narrator, overcome by the pathos of his story, takes refuge in moralization:

> Swich is this world, whoso it can biholde:
> In eech estaat is litel hertes reste—
> God leve us for to take it for the beste!

How true! And how supremely, brilliantly, inadequate! It has been said that all experience does no more than prove some platitude or other, but one hopes that poetic experience will do more, or in any case that poetry will not go from pathos to bathos. This moral, the trite moral of the Monk's Tale—Isn't life awful?—which the Monk arrives at—again and again—*a priori* would be accepted by many a medieval man as a worthy moral for the *Troilus*, and the narrator is a medieval man. But the poet behind the narrator is aware that an experience that has been intimately shared—not merely viewed historically, as are the Monk's tragedies—requires not a moral, but a meaning arrived at *a posteriori*, something earned, and in a sense new. Moreover, the narrator seems still to be asking the question, Can nothing be salvaged from the wreck of the story? For he goes on once more to have recourse to epic enhancement of his hero, more successfully this time, since it is the martial heroism of Troilus, rather than his unhappy love, that is the subject: there follow two militant stanzas recounting his prowess and his encounters with Diomede. But again the epic impulse fails, for the narrator's real subject is not war but unhappy love, for which epic values will still do nothing—will neither salvage the dignity of Troilus nor endow his experience with meaning. In a wistful stanza, the narrator faces his failure to do by epic style what he desires to have done:

> And if I hadde ytaken for to write
> The armes of this ilke worthy man,
>   [But, unfortunately, *arma virumque non cano*]
> Than wolde ich of his batailes endite;
> But for that I to writen first bigan
> Of his love, I have said as I can—
> His worthy deedes, whoso list hem heere,
> Rede Dares—he can telle hem alle yfere.
>   (1765–71)

This sudden turn from objective description to introspection mirrors the narrator's quandary. Unable to get out of his hopeless predicament, he does what we all tend to do when we are similarly placed: he begins to wonder why he ever got himself into it. The sequel of this unprofitable speculation is likely to be panic, and the narrator very nearly panics when he sees staring him in the face another possible moral for the love poem he has somehow been unwise enough to recite. The moral that is staring him in the face is written in the faces of the ladies of his audience, the antifeminist moral which is at once obvious and, from a court poet, unacceptable:

> Biseeching every lady bright of hewe,
> And every gentil womman what she be,
> That al be that Criseide was untrewe,
> That for that gilt she nat be wroth with me.
> Ye may hir giltes in othere bookes see;
> And gladlier I wol write, if you leste,
> Penelopeës trouthe and good Alceste.

While anticipating the ladies' objections, the narrator has, with that relief only a true coward can appreciate, glimpsed a possible way out: denial of responsibility for what the poem says. He didn't write it in the first place, it has nothing to do with him, and anyhow he would much rather have written about faithful women. These excuses are, of course, very much in the comic mood of the Prologue to the *Legend of Good Women* where Alceste, about whom he would prefer to have written, defends him from Love's wrath on the grounds that, being no more than a translator, he wrote about Criseide "from innocence, and knew not what he said." And if he can acquit himself of responsibility for Criseide by pleading permanent inanity, there is no reason why he cannot get rid of all his present tensions by funnelling them into a joke against himself. This he tries to do by turning upside down the antifeminist moral of the story:

> N'l saye nat this al only for thise men,
> But most for wommen that bitraised be ...

And I haven't recited this exclusively for men, but also, or rather but mostly, for women who are betrayed

> Thrugh false folk—God yive hem sorwe, amen!
> That with hit grete wit and subtiltee
> Bitraise you; and this commeveth me
> To speke, and in effect you alle I praye,
> Beeth war of men, and herkneth what I saye.

The last excursion into farce—in a poem that contains a good deal of farce—is this outrageous inversion of morals, which even so has a grotesque relevance if all human love, both male and female, is in the end to be adjudged unstable. With the narrator's recourse to comedy the poem threatens to end. At any rate, he asks it to go away:

> Go, litel book, go, litel myn tragedye,
> Ther God thy makere yit, er that he die,
> So sende might to make in som comedye....

(Presumably a comedy will not blow up in his face as this story has, and will let him end on a note like the one he has just sounded.) There follows the celebrated injunction of the poet to his book not to vie with other poetry, but humbly to kiss the steps of Virgil, Ovid, Homer, Lucan, and Statius. This is the modesty convention again, but transmuted, I believe, into something close to arrogance. Perhaps the poem is not to be classed with the works of these great poets, but I do not feel that the narrator succeeds in belittling his work by mentioning it in connection with them; there is such a thing as inviting comparison by eschewing comparison. It seems that the narrator has abandoned his joke, and is taking his "little book"—of more than 8,000 lines—seriously. Increasing gravity characterizes the next stanza, which begins with the hope that the text will not be miswritten nor mismetred by scribes and lesser breeds without the law of final –*e*. Then come two lines of emphatic prayer:

> And red wherso thou be, or elles songe,
> That thou be understonde, God I biseeche.

It is perhaps inconsiderate of the narrator to implore us to take his sense when he has been so irresolute about defining his sense. But the movement of the verse now becomes sure and strong, instead of uncertain and aimless, as the narrator moves confidently towards a meaning.

For in the next stanza, Troilus meets his death. This begins—once again—in the epic style, with perhaps a glance at the *Iliad*:

> The wratthe, as I bigan you for to saye,
> Of Troilus the Greekes boughten dere.

Such dignity as the high style can give is thus, for the last time, proffered Troilus. But for him there is to be no last great battle in the West, and both the stanza, and Troilus's life, end in pathos:

> But wailaway, save only Goddes wille:
> Despitously him slow the fierse Achille.

Troilus's spirit at once ascends into the upper spheres whence he looks down upon this little earth and holds all vanity as compared with the full felicity of heaven. The three stanzas describing Troilus's afterlife afford him that reward which medieval Christianity allowed to the righteous heathen. And in so doing, they salvage from the human wreck of the story the human qualities of Troilus that are of enduring value—most notably, his *trouthe*, the integrity for which he is distinguished. Moreover, this recognition by the plot that some human values transcend human life seems to enable the narrator to come to a definition of the poem's meaning which he has hitherto been unwilling to make. Still close to his characters, he witnesses Troilus's rejection of earthly values, and then, apparently satisfied, now that the mortal good in Troilus has been given immortal reward, he is willing to make that rejection of *all* mortal goods towards which the poem has, despite his resistance, been driving him. His rejection occurs—most unexpectedly—in the third of these stanzas.

Troilus, gazing down at the earth and laughing within himself at those who mourn his death,

> ... dampned al oure werk that folweth so
> The blinde lust, the which that may nat caste,
> And sholden al oure herte on hevene caste.

Up until the last line Troilus has been the subject of every main verb in the entire passage; but after he has damned all our work, by one of those syntactical ellipses that make Middle English so fluid a language, Troilus's thought is extended to include both narrator and reader: in the last line, *And sholden al oure herte on hevene caste*, the plural verb *sholden* requires the subject *we*; but this subject is omitted, because to the narrator the sequence of the sense is, at last, overpoweringly clear. When, after all his attempts not to have to reject the values inherent in his love story, he finally does reject them, he does so with breath-taking ease.

He does so, indeed, with dangerous ease. Having taken up arms against the world and the flesh, he lays on with a will:

> Swich fin hath, lo, this Troilus for love;
> Swich fin hath al his grete worthinesse;
> Swich fin hath his estaat real above;
> Swich fin his lust, swich fin hath his noblesse;
> Swich fin hath false worldes brotelnesse:
> And thus bigan his loving of Criseide,
> As I have told, and in this wise he deide.

But impressive as this stanza is, its movement is curious. The first five lines express, with increasing force, disgust for a world in which everything—not only what merely *seems* good, but also what really *is* good—comes to nothing in the end. Yet the last two lines,

> And thus bigan his loving of Criseide,
> As I have told, and in this wise he deide.

have, I think, a sweetness of tone that contrasts strangely with the emphatic disgust that precedes them. They seem to express a deep sadness for a doomed potential—as if the narrator, while forced by the evidence to condemn everything his poem has stood for, cannot really quite believe that it has come to nothing. The whole lovely aspiration of the previous action is momentarily recreated in the spare summary of this couplet.

The sweetness of tone carries over into the next two stanzas, the much-quoted ones beginning

> O yonge, freshe folkes, he or she,
> In which that love up groweth with youre age,
> Repaireth hoom fro worldly vanitee,
> And of youre herte up casteth the visage
> To thilke God that after his image
> You made; and thinketh al nis but a faire
> This world that passeth soone as flowres faire.

The sweetness here adheres not only to what is being rejected, but also to what is being sought in its stead, and this marks a development in the narrator. For he does not now seem so much to be fleeing away, in despair and disgust, from an ugly world—the world of the Monk's Tale—as he seems to be moving voluntarily through this world *towards* something infinitely better. And while this world is a wretched one—ultimately—in which all love is *feined*, 'pretended' and 'shirked', it is also a world full of the young potential of human love—'In which that love up groweth with *oure* age'; a world which, while it passes soon, passes soon as flowers fair. All the illusory loveliness of a world which is man's only reality is expressed in the very lines that reject that loveliness.

In these stanzas the narrator has been brought to the most mature and complex expression of what is involved in the Christian rejection of the world that seems to be, and indeed is, man's home, even though he knows there is a better one. But the narrator himself remains dedicated to simplicity, and makes one last effort to resolve the tension in his mind between loving a world he ought to hate and hating a world he cannot help loving; he endeavours to root out the love:

> Lo, here of payens cursed olde rites;
> Lo, here what alle hir goddes may availe;
> Lo, here thise wrecched worldes appetites;
> Lo, here the fin and guerdon for travaile
> Of Jove, Appollo, of Mars, of swich rascaile;
> Lo, here the forme of olde clerkes speeche
> In poetrye, if ye hir bookes seeche.

For the second time within a few stanzas a couplet has undone the work of the five lines preceding it. In them is harsh, excessively harsh, condemnation of the world of the poem, including gods and rites that have played no great part in it. In brilliant contrast to the tone of these lines is the exhausted calm of the last two:

> Lo, here the forme of olde clerkes speeche
> In poetrye, if ye hit bookes seeche.

There is a large imprecision about the point of reference of this couplet. I do not know whether its *Lo here* refers to the five preceding lines or to the poem as a whole, but I suppose it refers to the poem as a whole, as the other four *Lo here*'s do. If this is so, then the form of *olde clerkes speeche* is being damned as well as the *payens cursed olde rites*—by parataxis, at least. Yet it is not, for the couplet lacks the heavy, fussy indignation of the earlier lines: instead of indignation there is, indeed, dignity. I suggest that the couplet once more reasserts, in its simplicity, all the implicit and explicit human values that the poem has dealt with, even though these are, to a medieval Christian, ultimately insignificant. The form of old clerks' speech in poetry is the sad story that human history tells. It is sad, it is true, it is lovely, and it is significant, for it is poetry.

This is the last but one of the narrator's searches for a resolution for his poem. I have tried to show how at the end of *Troilus* Chaucer has manipulated a narrator capable of only a simple view of reality in such a way as to achieve the poetic expression of an extraordinarily complex one. The narrator, moved by his simple devotion to Troilus, to Pandarus, above all to Criseide, has been vastly reluctant to find that their story, so full of the illusion of happiness, comes to nothing—that the potential of humanity comes to nothing. To avoid this—seemingly simple—conclusion he has done everything he could. He has tried the epic high road; he has tried the broad highway of trite moralization; he has tried to eschew responsibility; he has tried to turn it all into a joke; and all these devices have failed. Finally, with every other means of egress closed, he has subscribed to Troilus's rejection of his own story, though only when, like Gregory when he wept for Trajan, he has seen his desire for his hero's salvation confirmed. Once having made the rejection, he has thrown himself into world-hating with enthusiasm. But now the counterbalance asserts its power. For the same strong love of the world of his story that prevented him from reaching the Christian rejection permeates and qualifies his expression of the rejection. Having painfully climbed close to the top of the ridge he did not want to climb, he cannot help looking back with longing at the darkening but still fair valley in which he lived; and every resolute thrust forward ends with a glance backward. In having his narrator behave thus, Chaucer has achieved a meaning only great poetry can achieve. The world he knows and the heaven he believes in grow ever farther and farther apart as the woeful contrast between them is developed, and even closer and closer together as the narrator blindly unites them in the common bond of his love. Every fake start he has made has amounted, not to a negative, but to a positive; has been a necessary part of the experience without which the moral of the poem would be as meaningless and unprofitable as in the form I gave it a little while ago. The poem states, what much of Chaucer's poetry states, the necessity under which men lie of living in, making the best of, enjoying, and loving a world from which they must remain detached and which they must ultimately hate: a little spot of earth that with the sea embraced is, as in Book Three Criseide was embraced by Troilus.

For this paradox there is no logical resolution. In the last two stanzas of the poem Chaucer, after asking Gower and Strode for correction, invokes the power that, being supra-logical itself, can alone resolve paradox. He echoes Dante's mighty prayer to the Trinity, 'that al maist circumscrive', and concludes with the lines:

> So make us, Jesus, for thy mercy digne,
> For love of Maide and Moder thyn benigne.

The poem has concerned a mortal woman whose power to love failed, and it ends with the one mortal woman whose power to love is everlasting. I think it is significant that the prayer of the poem's ending leads up, not to Christ, son of God, but to his mother, daughter of Eve—towards heaven, indeed, but towards heaven through human experience.

ROBERT WORTH FRANK, JR.

The Prologue to
The Legend of Good Women

The much admired Prologue to the *Legend of Good Women* is all of the *Legend* that the mid-twentieth century is willing to take to its bosom. It is famous for its charm. Or it is if one selects the proper passages. This is not a sneer; I simply wish to point out that some of the time Chaucer appears to be talking seriously so charm is not the whole business of the Prologue. Unfortunately, the charm both distracts us from the seriousness and encourages us to read only the Prologue, making it an end instead of what it really is—a beginning.

The Prologue is also famous because for many years it was the object of controversy. It exists in two versions, labeled nowadays F and G, and the question of which came first has received an extraordinary amount of attention.[1] There is today a consensus that F is the earlier, and I shall act on that assumption, basing my discussion primarily on F and referring to G only when necessary. The debate over priority is another factor that has tended to isolate the Prologue from the legends.

The main function of the Prologue in the total although incomplete work we call the *Legend of Good Women*, would seem, however, to be that of introduction. It is this function which I wish to discuss. This is not to deny the Prologue some of the qualities of an aesthetic entity; it is merely that this matter is not my concern. I wish to examine the Prologue for such clues as it may give us as to Chaucer's purposes in the legends themselves, in the project

---

From *Chaucer and The Legend of Good Women*: pp. 11–36. © 1972 by the President and Fellows of Harvard College.

as a whole. What he felt to be the significance of this work may in some part be revealed here, and that would be worth knowing.

In the chronology of the Chaucer canon the Prologue appears to be a throwback; as a dream vision it is a momentary regression to a form and manner already abandoned in the *Troilus* and the *Knight's Tale* and never used in the *Canterbury Tales*. Critics have commented on the Prologue's conventionality,[2] but the appearance of orthodoxy is misleading, probably deliberately so, for Chaucer's apologia in the Prologue, his explanation and defense of what he is about to do, is not merely conventional. True, the Prologue has its conventional furniture: the reference to books, the typically Chaucerian figure of the comically placed narrator, the talk of love and the God of Love, and the dream form itself. But Chaucer has not made merely servile use of these elements on other occasions, and he does not humbly crook the knee to them here. The conventions are, in fact, cajoled into performing services never dreamed of.

The reference to books has its customary function: it suggests a learned substructure for what is to be the fabric of his creations. Just how seriously we are to take this defense of "olde appreved stories" may not at once be clear. Since its immediate purpose seems to be to contrast with the artificially "natural" world of May mornings and simple daisies ("Farewel my bok, and my devocioun!"), the first reaction may well be to take lightly the bookish talk by this bookish writer. But the daisy blooms here only for a summer's day, we should observe. Critics sometimes talk of the Prologue as if it were nothing but daisies, daisies, daisies all the way, but it is not. Books win out in the end. There will be a *balade* about famous ladies to be met only in story; the conversation in the vision is to center on Chaucer's writing; the Prologue is a prelude to an open raid on the literature of the past. Perhaps the first thirty-five lines should be taken more seriously rather than less.

There is good reason for thinking Chaucer might have been writing these opening lines in other than a flippant mood. He was about to retell stories from the classical treasury of myth and poetry; he would be using Ovid extensively, and the Virgilian tale of Dido, if not Virgil himself. His love and reverence for writers of the classical past were deeply felt. The devout mood at the conclusion of *Troilus and Criseyde* is revealing:

> But litel book, no makyng thow n'envie,
> But subgit be to alle poesye;
> And kis the steppes, where as thow seest pace
> Virgile, Ovide, Omer, Lucan, and Stace.
>   (V, 1789–1792)

Then, too, in Chaucer's day the reworking of classical material was in some part an act of piety, for it was an act of preservation and propagation. In telling of Dido and Thisbe, Lucrece and Medea, Chaucer would be helping to keep a heritage alive. It is unlikely that he was emulating the scholarly and educative performance of Boccaccio in *De Casibus Virorum Illustrium* and *De Claris Mulieribus*;[3] his free treatment of sources implies no concern for a comprehensive erudition, no intention to create an encyclopedic work of reference like Boccaccio's. And yet he knew he was serving as a transmitter of the past, even if his method was only to "reherce of al hir lyf the grete." His book, too, would become in its fashion a key of remembrance.

It is not as a historian or scholar, but as an artist that Chaucer demands to be taken seriously here. The demand is made obliquely, but it is revealed in the larger strategy of the Prologue as a whole. The demand appears in the opening lines and it determines the "plot" of the Prologue. The attention paid to "stories" and the writing of them and the artful pressure exerted on his audience to persuade it to follow him in what he as a writer of stories is about to do suggest sincerity of intention and an awareness of innovation.

What he is about to do, to put it quite baldly, is to tell a series of tales coming out of the classical pagan past and tell them for their own sake. The fiction of a martyrology of lovers supplies a very general theme, but it does not really explain the act of composing these tales. It helps to place them within a recognizable and acceptable convention, that of idealized love, which ostensibly explains their creation and makes easier their reception. But the rituals of courtly love rarely intrude in the narratives themselves.

The theme of "the praise of good ladies" will operate to the extent that Chaucer will make Cleopatra an innocent such as she never was before or has been since, and he will pass in silence over events in Medea's history which reek too much of blood or witches' brew. But he does not so treat his material that the characters emerge transformed from their classical originals into recognizably medieval agents in a courtly love drama. Pyramus and Thisbe are not a Tristram and Isolde; the story of Lucrece illustrates no principle from Andreas Capellanus. One has only to compare Chaucer's treatment of the Thisbe story with the Anglo-Norman version incorporated into the *Ovide moralisé*, or his telling of the tale of Philomena with Chrétien de Troyes's *Philomena*, also absorbed into the *Ovide*, to see what metamorphoses can be wrought in Ovid's materials by medievalization in the cause of *fine amours* and to distinguish what Chaucer himself did and did not do with his material.

If the offering of the narratives on the altar of the God of Love is at best a pretence, it is nonetheless the only nod to didactic convention which Chaucer makes. He eschews completely any moral or theological purpose and claims for his tales a purely secular intention. Two fourteenth-century treatments of much the same material that he used here make an instructive contrast. The *Ovide moralisé* retells the *Metamorphoses*, medievalizing freely as it goes. The Ovidian narratives, when they are on stage, are quite obviously presented for the sheer enjoyment and fascination of the stories themselves. But the narratives are at the same time embedded in a moralistic matrix: the figures and events of the narratives are given allegorical interpretations, and moral comment is provided. Similarly, Chaucer's friend John Gower, in his *Confessio Amantis*, placed his tales, many of them from Ovid, in a double framework of convention: courtly love and morality. Though Gower normally allows the narrative to go its own way during the telling, it is always accompanied by comment which makes it an exemplum of a principle in either courtly love or orthodox morality, or both.

This treatment of Ovid was not only completely acceptable to medieval taste, it was also in harmony with one medieval view of Ovid, and for practical purposes we may take Ovid as the core of the *Legend*. There were divided attitudes toward Ovid in the later Middle Ages, and as a consequence there were several Ovids.[4] One was the "moral Ovid." This is the Ovid we see in the Ovidian allegorizations, of which the *Ovide moralisé* is only the most extended example,[5] and in the sententious comments culled from his writings.[6] Even the plain Latin text of the *Metamorphoses* could be accompanied by moralistic glosses or prefatory *accessus* introducing him as a moralist whose "final cause" was to urge us toward virtue and deter us from vice and showing us through his stories of transformation that worldly things are but transitory.[7] The *Heroides* might be met in similar guise.[8]

Chaucer's Ovid, however, is not this moral teacher, but the master of poetic narrative. The absence from the *Legend* of the kind of moral comment or allegorical interpretation so often found with Ovidian material is sufficient indication that Chaucer is not presenting the moral Ovid here. I am not suggesting that this makes the *Legend* superior to the poetry of moral comment, only that this makes it different. When, as in Gower, moral poetry accompanied narrative, it could add a useful and enriching dimension to the work as a whole and, often, to the narrative itself. Aside from its qualities as moral verse—a distinctive type of verse to be judged by distinctive standards—it had a supportive value for audience and artist. It made what might seem troubling or offensive comfortable and pleasing, what might seem strange ultimately familiar, what might seem pointless or irreverent happily instructive. But Chaucer abandons such support for his performance. He sets out to achieve independence of treatment, relying on "these olde appreved stories" with no extraneous propping. All that his stories will "prove" is that particular women, and by implication many women, are faithful. Since there are playful overtones to this dictum throughout and since in the development of some of the tales even this moral is subordinated, his audience will enjoy precious few moments of moral *frisson*, however ardently they worship the God of Love.

To illustrate the point at issue, let us anticipate by taking a passage from the last story he tells, the *Legend of Hypermnestra*. On her wedding night Hypermnestra has been ordered by her father under pain of death to slay her bridegroom, Lyno.

> The nyght is wasted, and he fyl aslepe.
> Ful tenderly begynneth she to wepe;
> She rist hire up, and dredfully she quaketh,
> As doth the braunche that Zepherus shaketh,
> And bust were alle in Argon that cite.
> As cold as any frost now waxeth she;
> For pite by the herte hire streyneth so,
> And drede of deth doth hire so moche wo,
> That thryes doun she fyl in swich a were.
> She rist yit up, and stakereth her and there,
> And on hire hondes faste Ioketh she.
> "Allas! and shal myne hondes blody be?
> I am a mayde, and, as by my nature,
> And bi my semblaunt and by my vesture,
> Myne handes ben nat shapen for a knyf,
> As for to reve no man fro his lyf.
> What devel have I with the knyf to do?
> And shal I have my throte korve a-two?
> Thanne shal I blede, allas! and me beshende!
> And nedes-cost this thyng moste have an ende;
> Or he or I mot nedes lese oure lyf.
> Now certes," quod she, "syn I am his wif,
> And hath my feyth, yit is it bet for me
> For to be ded in wifly honeste
> Than ben a traytour lyvynge in my shame.
> Be as be may, for ernest or for game,
> He shal awake, and ryse, and gon his way,
> Out at this goter, or that it be day"—
> And wep ful tenderly upon his face,
> And in hyre armes gan hym to enbrace,
> And hym she roggeth and awaketh softe.
> And at a wyndow lep he fro the lofte,
> Whan she hath warned hym, and don hym bote.
>   (F 2678–2710)

The passage, whether a success or failure (to my mind, it is admirable), is surely what we can call total narrative. It stands or falls on the author's ability to compel our awareness of the scene and create a sympathetic or empathetic reaction by a selective visualization of the event, by action, by speech (a kind of soliloquy or interior monologue here), and by language. There is no appeal to any handy external code to secure a reaction. To be sure, the tale is a few lines short of conclusion, but there is no reason to think this ending would have been different from the others. It would have been another comment on the faithfulness of women—a sentiment obviously inadequate to support the tale. Hypermnestra stands in an area of imagined experience outside the code of courtly love and outside the dogmas of Christian morality. She is interesting and moving, if at all, as a fragile, isolated, frightened creature trapped in a fearful dilemma. There is perhaps some general, external motivation in her decision "to be ded in wifly honeste." But the reflection is part of the internal drama and serves mainly to show the movement of her thought. The next lines discard even this, however: "Be as be may, for ernest or for game, / He shal awake"—so that the decisive action seems finally to spring from some instinct of devotion below consciousness.

I repeat, the success or failure of the scene is not the issue here. The issue is the method Chaucer has deliberately chosen: to present a narrative without reference to the conventions or moralizings ordinarily appealed to. The drama inherent in the human experience being witnessed and the skill with which the experience has been realized for our witnessing are his sole counters in the game.

To move now to the opening lines of the Prologue is to see what Chaucer is preparing the ground for. He is about to tell stories from a past and alien age outside ordinary experience, certainly outside ordinary literary experience. If the phrase were not so hackneyed and an appeal to it not so grotesquely anachronistic, one might say he is suing for the willing suspension of disbelief. Certainly it is belief he is pleading for.[9] He puts the matter quite explicitly some lines later, when he is repeating his argument:

> But wherfore that I spak, to yive credence
> To olde stories and doon hem reverence,
> And that men mosten more thyng beleve
> Then men may seen at eye, or elles preve,—
> That shal I seyn, whanne that I see my tyme ....
>   (F 97–101)

In the opening lines, very boldly, he alludes to the common belief in heaven and hell in spite of the absence of ocular proof—boldly, because there will certainly be no appeal to Christian faith in the legends which follow.[10] But belief in things not seen is a fact in men's lives, and he appeals to it now to claim a hearing for his narratives:

> But God forbede but men shulde leve
> Wel more thing then men han seen with ye!
> Men shal not wenen every thing a lye
> But yf himself yt seeth, or elles dooth;
> For, God wot, thing is never the lasse sooth,
> Thogh every wight ne may it nat ysee.
> Bernard the monk ne saugh nat all, pardee!
>   (F 10–16)

In petitioning for belief in the tales found in old books, Chaucer seems particularly interested in a range of human experience found there somewhat wider than was normally accommodated in courtly literature:

> Than mote we to bokes that we fynde,
> Thurgh whiche that olde thinges ben in mynde,
> And to the doctrine of these olde wyse,
> Yeve credence, in every skylful wise,
> That tellen of these olde appreved stories
> Of holynesse, of regnes, of victories,
> Of love, of hate, of other sondry thynges,
> Of whiche I may not maken rehersynges.
> And yf that olde bokes were aweye,
> Yloren were of remembraunce the keye.
> Wel ought us thanne honouren and beleve
> These bokes, there we ban noon other preve.
>   (F 17–28)

"These olde appreved stories"—note the skillfully loaded participle— "Of holynesse, of regnes, of victories, / Of love, of hate, of other sondry thynges...." It is a challenge, and at the same time a waving of most attractive bait to an audience he wishes to lure onto unfamiliar territory. And they are, I insist, asked to believe, to "yeve credence." The pseudoauthority of the dream will not be invoked for the narratives themselves. Praise of ladies and in some general way of the power of love there will be, but not the familiar French courtly love poem. Later in the Prologue he makes this explicit:

> Ne I not who serveth leef, ne who the flour.
> Wel browken they her service or labour;

> For this thing is al of another tonne,
> Of olde storye, er swich stryf was begonne.
>   (F 193–196)

And finally, as I have said, he was discarding the moralizing matrix which might ease these stories into acceptance and transform them into didactic dramas whose substantiality could be denied once the pleasure of their telling had been enjoyed. These were to be presented as stories of real events occurring in the past. They were to be accepted as records of believable human experience, wondrous and perhaps troubling because human and because strange. The range of this experience and its substantiality and secularity are insisted upon: "Bernard the monk ne saugh nat all, pardee!"

But what of the worship of the daisy? There is no gainsaying the charm of the marguerite passages, and no wish to gainsay it. One must, however, suspect Chaucer most when he is being most guileless and simple-seeming. The Prologue, and especially the daisy sequence, we know with the wisdom of hindsight, was a farewell performance. He would never use the vision form again; he would never write "courtly" poetry or treat courtly love seriously again. The sequence is reminiscent of some of the most delightful moments in the *Parliament of Birds* and might suggest that he is still preoccupied with the phenomenon of courtly love, however amused his attention may be. There is some of that.

But note one thing. The daisy passages skirt dangerously close to the shoals of parody. We may allow for the ritual of the flower and the leaf and still find an exaggeration here that flirts with mockery. He does, in fact, entreat us to consider his case apart from these playful cults. If his plea avoids the necessity of taking sides, it also denies involvement. Further, the rival cults were related to forms of love and ultimately to certain values.[11] The narrator's worship of the daisy, however, has no such dimensions; it appears to be an end in itself. Unlike the French "Marguerite" poems, there is no evidence of a lady hovering in the background. What is most to the point, the daisy sequence serves to keep the narrator within an area cleanly removed from the experience of courtly love. The sequence uses all the language and postures of courtly love, not for the proper object of love, but for a daisy.[12]

It is possible, it seems to me, to read the praise of the daisy both as a beguiling tribute to a modest, charming flower and as a sly and cheeky mockery of the worshipful lover and the worship of love. The hyperbolic language and postures are typical for devotion to ladies, but comic for devotion to daisies. He is up at dawn to see the flower unfold in the sun: "That blisful sighte softneth al my sorwe" (F 50). He does her reverence, "As she that is of alle floures flour, / Fulfilled of al vertu and honour" (53–54). Here the hackneyed metaphor acquires a comic truth—this really is a flower.[13] He will love it till he dies, he swears he will, he is not lying: "They loved no Wight hotter in his lyve" (59). And at evening he runs to see her go to rest. Alas, he has not sufficient English, rhyme or prose, to praise it properly!

> She is the clernesse and the verray lyght
> That in this derke world me wynt and ledeth.
> The hert in-with my sorwfull brest yow dredeth
> And loveth so sore that ye ben verrayly
> The maistresse of my wit, and nothing I.
> My word, my werk ys knyt so in youre bond
> That, as an harpe obeieth to the bond
> And maketh it soune after his fyngerynge,
> Ryght so mowe ye oute of myn herte bringe
> Swich vois, ryght as yow lyst, to laughe or pleyne.
> Be ye my gide and lady sovereyne!
> As to myn erthly god to yow I calle,
> Bothe in this werk and in my sorwes alle.
>   (F 84–96)

It is the familiar lexicon of love, with more to come: "gledly desir," fire in the heart, "dredful hert and glad devocioun." He kneels before it (117), he sinks down leaning on his elbow to gaze at it all day (178–183) and rushes home once more when the flower closes so that he can be out in the morning to see it open. But in this last detail, as in one or two others, the daisiness of the daisy emerges through the ritualistic language. We are not far from the technique employed for Pertelote, where the language of gallantry competes frantically with the gallinaceous.

If there were ultimately some transference of this intensity of devotion to a lady or to the cause of Love in some fashion, all might yet be well. But there is none. The daisy worship, to be sure, has a function in the necessary psychology of the literary dream. It is the waking preoccupation which, acting as a tripping mechanism to set the dream in motion, will appear splendidly transformed but still recognizable within the content of the dream. The daisy becomes, of course, the key figure, Alceste, whose "habit grene," gold fret in the hair, and white crown with "flourouns smale" make of her a living, walking daisy. But she is never presented as the object of the kind of personal feeling presumably expressed in the adoration of the daisy before the dream begins. The dreamer's relationship with Alceste is formal. He praises her beauty, but his attitude is not the tribute of an adoring lover.

Indeed, since he is represented as not knowing who she is until he is told, there can be no question of anything of the kind. He is grateful for her intercession (F 271–281, 455–474) and he reverences her goodness when he learns who, in fact, she is.[14] Throughout the scene, however, the issue is Chaucer's role as a poet, not his relationship with Alceste or any other lady. What is established between the daisy and Alceste is a pictorial equivalence, not an emotional one.

The daisy unquestionably plays a role in the vision as a whole. It dissolves into Alceste and explains in part her intercession for the poet: "Wel hath she quyt me myn affeccioun, / That I have to hire flour, the dayesye" (523–524). But it is questionable whether these functions demand the kind of language and the intensity of feeling expressed. Since the emotion is not transferred to a more worthy object but remains focused on the daisy, the suspicion of parody remains.

Working against these considerations, however, is the welcome to spring passage which in F comes between the morning and the evening worship of the daisy, immediately preceding the dream (125–177). I can find no mockery in the rejoicing of the birds at winter's end and their survival, in their mating, or in the brief survey of key values in the code of love: Danger, Pity, Mercy, Right, Courtesy.[15] In G, the personifications are removed, and the coming-of-summer passage is shifted to the opening moments of the dream proper. The passage then becomes introductory background and prepares appropriately for the entrance of the God of Love and Alceste. This may have been the intended function of the passage in F; if so, it is rather awkwardly placed. If taken seriously, that is conventionally, as part of the pre-dream experience, it reduces the sense of parody lurking about the daisy passages. (The changes in G make parody a stronger possibility, I should say.) We shall have to settle for the smaller portion: The daisy sequence, however much it may invoke the language of love, places Chaucer quite outside any involvement with love. His involvement, like Ferdinand the Bull's, is with flowers. And this artfully contrived separation from love is of some importance in understanding the meaning of the dream itself. The parody, if it be there, merely pushes harder in the same direction.

The dream—Chaucer's last literary vision—is the most paradoxical of all Chaucer's creations. It is more paradoxical than the daring, experimental dream in the *House of Fame*, for that vision, once it sets off in its novel manner in an unexpected direction, follows a consistent course. (Coincidentally, perhaps, in that poem, too, we are invited to consider, though much more briefly, Chaucer, the poet.) The paradox here, however, is more extreme. All the trappings are conventional for the love vision and are conjured up with dazzling mastery: the glittering God of Love with his two fiery darts as red as coals and his wings spread angel-like; Alceste, the delicate, beautiful, and tenderhearted queen, green and gold and white, with her crown "of o perle fyn, oriental"; the charming *balade*; the troop of ladies making their gracious obeisance to the daisy; the easy ordering of the whole company according to rank; the dramatic and sustained silence. Never had Chaucer created with such strokes the milieu of the courtly love poem and the exquisite ambiance peculiar to that literary mode.

But this delicate, sugary creation is allowed to go to waste, like an elegant wedding cake left melting in the hot sun. The substance of the vision is the charge against the poet, the discussion which ensues, and the imposing of penance. It is a literary conversation concerning the work of a particular writer, and it might have been conducted against any background. This setting is perhaps the most appropriate for the specific topic of conversation, but it needed only a sketching in. The unusual magic Chaucer creates in evoking the world of love promises an experience that is never realized. It sustains the fictional figures of the God of Love and Alceste and the fiction of a charge of heresy against love. It also helps sustain the fiction that the tales which follow are comfortably within the courtly love tradition; that, perhaps, is its most potent purpose. The magic of the early moments of the dream is such that it has led readers, including most scholars, to overestimate the subservience of the legends to the code. Agreed, the legends tell of true women and faithless men, but they speak of love not as it is envisioned in the code or in the *Book of the Duchess*, the *Troilus*, and the *Knight's Tale*, or in Froissart and Machaut, but as a force more powerful and more protean in its forms and consequences than Troilus, or Criseyde, or even Diomede had dreamed of. Rape, suicide, abandonment, despair, callous abuse, and cynical seduction are the matter of his legends. The lady's Mercy and Pity and Danger have nothing to do with the world Chaucer is about to unfold. The rose garden has vanished, and the green meadow of the Prologue will win by its illusory art the pardon that he needs to escape over the garden wall from what has threatened to become a prison.

The contrast between the promise and the performance is not ironic. The fact is simply that the vision is largely preoccupied with matters alien to the surface considerations that have preceded it. Having shown how well he could do the old soft shoe number, Chaucer goes on to what here really concerns him, his career as a writer, and the kind of material he wishes to be free to work on. The basic image of the vision is suggestive: he is charged with heresy against love, and he is obliged to do penance. The image suggests feelings of guilt: he has to a degree violated the code, he wishes to be even more free of its limitations, and he will be. And the image suggests feelings of restriction: to write within the code is punishment. This is to be heavy-handed about a very light matter indeed, but if the basic images have any deeper significance than the merely playful, this is the direction in which it seems to me they point.

The literary discussion in the vision goes rather more directly toward much the same issue: what a writer may or should write about. Beneath the metaphor of heresy is a serious literary question. We know nothing about specific censorship or a royal directive or a queen's request. Even if we did, the conversation would still be worth analyzing for it shows us Chaucer's mind at work on a matter of great concern to him as an artist. The charge is that he has spoken against Love (322–331) and that he has slandered women (332–334). The form his penance takes is to write about true women and thus presumably to support Love (435–441, 481–491). The defense Alceste advances for the poet is, as Robert Payne has observed, really no defense at all.[16] It is all a glorious wriggling out from under. A god should be merciful. Perhaps Chaucer has been slandered; perhaps, since he is rather simpleminded ("nyce": 362, he didn't realize what he was doing or he was simply obeying someone's command; perhaps he repents now. After all, he was only translating what older clerks had written, which is not the same as writing it himself out of malice. Rather more pertinent is her observation that in many of his poems he has served the God of Love and that he also has translated works of "holynesse." Chaucer's own defense is still more to the point: he is not guilty. Whatever his author meant (that is, the man whose work Chaucer was translating), in *Troilus and Criseyde* and the *Romance of the Rose* his intention was to further "trouthe" in love and to warn against falseness. But his rational observation is cut short in a manner typical of the arbitrariness and irrationality of love:

> Lat be thyn arguynge,
> For Love ne wol nat countrepleted be
> In ryght ne wrong; and lerne that at me!
> (475–477)

Perhaps we can take this as a self-contained if playful argument and let it go at that. But the issue that runs through the argument and that appeared earlier, before the dream began, is the issue of the writer's material and the role of the writer in relation to his matter. Robert Payne is surely correct when he observes that the Prologue is preoccupied with literary matters, that it is what he calls something close to a treatise on the art of poetry.[17] I do not agree, however, that the issue is the quality of Chaucer's artistry.[18] That is not a subject he can properly write about, and he dismisses that question with a

joke as always: "Al be hir that he kan nat wel endite ..." (414). I do agree with
Payne that Chaucer is discussing the matter which the artist uses, but I do not
think that the question is the relation of reading or tradition to experience.
Or, if so, it is only indirectly or incidentally. The question is rather the proper
or allowable matter which a writer may use in his composition, the source
materials he may work with. In practical terms, this becomes the question of
what a writer may write about, "may" meaning what he finds important as a
subject for imaginative treatment and what he can persuade his audience to
accept as an important and allowable subject for their attention.[19] Literary
history is in part a record of the struggle with their audiences which writers
must periodically engage in to get a hearing for unfamiliar or unwelcome
material. In our time it has been the battle by twentieth-century writers to
include sexual experience as a legitimate subject for treatment, but the long
struggle from roughly the 1740s to the 1840s to secure a hearing for poetry
focusing on personal, private emotion is equally dramatic.

For Chaucer (and for late medieval writers in general), the evidence
suggests that this question took a special form. The poet is not so much an
"inventor," a spontaneous creator, as he is a transmitter and reworker of already
existing materials. He provides "the key of remembrance," as Robert Payne
has reminded us, and the phrase is Chaucer's in this Prologue. The attitudes
expressed and the language used in the Prologue are revealing on this score
and lead to the heart of the issue. "Translating" is an important activity of
a medieval writer; in a sense, it *is* the activity of the writer. The distinction
between Chaucer's translation of the *Roman de la rose* and his creation, from
Boccaccio's *Il Filostrato*, of the *Troilus* is, we should notice, blurred. The charge
is that Chaucer has hindered Love's servants with his "translacioun":

> For in pleyn text, withouten nede of glose,
> Thou hast translated the Romaunce of the Rose,
> That is an heresye ayeins my lawe,
> And makest wise folk fro me withdrawe;
> And of Creseyde thou hast seyd as the lyste,
> That maketh men to wommen lasse triste....
> (328–333)

There is perhaps a slight distinction in the language used about the two works
here, but Chaucer's responsibility is the same for both. Alceste's language,
however, suggests no distinction between the two:

> And eke, peraunter, for this man ys nyce,
> He myghte doon yt, gessyng no malice,

> But for he useth thynges for to make;
> Hym rekketh noght of what matere he take.
> Or him was boden maken thilke tweye
> Of som persone, and durste yt nat withseye;
> Or him repenteth outrely of this.
> He ne hath nat doon so grevously amys,
> To translaten that olde clerkes writen,
> As thogh that he of malice wolde enditen
> Despit of love, and had himself yt wroght.
>   (362–372)

Here, both works appear to be things "made," and also things "translated." A distinction between these two works (*Troilus* and the *Romance*) and things he himself might have "wroght" is suggested, but it is not clear what things "wroght" would be. Entirely original works? Such works as the *House of Fame*, perhaps? A few lines later, however, Alceste makes no distinction between this work and a number of others, including Chaucer's reworking of Boccaccio's *Il Teseide*: "He made the book that hight the Hous of Fame," and also the *Book of the Duchess*, the *Parliament of Birds*, "And al the love of Palamon and Arcite," and "many an ympne ... / That highten balades, roundels, virelayes" (417–423). In matters of holiness "He hath in prose translated Boece, / And maad the lyf also of Seynt Cecile." The distinction implied by the language here is almost meaningless. The Life of St. Cecilia, at least as we have it in the Second Nun's Tale, is a poetic translation.[20] It is, to be sure, a somewhat free, poetic translation, as opposed to the more literal prose translation of Boethius, but any hope that this fact will fully account for the verb "maad" is somewhat dashed when we note that elsewhere Chaucer himself (or, rather, the Second Nun) calls it a "translacioun."[21] And in the next line of the Prologue Alceste says, "He made also, goon ys a gret while, / Origenes upon the Maudeleyne," a lost work which almost certainly was a translation.[22] Finally, in the G version (344) Alceste says, "he wrot the Rose and ek Crisseyde."

This blurring of distinctions which a nineteenth-century writer, say, would certainly maintain implies a somewhat different attitude toward the literary process from our attitude today. It does not necessarily imply that Chaucer was not aware of any difference between translating the *Roman de la Rose* and transforming *Il Filostrato* into *Troilus and Criseyde*. But it does imply that in some way he thought of the two activities as similar, even identical. One important similarity, I suggest, is that both involved transmission of already existing "matter" from another language, with such additions and subtractions as might seem necessary.

This in turn suggests the importance of the "matter" for the medieval writer, and an attitude toward it. It consists, roughly speaking, of the written materials—literature, history, moral writings, and so forth, inherited from the past, both distant and recent. The literary artist is the transmitter of this heritage. Or, to put it less passively, this heritage is a principal source of his own art and his own inspiration. He selects what he will write about, not from "experience" or "imagination," but from this accumulated body of tradition. The act of "creating" is not primarily the creating of the material. Chaucer, in his greatest poetry, has clearly not set out to "invent" in this sense. The creative activity, or at least an important part of it, is of another kind. The artist must *find* his material, somewhere, somehow. The act of finding material involves not merely the poet's learning or the act of discovery through reading but the act of selecting, the act of choice. What this becomes, finally, is an act of intense imaginative response. It is, in its own way, much like "inspiration." In a long addition to G (267–312), the God of Love very pointedly discusses this problem of choice:

> Was there no good matere in thy mynde,
> Ne in alle thy bokes ne coudest thow nat fynde
> Som story of wemen that were goode and trewe?
>   (G 270–272)

He proceeds to enumerate some of these sources, noting particularly the Roman and Greek authors in his library of sixty books, and concludes by emphasizing the problem of choice once more:

> But yit, I seye, what eyleth the to wryte
> The draf of storyes, and forgete the corn?
>   (G 311–312)

In F, Alceste's charge of simple-sooth foolishness implies the same problem, though more obscurely: "Hym rekketh noght of what matere he take" (365). *Take* is the operative word here.[23]

The matter an artist takes is an important part of the creative process. It still is, of course. But for a medieval writer intent on "creating" a work of some value, more frequently than for writers of later generations, the choice would be from traditional matter, "olde bokes." So talk about the sources to be used involves also the themes and the areas of human experience which a writer will be treating and which he will be asking his audience to accept as worthy of their attention. It is also, as I have said, a question of what his imagination responds to most intensely. This is the issue, I believe, in the heresy scene.

The weight of this scene, the sheer amount of time spent reviewing what Chaucer has written and discussing what he ought to write (for ought, read what he is planning to write), demands such an interpretation. Ordinarily Chaucer is dramatically self-effacing. Here, even though he makes himself the butt of a joke, I cannot believe he thrusts himself forward merely to prance about comically in the limelight. He is using himself in this way in order to announce what he is going to do in the *Legend* and to justify it. There would be no need to spend all the time he does on the announcement if the legends were, in fact, what he makes them appear to be, merely orthodox items in the literature of courtly love. The G addition suggests several characteristics in his material which might disturb his audience. One is the violence of the tales (see F 22–24):

> They chose to be ded in sondry wyse,
> And deiden, as the story wol devyse;
> And some were brend, and some were cut the hals,
> And some dreynt, for they wolden not be fals.
>   (G 290–293)

Another is their purely pagan character; they operate outside the familiar morality of both Christianity and courtly love:

> And this thing was nat kept for holynesse,
> But al for verray vertu and clennesse,
> And for men schulde sette on hem no lak;
> And yit they were hethene, al the pak....
>   (G 296–299)

The charge of heresy and the imposition of penance work then to this purpose: They suggest impatience with the more orthodox poetry of courtly love, and a "guilty" intention to abandon this for other kinds of writing (an abandonment already foreshadowed in the *Troilus*). The device enables him to suggest some of his problems as an artist, primarily the problem of "creative" choice. It lends an illusion of orthodoxy to the new kind of story he is introducing, which is written at the command of the God of Love and his queen as an act of penance. Unless he behaves too outrageously in the stories that follow, he can, under cover of the fiction he has contrived, do almost anything he wishes. The selection of the theme of "faithful women" permits him to use freely material in Ovid and other writers, gives him the frame he needs as a vehicle for the "publication" of a series of tales, and leaves him with a toehold on the old orthodoxy of courtly love. He apparently has achieved the maximum maneuverability he felt he could win for himself, granted the character and tastes of his audience and the role he had played as a writer heretofore. All in all, it seems a successful, even a brilliant device, but we must see it for what it is and not be deluded by it.

We should be careful, also, not to minimize the importance of the strategic victory which Chaucer wins by this means. It is a quiet declaration of independence on an issue of central importance in the creative activity of a medieval writer. The material Chaucer selects for the legends which follow is essentially alien to the code of courtly love. By ignoring its prescriptions and treating love as a varied human experience rather than a ritualized process (however psychologically relevant this may be), the tales are an oblique challenge to the code. Once freed, Chaucer could work with material yet more alien, material even richer in possibilities for an artist of his widely ranging interests and varied talents: secular legend, folk tale, beast fable, fabliau. The *Legend* does reveal the development of several techniques of his art, as we shall see. But if we consider for the moment only the kind of material used, we can see that to step from the *Troilus* to the *Legend* to the *Canterbury Tales* is easier than to step from the *Troilus* directly to the *Canterbury Tales*. A struggle for freedom of choice in the materials of his art is waged and, under the guise of capitulation, won in the Prologue. Charm is used here, as it has been used on many occasions, in the interests of seduction and conquest. And Chaucer's battle sign has been not a dragon or a lion or even a rose, but the ordinary daisy. Some centuries later Walt Whitman went him one better and used grass for much the same purpose. The analogy, I suggest, is worth reflecting on. In its simplicity and "naturalness," in its commonplace quality, the daisy is not unlike Whitman's leaves of grass. It serves to break through not to a democratic poetry, but to a poetry more of the world and less of the garden, to a realm of experience beyond the patterned and polite, the limited and predictable emotions and movements of courtly love. Given this significance, the daisy is a proper object for Chaucer's passion, the artist's passion for his freshest vision.

Notes

1. For an admirably succinct review of the controversy over the question of priority up to 1907, see Eleanor P. Hammond, *Chaucer: A Bibliographical Manual* (New York, Macmillan Company, 1908), pp. 381–382. For later bibliography on the controversy, see Dudley David Griffith, *Bibliography of Chaucer: 1908–1953* (Seattle, University of Washington Press, 1955), pp. 272–282. The case for the priority of F (formerly called B) over G (formerly called A) was argued by John Livingston Lowes in two magisterial

articles: "The Prologue to *The Legend of Good Women* as Related to the French *Marguerite* Poems and the *Filostrato*," *PMLA*, 19 (1904), 593–683, esp. pp. 635–683; and "The Prologue to *The Legend of Good Women* Considered in Its Chronological Relations," *PMLA*, 20 (1905), 749–864. The latter assigns dates for the two Prologues: the summer or autumn of 1386 for F (see pp. 753–779); sometime, possibly soon, after Anne of Bohemia's death on June 7, 1394, for G (see pp. 780–781). Lowes's additional supporting arguments for this approximate date of G (see pp. 782–801) are less substantial; his argument that the legends themselves were all or largely written before the (F) Prologue to the *Legend* (pp. 802–818) is subjective and has never been accepted. The argument for the priority of F, however, has never been convincingly challenged.

2. For example, George Lyman Kittredge, *Chaucer and His Poetry* (Cambridge, Mass., Harvard University Press, 1915), p. 152; John Livingston Lowes, *Geoffrey Chaucer* (Oxford, Eng., Clarendon Press, 1934) p. 126.

3. Aage Brusendorf suggested that the Latin titles of the individual legends were modeled on Boccaccio's chapter headings in *De Claris Mulieribus*; see *The Chaucer Tradition* (London, Humphrey Milford, Oxford University Press, 1925), pp. 144–145.

4. For a quick glance at medieval attitudes toward Ovid, see L. P. Wilkinson, *Ovid Recalled* (Cambridge, Eng., Cambridge University Press, 1955), pp. 366–398. See also F. Munari, *Ovid im Mittelalter* (Zurich, Artemis Verlags-AG, 1960), and Simone Viarre, *La survie d'Ovide dans la littérature scientifique des XII*e *et XIII*e *siècles*, Centre d'Études Supérieures de Civilisation Médiévale (Poitiers, 1966).

5. For details, see Lester K. Born, "Ovid and Allegory," *Speculum*, 9 (1934), 362–379, esp. 370–379. The attitude toward allegory expressed there is somewhat out of date.

6. See *ibid.*, p. 371, for one instance. In the *Speculum Historiale* of Vincent de Beauvais, chaps. cvii to cxxii of Book VI consist of *flores* and *flosculi* from Ovid's writings.

7. Some of these accessus are printed in Karl Young, "Chaucer's Appeal to the Platonic Deity," *Speculum*, 19 (1944), 1–13, specifically 4–10. See also Gustaw Przychocky, *Accessus Ovidiani*, in Polska Akademia Umiejetnosci Cracow, Wydzial Filologiczny, Rozprawy Akademia Umiejetnosci, ser. III, 4 (1911); Edwin A. Quain, "The Medieval Accessus ad Auctores," *Traditio*, 3 (1945), 215–264; and R. B. C. Huygens, *Accessus ad Auctores*, Collection Latomus, XV (Berchem-Bruxelles, 1954).

8. Born, "Ovid and Allegory," p. 377, provides one example. And a brief moral lesson directed to the business of love is suggested in the "Prologo" which introduces almost every epistle in the Italian translation of the Heroides by "Filippo," which Chaucer may have used: *Volgarizzamento delle Pistole d'Ovidio* ... (Florence, 1819), pp. 1, 27, 40–41, 49, 60, 80, 100, 107, 121, 139, 156, 171(?), 196. An example from the prologue to Medea will suffice: "La 'ntenzione d'Ovidio principalmente ene di riprendere li sperguiri amanti, i quali sono piu vaghi della grolia vana, che di mantenere la chiara veritade. E spezialmente intende di riprendere li nobili e possenti uomini, le cui opere sono tutte in essemplo ..." (pp. 107–108). Chaucer's martyrology is not this tendentious, even within the framework of its concern for love.

9. For example, "men shulde leve," "Yeve credence," "yive I feyth and ful credence": F 10, 20, 31.

10. Cf. G 296–300, where he calls attention, through the God of Love, to the fact that the women he is being urged to write about were pagans: "And yit they were hethene, al the pak...."

11. See Derek A. Pearsall, "Introduction," *The Floure and the Leafe* ... (London, Thomas Nelson and Sons, Ltd., 1962), pp. 22–33.

12. If the passage expresses a devotion to Queen Anne, as has been suggested see F. N. Robinson, *The Works of Geoffrey Chaucer*, 2nd ed. [Boston, Houghton Mifflin Company, 1957], pp. 839–840) she also is an object removed from the realm of courtly love, and the language is a recognizable rhetoric for praising her, nothing more. That Chaucer is referring to his lady, whoever this might be, seems an unlikely reading of the text. Those few lines which might suggest a real woman (i.e., F 94) do not necessarily bear this meaning. The whole weight of Chaucer's talk of love is directed toward the daisy. No real lady ever emerges from behind the flower; if she was there, she was sadly ignored. Nor is Alceste, the figure related to the daisy, his lady. See below, n. 14. Dorothy Bethurum's cry of vexation is understandable but mistaken; it reveals how far beyond the believable toward parody Chaucer has pushed matters: "The daisy is, of course, some woman; not even Wordsworth could find in that miserable little English daisy 'the clernesse and the verray lyght / That in this derke world me wynt and ledeth.'" See "Chaucer's Point of View As Narrator in the Love Poems," *PMLA*, 74 (1959), 516.

13. It is repeated at F 185, but omitted in G. Peter Dronke discusses the history of the image, with many examples, in *Medieval Latin and the Rise of European Love Lyric*, 2 vols., 2nd ed. (Oxford, Eng., Clarendon Press, 1968), I, 181–192. (On the range of experience encompassed by Ovid's *Heroides* [and *Amores*], see *ibid.*, I, 163.)

14. The "my lady" of the refrain in F (255, 262, 269) and the phrase "my lady sovereyne" used by the poet a few lines later (F 275) is either a direct translation of the "ma dame" in his French original (see Robinson, *Chaucer*, note on these lines, p. 843), or more probably the formal "my lady"; she is not his "lady" in the courtly love sense. The G text does not contain this possible ambiguity. Elsewhere in F Alceste is "a quene" (213), "this lady" (248, 341), "his quene" (302). The God of Love calls her "my lady" at 454.

15. In the context of the "natural" world evoked by the daisy itself, it is just possible that these other elements from the natural world, the birds, are in some danger of shedding their conventional character and becoming real birds again. In which case, the conventions of love are set against realities of nature, and their artificiality is threatened with comic exposure. There is some insistence in the passage on their bird nature: e.g., the reference to the fowler (conventional enough in other contexts but not inevitably so here), and especially the lines whose tone is otherwise rather puzzling:

> Yeldyng honour and humble obeysaunces
> To love, and diden hire other observaunces
> That longeth onto love and to nature;
> Construeth that as yow lyst, I do no cure.
>   (F 149–152)

The illusion does seem at moments to be under attack.

16. Robert Payne, *The Key of Remembrance: A Study of Chaucer's Poetics* (New Haven, Connecticut, Yale University Press, 1963), p. 103.

17. *Ibid.*, pp. 56, 63–66, 91–111.

18. *Ibid.*, pp. 99, 101.

19. We know very little about Chaucer's relationship with his audience and about the composition of that audience. Ruth Crosby worked out some of the influences of oral presentation on his poetry in two articles, "Oral Delivery in the Middle Ages," *Speculum*, 11 (1936), 88–110, and "Chaucer and the Custom of Oral Delivery," *Speculum*, 13 (1938), 413–432. So did Bertrand Bronson in "Chaucer's Art in Relation to His Audience," in

Five Studies in Literature, University of California Publications in English, Vol. 8, No. 1 (Berkeley, University of California Press, 1940), pp. 1–53. A strong sense of Chaucer's sensitivity to his audience emerges from the studies, but we learn very little about the nature of his audience, except for Bronson's praise of its sophistication (pp. 52–53). There are some revealing moments in his poetry, however, in which we catch Chaucer being very much concerned about his audience's reaction and working adeptly to win their acceptance or at the very least to ward off their displeasure. *Troilus*, based on an Italian original (not something from the familiar and accepted French literary culture) and studying with unusual intensity and detail a courtly love affair without the usual accompaniment of battle and adventure, apparently struck Chaucer as sufficiently unfamiliar fare to make advisable meeting the objections he anticipated; hence his comments to his audience at the beginning of Book II, lines 22–49. For all his lightness of tone, he is clearly concerned about the reaction of the women in his audience to his story of Criseyde's unfaithfulness when the narrative is ended (V, 1772–1785). Pushing into unknown waters in the *Canterbury Tales*, he prepares his audience most carefully for the novel kinds of narrative and especially for the crude action and crude language of some of the tales to come in his apology at the end of the *General Prologue*, A 725–746. When the first of these ungenteel narratives, the *Miller's Tale*, is about to begin, he prepares his audience again, making it quite clear what kind of story this and the *Reeve's Tale* following will be, repeating his apology and warding off any objection by suggesting to his audience that they can choose another tale instead (A 3167–3186). There is no mistaking how intently and how ingeniously Chaucer labors here to lead his audience into his material and to control their reaction. When the *Miller's Tale* is finished, he is very careful to say that the tale amused most of the pilgrims (several of whom were "gentils") and grieved none but Oswald the Reeve, and that was of course for purely personal reasons. Thereafter he feels no need to intervene. All of this suggests that, when Chaucer did something new, he felt obliged to persuade his audience to move with him. It also suggests a somewhat conservative audience or a Chaucer not completely confident that he can present anything he wishes to his audience, or both. Alfred David has some interesting comments on this question in "The Man of Law vs. Chaucer: A Case in Poetics," *PMLA*, 82 (1967), 217–225. Boccaccio's defense, at the opening of Book IV of *Il Decamerone*, of the kind of tales he was telling, and his "apology" in his Epilogue, both directed especially at hostile comments from the ladies in his audience, are a tempting parallel. See Aldo D. Scaglione, *Nature and Love in the Later Middle Ages* (Berkeley and Los Angeles, University of California Press, 1963), pp. 102–113, 198–201. But Italian culture is too distant in space and tradition to permit us to draw any hard conclusions.

20. For Chaucer's sources see G. H. Gerould, "The Second Nun's Prologue and Tale," in *Sources and Analogues of Chaucer's Canterbury Tales*, ed. W. F. Bryan and Germaine Dempster (New York, The Humanities Press, 1958), pp. 664–684.

21. *Canterbury Tales*, G 24–25; see also 79–83.

22. Robinson, *Chaucer*, p. 845, note on 417ff. See also John P. McCall, "Chaucer and the Pseudo Origen *De Maria Magdalena*: A Preliminary Study," *Speculum*, 46 (1971), 491–509.

23. In the F Prologue the God of Love touches on the problem of the writer's choice just before the vision ends:

> Thise other ladies sittynge here arowe
> Ben in thy balade, yf thou kanst hem knowe,
> And in thy bookes alle thou shalt hem fynde.
> Have hem now in thy legende al in mynde;

I mene of hem that ben in thy knowynge.
For here ben twenty thousand moo sittynge
Than thou knowest, goode wommen alle,
And trewe of love, for oght that may byfalle.
Make the metres of hem as the lest—
　　(F 554–562)

This passage is omitted in G, and I suspect that the lengthy passage added in G, the one I have been discussing, replaces it and expands upon it. The issue is also present by implication from the beginning of the Prologue in F as well as G in the introductory discussion of "olde bokes."

RICHARD NEUSE

Epic Theater:
The Comedy *and* The Canterbury Tales
(The Knight and the Miller)

In terms of genre, I have argued so far, *The Canterbury Tales* takes its place in the line of epic, particularly as that has been redefined by Dante's allegorical poem. In this chapter I want to pursue the argument by exploring another feature common to both poems. This is also part of epic tradition—hence my use of the phrase "epic theater"[1]—but in the works under consideration it is developed, as I intend to show, to a point of special structural and thematic significance.

When Aristotle praised Homer for the basically dramatic character of his epics, the link between epic and drama was perhaps not altogether obvious. Homer, Aristotle writes,

> deserves our admiration for many reasons, but particularly because he alone of the (epic) poets is not unaware what it is one should be composing [himself]. Namely, the poet himself ought to do as little talking as possible; for it is not by virtue of that that he is a poet. Now the others are on stage themselves, in competition, the whole time, and imitate but little and occasionally, whereas he, after a few words by way of preface, immediately brings on stage a man or a woman or some other character, and not one characterless but (all) having character.[2]

From *Chaucer's Dante: Allegory and Epic Theater in* The Canterbury Tales: pp. 105–139. © 1991 by The Regents of the University of California.

Whether Dante or Chaucer ever read this passage we do not know, but they might have done so in William of Moerbeke's Latin translation of the *Poetics* (1278).[3] In any case, the idea that the Homeric epics represent the true origin of Greek drama was probably familiar to them from a text like Evanthius's *De Fabula* (fourth century A.D.), which was widely known in the Middle Ages.[4] Evanthius wrote that

> although ... those who have gone through ancient documents find that Thespis was the first inventor of tragedy and believe that Eupolis together with Cratinus and Aristophanes is the father of old comedy, nonetheless Homer, who is the most ample source of almost all matters poetical, also provided the examples for these songs and prescribed, as it were, a certain law for their works: he is shown to have made the *Iliad* on the model of a tragedy, the *Odyssey* in the image of a comedy. For after he established such a great example, highly ingenious imitators reduced to order and divided up what until then was being written with boldness but without polish or any of the seemliness and lightness of touch that became the practice afterward.[5]

The original reason for considering the Homeric narratives the very model and fountainhead of drama would seem to be their role in bridging the gap, as it were, between an oral and a literate stage in Greek society. A modern scholar comments on the *Poetics* passage as follows:

> To Aristotle's mind *Homer is not really so much a narrator as a dramatist*. He is just that epic poet who narrates least and dramatizes most. Aristotle does not dodge the paradox, he states it boldly—even, perhaps, with a little too much *insouciance*. Homer, he says, uses straight narrative only for a brief prologue, then immediately "brings on stage" a "character" (who then takes over and speaks for himself). The other poets remain on the stage themselves all the way through. But how else, after all, *should* a narrative poet behave? The paradox is certainly not a sign of different "strata" in the *Poetics*. It is inherent in Aristotle's conception of Homer as a man between two worlds: epic poet, but also precursor and in a sense inventor of the drama. If this is treason to the epic as such, it springs from allegiance to a greater cause, that of poetry as a whole, of which tragedy is the exemplar and Homer was the first prophet.[6]

As "a man between two worlds" Homer represents for Aristotle a link with an earlier stage of the culture when the verbal arts were regarded as essentially performative. The special status of the Homeric epics in Athenian society is accordingly attributable to their dramatic character, the fact that they bring to life *and keep alive in the present*, as only dramatic tragedies will be able to do, a heroic past in its human individuality, where no one is characterless but all have character (*ouden aethes all' echonta ethos*). The polemic against Homer of Aristotle's teacher Plato would seem to support this idea. It is based on the conviction (as Eric Havelock has argued) that Homer stands for a concrete, rhythmic mode of cultural transmission that Plato sought to replace by a more abstractly philosophic *paideia*.

Plato's attack, accordingly, focuses on Homer's *mimesis*, by which he understood, in Havelock's words, the oral poet's

> power to make his audience identify almost pathologically and certainly sympathetically with the content of what he is saying. And hence also when Plato seems to confuse the epic and dramatic genres, what he is saying is that any poetised statement must be designed and recited in such a way as to make it a kind of drama within the soul both of the reciter and hence also of the audience. This kind of drama, this way of reliving experience in memory instead of analysing and understanding it, is for him "the enemy."[7]

The very characteristic, in other words, that for Plato is an objectionable survival of preliteracy becomes for his disciple Aristotle a mark of Homer's superiority to later epic poets, who lacked his understanding of "the poet's duty: that is, to imitate (*mimeisthai = poiein*), not merely to talk (*legein*)."[8]

In the Europe of Dante's and Chaucer's time a shift similar to that marked by the Homeric poems was taking place, from a largely oral to a largely literate kind of society. If this rough parallel allows for any inferences regarding the "mimetic" character of the *Comedy* and the *Tales*, they seem rather more plausible for the latter than for the former. In *The Canterbury Tales* the Chaucerian poet presents himself at once as minstrel performing for a "popular" audience (*Sir Thopas*) and as bookish *translateur* (*Melibee*). The poet of the *Comedy* does of course speak, and stage himself, to his audience, but he usually addresses it as "reader." What I have called the theatrical character of these works is thus an effect less of their cultural-historical situation than of a particular poetics. One of the "norms" of epic narrative, as Thomas Greene has shown, is its alternation of different kinds of dramatic scenes.[9]

My discussion of "epic theater" accordingly focuses, in the first instance
on the inner constitution of the works concerned and largely slights their
historical context, including such intriguing questions as their relation to the
actual drama of the time and late-medieval ideas about the staging of plays,
especially Seneca's, in antiquity. An example of the latter especially relevant
to my notion of epic theater is to be found in the early-fourteenth-century
commentary on Seneca's *Hercules Furens* by the English Dominican Friar
Nicholas Trevet:

> And note that tragedies and comedies were customarily recited
> in the theater in the following manner. The theater was a
> semicircular platform in the midst of which there was a small
> structure called the stage, consisting of a scaffold on which the
> poet declaimed verses; beyond this scaffold there were mimes
> who imitated the declamation of the verses by corporeal gestures,
> adapting them to whatever character might be speaking.[10]

The spectacle of the poet on a scaffold stage declaiming his verses while
mimes act out their different roles by bodily movements—this fits well
with our discussion in the preceding chapter of the poet's allegorical
self-multiplication. In addition, the mimes serve as an apt metaphor
for the audience that simultaneously reads and participates in the epic
theater.

The distinction between "mimetic" and "diegetic" narrative, to use
the Aristotelian terms,[11] can be clarified by the distinction Keir Elam draws
between what he calls the "ostended" world of drama and the "represented"
world of narrative:

> Classical narrative is always oriented towards an explicit *there
> and then*, towards an imaginary "elsewhere" set in the past and
> which has to be evoked for the reader through predication and
> description. Dramatic worlds, on the other hand, are presented to
> the spectator as "hypothetically actual" constructs, since they are
> "seen" in progress "here and now" without narratorial mediation.
> Dramatic performance metaphorically translates conceptual
> access to possible worlds into "physical" access, since the
> constructed world is apparently *shown* to the audience—that is,
> ostended—rather than being stipulated or described.[12]

The epic obviously cannot dispense with "narratorial mediation," but it does
have various ways of creating a textual counterpart of an "ostended world."

One is the elaboration of larger-than-life characters, the mere invocation of whose names can import into the narrative, Atlas-fashion, the aura of an entire world. Then there are the gods, not only participants in the action, but also spectators; hovering over the reader as well as the heroes, they hint at a world theater encompassing all.

Indeed, central to "epic theater" is the idea of an action presented as being observed even as it takes place, and the awareness of being observed of those involved in the action. The action, in other words, is also a transaction with an audience of gods or other characters. And this transaction parallels in various ways the implicit relationship between the narrative and its audience of readers or listeners. There is of course never more than a parallel here; the narrator never quite "disappears" into the characters, the reader never quite merges with the fictive audience. But in its relation to the reader the text will constantly strive for a self-exhibition like that of its characters; like them it will, in Aristotle's words, always have character and never be characterless (i.e., a mere function of the plot).

Narrative theatricality, in other words, involves a heightened reflexiveness, a heightened self-consciousness; and this self-consciousness in turn generates a more than usual "audience participation," permitting readers to accept characters as analogues of themselves, physical, social, yet inward and desiring they know not what or why.[13] Thematically, the epic theater of the *Comedy* and *The Canterbury Tales* points to a goal beyond the human image, to an apprehension of the human person or subject in its concrete, worldly manifestation.

What, now, is the place of the *Comedy* in the line of descent from the "theatrical" Homeric epic? With the advent of Christianity we would expect the spectator gods to be displaced by the all-seeing eye of God, the "sighte above," as the Knight calls it (I.1672). But that is not exactly what happens in Dante's poem. By the end of the *Paradiso* it is apparent that the tripartite cosmos is also a world theater (like Seneca's, cited in the next chapter), except that the spectators now are not the gods but the saints seated in the celestial Rose, which is really a vast amphitheater or colosseum,[14] where they have an unobstructed view of everything: looking up, they see God's face; looking *down*, they can observe the human scene.

This last detail is, however, already made evident in canto II of the *Inferno*, during the so-called "prologue in heaven," which unobtrusively points ahead to the amphitheater of the *Paradiso*. There Lucy asks Beatrice:

> ché non soccorri quei che t'amò tanto,
> ch'uscì per te de la volgare schiera?
> Non odi to la pieta del suo pianto,

non vedi tu la morte che 'l combatte
su la fiumana ove 'l mar non ha vanto—?
(104–8)

(why have you not helped him who loves you so
that—for your sake—he's left the vulgar crowd?
Do you not hear the anguish of his cry?
Do you not see the death he wars against
upon that river ruthless as the sea?)

Her questions indicate that in their activities, in their struggle with visible and invisible foes, even in the expression of their most intimate feelings, the inhabitants of the *Comedy*'s cosmos are seen and heard by a heavenly audience.

That heavenly audience is important. It means, in the first place, that the various scenes which the Pilgrim confronts, and by which the *Comedy*, like the classical epic, advances, are a drama that is judged by human, not by fixed unearthly standards. In the second place, it means that it is not just a "drama of the mind," in Francis Ferguson's phrase,[15] but a historical drama of sorts with a cast of thousands, though it has its origin and, we might say, its raison d'être, in the autobiographical fiction that is its central plot. Let us look more closely at this fiction.

It looks at first as though what is involved is a simple split—common in autobiographical and confessional literature—of the Dantean "subject" into two, an earlier and a later, Pilgrim and Poet. This is essentially how Singleton and those, like Gianfranco Contini, who follow him, view the matter. For them the "I" of the *Comedy* is divided into an allegorical Everyman figure and a real individual on a literal journey through the otherworld. I cite at length from Singleton's well-known discussion of this point, first, because he endorses the idea for which I am arguing here of Dante's basically dramatic approach to his fiction, and second, to show that his simple dichotomy of the *Comedy*'s subject does not do full justice to Dante's fiction.

In a sense it might be regretted that somehow a curtain does not fall at the end of Canto II *Inferno* to mark off the first two cantos of the poem for the prologue which they are. Such a marker would serve to point up some fundamental distinctions as to time and place in the poem, distinctions which must be grasped if we are to see the true nature and outline of its allegory. Just there, at that point, some such device would help us to realize that in the prologue scene we are set up on the stage of this life; that on this first stage we may speak of the actor or actors in the first person plural, as "we," even as the poem suggests in its first adjective. This is the way of our life, the life of soul, this is our predicament. It ought to be the scene we know best, the most familiar scene in the world—and in the poem. Here lies the way of our life. The features of it, the things here that we can make out; a hill, a wood, these beasts, all have their existence there where the *fiumana* runs which Lucia sees from Heaven.... Here we are in no space-occupying place. Then: curtain—to rise again on the first act of this play, on a scene before the doorway to Hell which is an abyss that is space-occupying and which, on Dante's map, may be located. The change in scene is not only a change in place. Time has changed. For we do not forget that this is a remembered journey (and hence may not really be given in dramatic form). The man who went that way has now returned. His journey was there and it was then. And time in yet another sense has changed. Of the scene and of the journey in the prologue we might say "our life." Not so beyond the door. The journey beyond is too exceptional an event to bear any but a singular possessive. It was then, and there, and it was his journey. Whereas in the prologue (even though the tense is past) in so far as we might see this as "our" journey, it takes place, as to time, in a kind of "ever-present," with Everyman as actor.

And yet, no sooner have we imagined a curtain at this point than we could wish it away. It might help us with certain essential distinctions. But the poet has not wanted there any such discontinuity as it might suggest. His problem was not Augustine's "how shall I tell of movements of soul in concrete images." His language is already given to the poet and he uses it with full assurance. His problem is to manage to leave this scene, which is not space-occupying, and to attain to that scene which is; to remove a wayfarer from this scene, where he functions in a mode open to a plural "we," on to a scene and a journey where his role is a most singular one. "Our" journey must become "his" journey, "his" must arise out of "our." A literal and very real journey of a living man, a man in a body of flesh and bone, is to be launched forth from a place that does not occupy space. A curtain cannot help, indeed can only defeat. Only a movement within poetic ambiguity at its fullest power could bring about an organic transition in these terms.[16]

As with almost everything else Singleton has written on the *Comedy*, this strikes me as extraordinarily interesting and illuminating even when, or precisely when, it provokes disagreement. Here he describes with great cogency how the opening cantos of the *Inferno* serve to establish a dual relationship between the reader and the Pilgrim-protagonist of the *Comedy*. On the one hand, that is, the reader is drawn into an identification with the Pilgrim as one of "us," and with Everyman, who finds himself where all, at one time or another, find ourselves. On the other hand, the reader is distanced from the Pilgrim by the sense that he is a literal other, "a man in a body of flesh and bone" who does not fit into any of the categories of a strictly (or radically) allegorical poem. The intriguing phrase by which Singleton seeks to explain the Pilgrim's transition from Everyman figure to mysteriously individuated character fits, I believe, with my discussion in chapter 1 of Dante's attempts to incorporate the human body into his poem. A "movement within poetic ambiguity at its fullest power" might well be an equivalent of the "gaps" that allow the reader to create an extratextual reality as a kind of "supplement" to the text.[17]

There are, nonetheless, certain aspects of Singleton's discussion that strike me as questionable. The first thing is his curious division between the first two cantos and the rest, with the claim that the former are allegorical, the latter literal. No sooner has he drawn the line than he goes on to erase it, for the obvious reason that, whatever else it may be, the otherworld journey is undeniably allegorical. But why should he want to insist on a distinction that is so clearly unfounded? Granted that the events and the landscape described in the "prologue" belong to the realm of allegory, it makes no sense to regard the "I" speaking there as distinct from the "I" speaking in the later cantos. And why should this "I" refer any less to a particular individual than the one speaking during the actual pilgrimage?

Singleton's division is designed, I believe, to establish the Dantean "I" as both in control of and controlled by the scheme of biblical allegory that he regards as determinative in the *Comedy* (see chapter 2). Thus he curtains off—even if he then wishes the curtain away—the *allegorical* (Everyman) self from the real (de Man's "empirical") self, because his theory compels him to find within the poem a "literal" Dante who remains uncontaminated, as it were, by the allegorical fiction. And once he has found this literal, real self, that is to say, the Pilgrim, within the poem, he can identify him with the Poet outside the poem, the only significant difference between the two being that one has completed the journey whereas the other is still on it. And the same maneuver that allows Singleton to insist on the fundamental identity of Pilgrim and Poet *in reality* also allows him—against the evidence, as we have seen in earlier chapters—to insist on the strict separation between Pilgrim and Poet throughout the *Comedy*, until they are finally "merged" at the conclusion.

Now, if we take seriously, as I believe we should, the idea of the narrative as a kind of theater, we arrive at the conclusion that, *given the autobiographical fiction*, the voice speaking to us in the first person is, from first to last, a voice inside the poem's imaginary theater, while we (readers) constitute an audience analogous to that seated in the celestial auditorium. Putting it in slightly different terms, from the very opening line of the poem the "I" that addresses us is merely one, if the most dominant, of a variety of roles played by the poem's subject: poet-narrator, Florentine citizen, pilgrim, Everyman or "man in general" (Contini), and so forth. Somewhere among or behind these roles there also lurks the "real," historical individual we refer to as Dante Alighieri, but at no point can we identify that individual with any one role or any combination of these roles.

This multiplex, indeterminate persona would seem to be implied in Virgil's remark to the Pilgrim after the latter's ecstatic vision on the third terrace of Purgatory:

> "Se to avessi cento larve
> sovra la faccia, non mi sarian chiuse
> le tue cogitazion, quantunque parve."
>   (*Purg.* XV.127–29)

> ("Although you had a hundred masks
> upon your face, that still would not conceal
> from me the thoughts you thought, however slight.")

A hundred masks is just what we would expect our Pilgrim-Poet to wear in the course of his journey through the hundred cantos of his poem. Here in Purgatory, where there is tremendous consciousness of the ways in which human existence is a matter of artifice, these masks can be acknowledged. And that masks are not mere playthings but are fraught with implications and consequences for their wearers is indicated in a simile applied to the flowers and sparks of the Empyrean changing before the Pilgrim's eyes,

> come gente stata sotto larve,
> che pare altro che prima, se si sveste
> la sembianza non sua in che disparve.
>   (*Par.* XXX.91–95)

> (just as maskers, when they set aside
> the borrowed likenesses in which they hide,
> seem to be other than they were before.)

In the *selva oscura* at the beginning of the *Inferno*, however, the crisis is precisely that of a man shocked by the realization of his masklike existence. He is filled with terror at the thought of having lost his authentic self somewhere along life's way, a terror—*paura* (I.6, 15, 19, etc.)—of his situation that Michael Goldman ascribes to the self-alienation of the actor:

> The actor's body is possessed by something other, that is at once the particular object of his mimesis and a vaguer, more numinous source. I would say that it corresponds to otherness itself in its threatening aspect, all that generality of terror man has tried, apparently from his earliest days, to enact so as to control.[18]

That generality of terror can in this case be seen as the Inferno, which the Pilgrim will shortly enter, though it will be the shades (*ombre*) there that will enact its threatening otherness. In making the Inferno the first stage of his epic theater Dante could draw on a tradition especially strong among early Christian writers like Lactantius and Augustine, which saw the theater as a place where demons take possession of the human soul and induce in the spectator "a miserable madness."[19]

By entering the Infernal theater, the Pilgrim risks madness and demonic possession, and certainly in the first canticle that risk never disappears altogether. But in the course of his engagement with the shades the Pilgrim-actor gradually overcomes his sense of self-alienation. By the end of the *Inferno* he has, like Macbeth, "supp'd full with horrors" and is capable of feeling a sense of community even with the inhabitants of that monstrous world. The Pilgrim experiences otherness less and less as a threat because in his growing self-awareness he recognizes his own Protean nature—"che pur da mia natura / trasmutabile son per tutte guise" ("who by my very nature am / given to every sort of change," *Par.* V. 98–99)—and above all an inescapable doubleness, the actor's self-consciousness but also the sign (Gemini) imprinted on his genius at birth:

> O gloriose stelle, o lume pregno
> di gran virtù, dal quale io riconosco
> tutto, qual the si sia, il mio ingegno.
>   (*Par.* XXII.112–14)

> (O stars of glory, constellation steeped
> in mighty force, all of my genius—
> whatever be its worth—has you as source.)

The Canterbury Tales continues the *Comedy*'s theatricality and thematizes it. I will discuss the tales of the Knight and the Miller as examples of this theatricality and of certain opposed views about the theater that continued into the fourteenth century and beyond. First, however, let us look at the basic features of *The Canterbury Tales* as "epic theater."

An obvious difference from the *Comedy* is the absence of an overtly autobiographical fiction, even though the role of the poet-pilgrim continues to be pivotal, as we have seen. Another obvious difference is that in place of an otherworld stage, Chaucer has the literal stage of inn and roadside familiar to fourteenth-century theatrical genres like the morality and mystery plays.[20] On this stage, which is a lot like Elam's "hypothetically actual" world in that it is "ostended" rather than described, Chaucer's pilgrims are alternately both players and audience. In the act of telling their tale, the pilgrims find themselves at "center stage" and confronting the others as audience. The tale becomes their script, by and through which they perform and in a sense exhibit themselves to their audience.[21] In the absence of stage directions this self-exhibition is of course limited and indirect. But a definitive indication that we are to think of them as physical presences in the course of their tale-telling is the General Prologue, whose portraits constitute an "illustrated" catalogue of the dramatis personae who will eventually appear "on stage." The gap between the pilgrims' portraits and their tales necessitates a conscious exercise of the reader's memory, and this might be considered an analogue to an audience's experience of a literal performance, in this sense at least, that the tale-teller is not a disembodied voice but an individual with a set of physical and other characteristics.

I have not forgotten the caveats in chapter 1 against treating literary characters as though they had an existence independent of the text. I am obviously contending that epic theater like that of *The Canterbury Tales* encourages, if not a confusion between characters in fiction and actual persons, at least an increased sense of an analogy between them. So it does not seem self-contradictory to think of the Canterbury pilgrims as standing in a variety of relations to their narrative. Some, for example, seem more "inside" their narrative than others, as though they were engulfed by it or were dreaming even as they were telling it. Something like this last seems to me the case with the Wife of Bath's Tale, which perhaps not so incidentally ends with a wish fulfillment in the bedroom. It is generally assumed that this wish is really the Wife's and that the Old Hag's becoming young again is her self-projection. But there are other possibilities. The young knight, for instance, and his enforced quest to discover what it is that women most desire, could well be an "unconscious" self-projection that subtly criticizes her Prologue's self-presentation with its pretense that she knows her desire.

Let us turn now to the group of pilgrims—Chaucer, the Second Nun, the Nun's Priest—that are not given a portrait. Of these Chaucer the pilgrim, reporter, and poet is obviously the most important and makes himself felt throughout as a presence, like Dante the pilgrim-poet, and in analogous fashion.[22] There has been considerable debate about this Chaucer, his character and his role in the poem, and that this debate is appropriate, that the reader is meant to treat Chaucer's "personality" as a puzzle alongside that of the other pilgrims, is evident from the scene in which the Host, who has apparently not noticed him before, turns to Chaucer with the abrupt question, "What man artow?" (VII.695). At this point Chaucer becomes another figure on the poem's stage, and the answer to the Host's ultimately unanswerable question is now his burden, as it is that of each pilgrim-teller to announce and reveal himself. The Host's question, in other words, is like an echo of the unspoken one that hangs over Dante's Pilgrim at the very beginning of the *Comedy* and causes him so much terror. In both poems it is the starting point of the pilgrimage, its tentative answer (or answers) the distant goal toward which the respective pilgrimages move.

The Host's words to Chaucer also give a hint of the latter's physical appearance, precisely what the reader has lacked so far to round out his sense of the poet as pilgrim and player:

> He in the waast is shape as wel as I;
> This were a popet in an arm t'enbrace
> For any womman, smal and fair of face.
>   (VII.700ff.)

The picture of a slightly rotund "popet" should not, perhaps, be taken entirely at face value, but the hint of a faintly ambiguous sexuality ("smal and fair of face" has two possible referents) allows us to "see" the poet's presence in *child* Thopas with his "lippes red as rose" and "semely nose" (VII.726, 729). That this is at least in part a comic mask, a playful self-caricature, is itself an important index to Chaucer's personality in *The Canterbury Tales*.[23]

The other two pilgrims with no portrait might of course have received one had Chaucer lived to complete his poem, though we cannot be sure of that. In any case, the absence of a portrait of the Second Nun would seem to have a certain logic. After forty-five lines in which the Prioress emerges in her full individuality and disregard for the rules of her order, the mere mention of her "chapeleyne" in a line and a half (I.163f.) suggests that here is someone who at any rate aspires to be equal to her nun's habit.

The case of the Nun's Priest is more complicated. Not only is there no portrait of him in the General Prologue, but there is even some question whether he is just one of three priests attending the Prioress.[24] The Host's words to him *after* he has told his tale (VII.3450ff.) do little to illuminate the mystery of the Priest's appearance, for they are markedly similar to his words earlier to the Monk (VII.1934ff.), surely a very different type. The Nun's Priest's Tale thus implicitly raises certain questions in relation to the theatrical principle of *The Canterbury Tales*. What kind of evidence, for instance, does a given tale provide about its teller? How necessary is collateral evidence— regarding appearance, social background, personal habits, attitudes—to confirm or at least corroborate the impression of a teller's character as derived from his tale?

The "disembodied" Nun's Priest accordingly serves a dual function in *The Canterbury Tales*. First, he helps to establish the ultimate undecidability of all these questions about character. Second, the bodiless Nun's Priest underscores, paradoxically, the importance of *physical* appearance as an index or basis of character. Where there is no body we are bound to invent one. Thus, though his tale is delivered by a voice seemingly from nowhere, we are at once grateful for and tantalized by the Host's reference, at the conclusion of the tale, to the Priest's large neck and chest (3456). Is it intended literally? ironically? How does it square with our sense of the Priest's physical dimensions as conveyed by his tale?

It may be that the Nun's Priest is intended as just that figure of indeterminacy that makes theatrical play possible, the "nobody" who can represent or "stand in" for anybody.[25] This capacity for theatrical representation is of course not purely negative, but must in turn appeal to the audience's sense of potentiality, such as is dramatized in Shakespeare's Bottom, who believes himself capable of playing any role he chooses (*A Midsummer Night's Dream* II.ii). The unspecified or "blank" persona of the Nun's Priest, in other words, acts as a lure for the reader, enticing him or her (!) to identify with it mimetically, to use Bruce Wilshire's terms.[26]

In her book *Narrative as Performance* Marie Maclean points out that aside from empathy, the theatrical performer is also subject to "the gaze and measurement of others,"[27] the others in the case of *The Canterbury Tales* being the pilgrims, who constitute the immediate or "narrative audience." This audience has behind it, or stands in for, a second or "authorial audience" consisting of the readers of the text. The complexity of interdependence that obtains between Chaucer's pilgrims and their twofold audience is caught perfectly by Maclean's observation about narrative performance, which according to her involves an intimate relationship which, like all such relationships, is at once a cooperation and a contest, an exercise in harmony and a mutual display of power. It is both "act" and interaction, and implies a contract, a recognition of obligation and expectation, thus acknowledging the rules which govern the interplay. The two parties to the agreement, the narrative performers and the narrative audience, must be seen in relationship to the text and to each other.

   (Pp. xii–xiii)

Co-operation and contest, exercise in harmony and mutual display of power—these phrases seem an apt characterization of the tale-telling game in *The Canterbury Tales*, and at the same time they make clear that this game can serve as model for the relationship between Chaucer's epic theater and the "live audience" of his readers. As there is among the pilgrims, so an implied contract or agreement governs the latter relationship, with the poet-narrator acting in the role of mediator or negotiator who anticipates the readers' resistance or calls upon their goodwill. For the contract is clearly a provisional one, constantly subject to renegotiation and reinterpretation, as befits the kind of theater that is being enacted, open-ended, improvisational, akin to carnival and various types of festival.[28]

   In what follows I focus on the tales of the Knight and the Miller and the way that by their very opposition they initiate this theatrical process. The opposition between the tales is more than stylistic; it is as if the Miller had suddenly entered the lists against the Knight in order to challenge his entire vision and version of self and society. And though the Knight himself does not respond—the Reeve, we might say, serves as his ironic proxy—the combat of wits will continue in one form or another throughout the pilgrimage and with all the weapons that the theatrical medium can supply. Significantly, furthermore, the opposition between the first two tales revolves to a considerable extent around their very different notions of theater.

   In the Knight's Tale, this notion is most fully represented by the amphitheater built for the tournament between Palamon and Arcite:

   swich a noble theatre as it was
   I dar wel seyn in this world ther nas.
   The circuit a myle was aboute,
   Walled of stoon, and dyched al withoute.
   Round was the shap, in manere of compas,
   Ful of degrees, the heighte of sixty pas,

> That whan a man was set on o degree,
> He letted nat his felawe for to see.
>   (1885–92)

In its monumental circularity and the unobstructed view it provides for its occupants, this theater recalls the celestial Rose that, as we saw above, is also a kind of colosseum from which the blessed can view the events in the world below. Both structures are obviously classical, that is, Roman, in inspiration and represent a microcosm of the human society in each poem.[29] Each structure also creates the idea of a "world theater" along the lines of the classical epic discussed at the beginning of this chapter. In the *Comedy*, as we have already seen, it is the whole of human history that is played out before the eyes of the elect, who themselves at one time were players on the world's stage. In the Knight's Tale the world theater has the much more limited function of being the staging ground for an aristocratic tournament "For love and for encrees of chivalrye" (2184) and for the benefit of the Athenian populace. Just as God the Prime Mover is above the Rose, so the gods are above Theseus's amphitheater,[30] and, more important, three of the principal gods have temples dedicated to them on the periphery of the amphitheater.

Rose and amphitheater, then, define the respective worlds of their poems, and I suggest that the parallels and contrasts between the two are sufficiently striking to raise the possibility that the Knight's Tale is in a number of ways an antithesis to the *Comedy*. In order to explain what I mean by this, I must digress for a moment and refer the reader to Francis P. Pickering's important but neglected thesis, first published in 1967,[31] that all medieval narrative, whether historical or fictional, involved a choice between two models: an Augustinian, the history of the City of God on earth, and a Boethian, also Christian in spirit, yet essentially secular and dynastic. The premises of the Augustinian model include these:

> That history began with the Creation, and that from the Fall of the Angels until beyond the Day of Judgment it is foreordained by the triune Godhead. God's providence is responsible for the course of all that happens in time. But the only events which ever become history within this system are those which the Church elects to remember, and on which it has passed its verdict. The memorable history of the world since Christ's Ascension is Church history, *sub specie aeternitatis* it is "Heilsgeschichte." In respect of datable events, there are for instance the Church's Councils and the victories of the faith itself over the heathen. There are the *res gestae* of those heroes which the Church canonised or declared martyrs.[32]

In this scheme, furthermore, Fortune is "little more than a talisman, of pagan Rome, now fallen and superseded by the Rome of Peter and Paul" (p. 177). The Boethian model, contrariwise, focuses precisely on the problems posed by a seemingly arbitrary Fortune and in so doing is able to deal with just the secular, dynastic history that Augustine in the *City of God* dismisses as irrelevant. But even though Boethius's focus is on the problematic, confused realm of secular history dominated by Fortune, he still finds in it a divine order as expressed by this descending "hierarchy of instances": *God* and his *Providence*; the *Fate* of all temporal things and beings—including man; *Fortune*; the *Free Will of Man*. And it is Pickering's contention that the Boethian model, derived from the *Consolation of Philosophy*, "was known to every medieval author as being the only one available for works of non-theological content, for the rational interpretation of 'real' history ... or for the composition and interpretation of all kinds of fictions" (p. 181 f.).

Pickering's thesis, with whose *general* applicability I am not here concerned, clarifies two fundamental points about the Knight. First, in the General Prologue he sees himself as part of the Augustinian paradigm of history, as a fighter for "the victories of the faith over the heathen," rather than for some spiritually ambiguous dynastic cause. Though he may have too much humility to present himself as a hero of *Heilsgeschichte*, he probably looks upon the "felaweshipe" of the Teutonic order, with which he banqueted and fought against the Russian infidels (I.52–55), the way the Arthurian Grail knights saw themselves, namely, as a portion of the City of God on earth.[33] Second, as tale-teller, the Knight makes precisely the kind of choice Pickering says a medieval author must make. His tale is "Boethian" in the sense that its pagan characters have, aside from their gods, only a philosophy outside the Christian theological framework to guide and console them.[34] And this accounts for the Knight's refusal to tell where Arcite's soul went upon his death:

> His spirit chaunged hous and wente ther
> As I cam nevere, I kan nat tellen wher.
> Therfore I stynte, I nam no divinistre;
> Of soules fynde I nat in this registre,
> Ne me ne list thilke opinions to telle
> Of hem, though that they writen wher they dwelle.
>   (2809–14)

Surely Dante is among those whose opinions the Knight prefers to ignore,[35] since his *Comedy* is always ready to raise doctrinal difficulties, especially regarding pagans, and to insist on the vital role that pagans play within a Christian framework of history. The Knight's Tale points entirely in the opposite direction, and the amphitheater is a perfect emblem of this opposition. Its temples and the gods enshrined in them define, as we have seen, the limits of the tale's pagan world. The Knight is intent on keeping the pagan world neatly framed and apart from his own.

The idea of history, furthermore, that is enacted in his theater differs fundamentally from the *Comedy*'s. In the latter, there are no privileged performers: all, high or low, Christian, Jew, or pagan, can be heroes or villains. In the Knight's Tale, on the contrary, the only players who count are aristocrats: others may have supporting roles, but for the most part they merely make up the multitude and serve as spectators for the aristocratic spectacle. And from the Knight's point of view this is a very consciously staged, ritualistic spectacle whose rules are well defined and strictly enforced. For all that, however, it involves an unpredictable, ominous element; indeed, an atmosphere of potential disaster hovers over the entire theater.

Its source is the gods, and their menace is portrayed in the temples on the periphery of the amphitheater. These temple interiors with their frequently sinister statues and murals have some of the atmosphere as well as some fairly specific echoes of Dante's *Inferno*. Accordingly, when the Knight, in describing the temples, suddenly resorts to the formula "Ther saugh I"—a frequent formula in the *Comedy*[36]—eight times in short succession (1995; cf. 2005, 2011, 2017, 2056, 2065, 2067, 2073), he takes on the air of a Dantean tourist in hell, with this difference: he does not need to descend to the otherworld, since as far as he is concerned hell is already where the pagan gods are. A further difference from Dante's pilgrim is that the Knight's gaze is entirely impassive; it merely registers and remains wholly unmoved by the horror or absurdity of what it beholds.

This unemotional, nonempathetic spectatorship characterizes, of course, the old warrior's entire attitude toward the world of his tale. He is clearly determined to keep it at a distance from himself, in part, at least, because of a suspicion of the theater—of which the temples are an integral part—and its potentially devastating effect upon the unguarded viewer. We are, in other words, in the intellectual and spiritual ambience of Tertullian and other early Christian polemicists who regarded the theater as an essentially pagan institution diabolic in origin.[37] In the *City of God* Augustine views it, in the words of one modern authority, as "a false temple, or anti-temple, standing in mocking antithesis to the true temple, ... inhabited by demons ... and dedicated to the overthrow of humanity."[38]

Against this threat, the Knight—whose Augustinianism we have discussed—must fortify himself with a coldly ironic stare, especially when the theater literally fulfills its demonic role, at Saturn's instigation, as a "furie infernal" bursts from the ground and causes Arcite's fatal fall from his horse.[39] This sudden *peripeteia*, followed by Arcite's final illness, his moving speech of farewell to Palamon and Emily (2765–97), his death and the violent grief of young and old (2817)—all this fits into the *pattern* of tragedy to be examined in the next chapter, and we can amplify the comments made there about the Knight's interruption of the Monk's tragedies. For it is clear that even Arcite's extremely simple "tragedy" is anathema to the Knight:[40] whenever his own voice enters by way of comment, it is to deflate the aura of tragedy and to demonstrate his own utter emotional detachment.[41]

This, the Knight seems to say, is the only way of dealing with the spectacle of pagan theater, or, in the larger perspective, of history. One must contemplate it with the calm objectivity of one who is totally uninvolved *because as a Christian he knows himself to be free of the demonic forces that, in the guise of the gods, can still enthrall the pagan soul.* But to know oneself free of them is of course not to say that they cannot once more take possession of one's soul, and it is therefore imperative to remain vigilant against that eventuality.

For all that the Knight attempts to seal off the world of his tale from any contact with his own experience, it is evident that what I have described as the spectacle of pagan history is in essence the Knight's vision of profane, secular history, the history that is distinct from Augustinian *Heilsgeschichte*, the struggle of the City of God in time. Profane history, in other words, is still, at bottom, demonic, or at least one where the "furie infernal" may erupt at any moment. In the face of that threat, however, the situation is not completely hopeless. There is one character capable, not of preventing the furies, but of controlling them. That is of course Theseus. Like the Knight, Theseus refuses to be drawn into the "tragedy" of Arcite's death. Instead, he proceeds by all means at his command to regain control of the "theater" that, as ruler of Athens, he directs and of which he is the center. Until the accident, Arcite and the tournament were part of this political "theater," and Theseus's chief concern now is to make them once again a part of it. So that the accident will not dampen the cheer of his guests (2703), therefore, he organizes all-night revels (2715ff.), decrees that all rancor and envy must stop (2731f.), gives gifts, holds a three-day feast, and then conveys the royal guests out of town (2735ff.). After the death, he is quickly comforted by his father's platitudes (2837) and loses no time in organizing the funeral pyre (2853ff.). While laying out the body, it appears for a moment as though he succumbs to the emotion of the occasion:

> He leyde hym, bare the visage, on the beere;
> Therwith he weep that pitee was to heere.
> And for the peple sholde seen hym alle,
> Whan it was day, he broghte hym to the halle,
> That roreth of the criyng and the soun.
>   (2877–81)

But stripped of their modern punctuation (in this case the period after 2878),[42] the lines more than hint at the theatricality of Theseus's tears.

It is difficult indeed to determine what attitude the Knight has to this kind of political theater. We may smile at Theseus's unwavering attention to its ceremonial niceties and its thinly veiled opportunism, as when he summons Palamon, who is still in mourning and has no inkling of what is going on (2977–78), to the Athenian parliament, "To have with certein contrees alliaunce, / And have fully of Thebans obeisaunce" (2973–74), by having him marry Emily. And we may smile at his theatrical posturing before delivering his oration to the same parliament (2981–86). But it does appear that Theseus, as the one who orchestrates the theater of which he is himself the principal focus, is a model for the Knight in his undertaking to master his narrative and his audience.

The first part of this undertaking need not concern us in any detail, since it has been discussed by a number of commentators. I am referring to the deliberate, rhetorically self-conscious ways in which the Knight *reduces* the *Teseida* not only in length but also, especially, in the vitality and dramatic autonomy of its characters.[43] Starting with his literal and symbolic conquest of "al the regne of Femenye" (866), the Knight's Theseus achieves an analogous dominance over the people around him. The second part of the Knight's undertaking, the mastery of his audience, has also received ample critical attention, especially his excessive use of *occupatio*, the rhetorical ploy of describing something while in the act of saying that one will not describe it. The many occasions when the Knight interrupts his narrative to address the pilgrims directly likewise demonstrate his desire, mingled with an ironic condescension, to hold their attention.[44] It is here that the Knight's ambiguous attitude to the pilgrim audience suddenly mirrors that of Theseus toward the Athenian crowd. This crowd is waiting outside the ducal palace for a proclamation while Theseus is "at a window set, / Arrayed right as he were a god in trone" (2529–30). Below, meanwhile, "an heraud on a scaffold made an 'Oo' / Til al the noyse of the peple was ydo" (2533–34), and then delivers Theseus's message. This brief scene is fleetingly recapitulated by the Knight, 140 lines later, in his own role as narrator. After he has described the crowd's frenzied reaction to Arcite's victory:

> Anon ther is a noyse of peple bigonne
> For joye of this, so loude and heighe withalle
> It seemed that the lystes sholde falle
>   (2660–62)

he goes on to admonish his own audience:

> But herkneth me, and stynteth noyse a lite,
> Which a myracle ther bifel anon.
>   (2674–75)

His words insinuate an ironic equation between the pilgrims and the Athenian crowd; both have the characteristics that make a theater audience so objectionable: incessant noisiness, readiness to be swayed by emotion, addiction to spectacle and the spectacular ("Which a miracle"!). But beyond these ironies there is also, surely, more than a slight hint of a connection between the Knight's exhibitionism as a performer and Theseus's near-blasphemous self-elevation.

The scene in which the Miller, over the objections of the Host, insists on his right to speak next, has been discussed earlier. Nonetheless, I want to refer to it yet again to underline how perfectly it exemplifies a kind of theater diametrically opposed to the Knight's, and one, furthermore, that will be fully exemplified by the Miller's own tale. In this theater, first of all, there are no performers who are elevated above all the other performers. By the same token, no performer is in complete control of the performance—first, because each performer has a chance to be at center stage and no role is absolutely fixed, and second, because there is no radical separation between performers and spectators, so that spectators can at any moment become a part of the performance.

It is not hard to imagine the Knight reacting to the Miller's intrusion into the Host's protocol as an example of "the cherles rebellyng" (2459), a matter for which, in the Knight's Tale, Saturn takes credit. "The multitude," as a recent observer of Western society might put it, though the Miller is of course nothing like Ortega's "mass man."[45] Technically, to be sure, "the Millere is a cherle, ye know wel this" (3182) and "told his cherles tale" (3169); but the poet-narrator's mock-apology on this point is, rather, a way of reinforcing the inclusiveness of the pilgrims' theater, its readiness to yield center stage to all, aristocrats, churls, and others. What the narrator does not say, and does not need to say, is that in "quiting" the Knight's Tale the "churl" initiates a transformation of social and literary values that marks *The Canterbury Tales* as a whole.

The characters of the Miller's Tale reflect his approach to theater as *play*, a form of inspired improvisation in which the performer seeks to engage the audience's active participation in the performance. Each of the characters at one point or another in the tale occupies center stage, making us see the world through his or her eyes. In addition, the characters represent a variety of social classes, from the "knave" Robin to the parish clerk Absolon, and the carpenter, John, who for all that he is "a riche gnof" (3188), knows himself inferior to the "poure scoler" Nicholas: "What! thynk on God, as we doon, men that swynke" (3490).

The lowly shot-window—it only reaches up to Absolon's chest (3696)—of the carpenter's house, might be said to function as "center stage" in the theater of the Miller's Tale. Early in the tale, indeed, when Absolon stations himself by this window to serenade Alison (3695), who is in bed with her husband, it functions rather like the window in the Knight's Tale at which we saw Theseus "set, / Arrayed right as he were a god in trone": it allows communication between performer and audience even as it establishes a discreet barrier between them. Later, however, on the fateful night when Absolon reappears at the window to beg a kiss, it still frames the performers like any proscenium arch, but now it also opens up to allow direct contact between the characters, who are, interchangeably, performers and audience. And here, at center stage, the three principals of the Miller's Tale take turns in making an entrance, as it were, and delivering a statement in truly theatrical fashion, that is, not just with words but also by physical gesture and action.

Alison's "statement" in sticking her rear out the window is clear enough, though we might question whether it is aimed just at the "romantic" Absolon or, ultimately, at all men and their unceasing quest for "taille" (VII.416). Absolon's response to her with the "hoote kultour" (3776) would seem to signify all the repressed anger men feel toward women and which, in the Knight's Tale, they express in violence toward the rivals for the object of their desire. Nicholas's statement, finally, seems akin to that of the demon Barbariccia in *Inferno* XXI, who "had made a trumpet of his ass" ("avea del cul fatto trombetta," 139); Singleton's comment on the conduct of the other demons in the preceding lines seems perfectly apt for Barbariccia's fart as well: a gesture, he calls it, "of complicity and delight at the prospect of the adventure ahead, in which the devils are going to trick Virgil and Dante."[46] Only a slight change in the wording is needed to fit this to the demonic Nicholas's performance at the window. He is expressing his complicity and delight at the apparently successful adventure in which he and Alison tricked the old carpenter and Absolon. There is further reason to suspect the invisible presence, in this scene, of Dante's demon, whose name means "curly beard": after planting his kiss Absolon "thoughte it was amys, / For wel he wiste a womman hath no berd" (3736–37), and Nicholas, who cannot very well have heard Absolon's unspoken reflection, exclaims "A berd! a berd! ... / By Goddes corpus, this goth faire and weel" (3742–43).

Nicholas is "demonic" in his apparent knowledge of the unspoken (and, we might add, of the unseen), and in the more precise sense of his systematic, meticulous way of inverting all the norms, sacred and profane, of his society. As such, he reflects an aspect of the Miller especially prominent in the General Prologue portrait, the physical features that make him like an embodiment of the infernal, demonic side of the mystery plays—like Noah's Flood—to which his tale alludes. His mouth is a virtual hell-mouth, traditionally represented by "a greet forneys" (I.559) in the mysteries. The various animal associations of his facial features suggest the animal masks worn by the "demons" in the mysteries. By his appearance, in other words, the Miller seems to stand for the comically profane and grotesque elements of the mystery plays that oppose and burlesque the sacred event, "Goddes pryvetee."[47] As a sideshow performer, too, the Miller comes to seem a comic subverter of social norms: at least his wrestling, his lifting doors off their hinges or breaking them down with his head, and his playing the "goliardeys" can easily be imagined as so many ways of exposing the *pryvetee* usually hidden under masks and conventions or kept behind locked doors.

In the perspective of the Miller and his tale the demonic is of course not perceived or felt as such, but is, rather, considered part of the *natural* order or course of things. Thus, what in the Knight's Tale is feared as a potential source of disaster—the spontaneous, the accidental, the erotic, like the sudden glance of a woman—is in the Miller's Tale simply a facet of the unaccountable plenitude of creation. Indeed, as the scenes at the shot-window demonstrate, it is precisely the fortuitous and seemingly demonic that cause poetic justice to prevail:[48] Nicholas and carpenter John are punished for their respective presumptions, and Alison is spared, since, as the Miller asserts in his prologue, a wife is an intimate part of "Goddes pryvetee" (3164).[49] Repudiating the Knight's opposition between Augustinian and Boethian accounts of the way of the world, the Miller remains true to the premises of the mystery cycles to which he owes much of his own being and presents in his tale a Boethian fortune working an apparently providential justice.

The Miller's *theatrical* critique of the Knight's Tale begins with a reduction of the latter's monumental political theater to the intimate dimensions of the carpenter's household, where literally everyone can play. The broader setting of the Miller's Tale suggests a comic *translatio studii* but also the reduction of the fabled center of ancient civilization to contemporary small-town Oxford with its humble "street-theater," whose spirit rules the tale. Of the various specific allusions to the mystery plays in the Miller's Tale the following is particularly significant because it is also one of a number of echoes of the Knight's Tale.[50] "Somtyme, to shewe his lightnesse and maistrye," Absolon "pleyeth *Herodes upon a scaffold bye*" (3383–84; my italics), recalling the moment when "an *beraud on a scaffold* made an 'Oo!'" (2533) to silence the Athenian crowd. The juxtaposition of these two scaffolds, one belonging to the homely "epic theater" (in the Brechtian sense!) of the mysteries, the other to the "political theater" of classical epic, defines the theatrical distance between the respective tales. And of course this is a matter, not just of the scaffolds, but also of acting styles and rapport with the audience. Playing the ranting tyrant of the mysteries, Absolon is like the "heraud" who is Theseus's mouthpiece, but his audience knows from his manner of playing the part—made more absurd, surely, by his high-pitched voices[51]—what kind of character he represents, something the Athenian audience could scarcely infer from the herald's decorous "Oo!" In the same vein, furthermore, Absolon's eagerness to impress his audience with his *lightnesse and maistrye* as an actor sums up in one phrase the paradoxical ambitions of the small-town dandy and the Athenian ruler.

Absolon's desire to demonstrate *maistrye* also serves broadly as a parody of the Knight's preoccupation with various kinds of mastery in his tale, his evident desire to impose himself on his audience,[52] his covert identification with Theseus, who so effectively dominates the world of the tale. And it is here that the Miller's Tale once again presents a startling contrast, for the Miller includes himself in his tale quite overtly *and* as a strictly marginal figure. I am referring to his namesake and mirror image, carpenter John's servant, Robin, "a strong carl for the nones," who lifts the door of Nicholas's room off its hinges. We already know the Miller's name from the Prologue to his tale (3129), and in the General Prologue we learned that the Miller is a "stout carl for the nones" for whom there "was no dore that he nolde heve of harre, / Or breke it at a rennyng with his heed" (545, 550–51). Assuming the Robin in the tale is a deliberate self-portrait, however, the Miller obviously sees himself in a rather different way from the brash figure presented in the General Prologue. This Robin is a humble "knave" who is himself somewhat of a dupe as he kneels outside Nicholas's door:

> An hole he foond, ful 'owe upon a bord,
> Ther as the cat was wont in for to crepe,
> And at that hole he looked in ful depe.
>   (3440–42)

His position is faintly anticipatory of Absolon's later at the window, and however deep he looks he sees only what Nicholas wants him to see. Later, speaking to the carpenter, Nicholas singles out Robin and the maid as among those excluded from the divine scheme of salvation:

> But Robyn may nat wite of this, thy knave,
> Ne eek thy mayde Gille I may nat save;
> Axe nat why, for though thou aske me,
> I wol nat tellen Goddes pryvetee.
> (3555–58)

Of course, it is just this humble pair who are saved, at least from the comic catastrophe at the carpenter's house, because by some irrational scruple John thinks to save them from the flood by sending them off to London on an errand (3630–31). It may be no more than a coincidence that the maid and Noah's wife in the Towneley cycle are both named Gill.[53] In any case, it seems entirely congruent with the spirit of the Miller's Tale to suggest that as this lowly pair trudge off to London we subliminally perceive them as a latter-day Mr. and Mrs. Noah embodying the fate of mankind.

For all its marginality, then, the figure of Robin in the Miller's Tale is of wide-ranging significance. It suggests the potentially multiple roles of the tale-teller as participant and spectator in his own tale. A final question concerns the contrast between this Robin, the apparent innocent, and Robin the extroverted, aggressive, crude "janglere" who tells the tale. Despite their outward similarities, are these not different, even antithetical characters? In a sense, that is certainly undeniable, yet I argue that they also belong together, that it is in fact the triumph of the theatrical conception of character that it can yoke apparently antithetical elements together in a believable union.[54]

Virtually from his first appearance on the road to Canterbury we see the two Robins in the figure of the Miller. When the Knight has finished his tale and the Host exclaims, "trewely, the game is wel bigonne" (3117), the Miller immediately seizes upon the theatrical implications of his words and

> in Pilates vois he gan to crye,
> And swoor, "By armes, and by blood and bones,
> I kan a noble tale for the nones,
> With which I wol now quite the Knyghtes tale."
> (3122–27)

The Miller here reenacts that union of game-playing and theater that V. A. Kolve's book on medieval drama has described so felicitously:

> When the drama [of the Church] moved into the streets and the
> market place, into a milieu already the home of men's playing and
> games, it was redefined as game and allowed to exploit fully its
> nonearnest, gratuitous nature.... It was a special kind of game ...
> in which a peasant is made a king or knight, and after it is over
> becomes once again a peasant.[55]

The Host has not yet caught on to the Miller's idea of game and attempts to
stop him on the grounds of social precedence. But when the Miller threatens
to "go my wey," the Host yields the stage to him: "Tel on, a devel wey! / Thou
art a fool; thy wit is overcome" (3134–35). If we now expect "a prototype
of the traditional raging, frothing, pompous Pilate," as K. B. Harder has
characterized him, we will be disappointed.[56] The "janglere and goliardeys"
eager to impress with his "lightnesse and maistrye" is only one side of the
Miller.

Or rather, the Miller has his lightness as well as his *maistrye*. I am
referring to the side of him that is humorous, humble, and reasonable and
able to articulate an astonishingly enlightened view of marriage, as witness
his diplomatic words to the angry Reeve. "Leve brother Osewold," he tells
him,

> Who hath no wyf, he is no cokewold.
> But I sey nat therfore that thou art oon;
> Ther been ful goode wyves many oon,
> And evere a thousand goode ayeyns oon badde.
> That knowestow wel thyself, but if thou madde.
> Why arrow angry with my tale now?
> I have a wyf, pardee, as wel as thow;
> Yet nolde I, for the oxen in my plogh,
> Take upon me moore than ynogh,
> As demen of myself that I were oon;
> I wol bileve wel that I am noon.
> An housbonde shal nat been inquisityf
> Of Goddes pryvetee, nor of his wyf.
> So he may fynde Geddes foyson there,
> Of the remenant nedeth nat enquere.
>   (3151–66)

I have quoted the entire speech because its irreverent, slightly blasphemous
banter can cause us to overlook just how extraordinary it really is. The idea of

marriage it implies, as the joke of the last four lines underscores, accords the
wife her full measure of independence, and—once we get beyond the purely
sexual equation[57]—godlike mystery. Marriage, in other words, is not like
the yoking together of two oxen before a plow, but a union of free persons
respecting the otherness of the other.

Even if the sentiment is not considered startling in itself, it surely is
coming from the Miller, to the point that it forces us to revise the impression
we have developed of him up to now. And for the purposes of this revision
there is perhaps no more appropriate model than the one the Miller presents
of marriage as a multiplicity—"Goddes foyson"—united into one without
losing the heterogeneity of its constituent parts. In the General Prologue
portrait these heterogeneous elements take on a self-proliferating, grotesque
life of their own, so that it is as though we were seeing multiple exposures of
the Miller at once. Using his head to break down a door (551), he becomes
the ram that is also his as a prize in wrestling (548). The wart on the tip of his
nose with its hairs "reed as the brustles of a sowes erys" (556), together with
the black and wide nostrils, the large mouth, and the "berd [that] as any sowe
or fox was reed" (552), creates the surreal effect of one face superimposed on
another. It is not until the final detail, the bagpipe played by the Miller, that
the entire portrait stands revealed as one great synecdoche, a mask. Made of a
sow's bladder, shaped like a gut and phallus, and classified by Machaut among
the "instrumens des hommes bestiaulx,"[58] it is the Miller's comic double,
another example of his self-multiplication. But the bagpipe makes clear that
the Miller's portrait is not just another Geryonic image.[59] Like a theatrical
mask, it is hollow and receives its animation from a source not its own but
behind and inside it: "A baggepipe wel koude he blowe and sowne, / And
therwithal he broghte us out of towne" (565–66). That blowing and sounding
is what transforms a mere image into a "living" character, just as Zephirus's
"sweete breeth" (5) brings to life the springtime landscape and arouses folk,
who suddenly "longen ... to goon on pilgrimages" (12).

In his comic apology before he starts his tale, the Miller speaks as one
who is aware of himself as wind instrument and mask, whose sound is not
entirely his own:

"Now herkneth," quod the Millere, "alle and some!
But first I make a protestacioun
That I am dronke; I knowe it by my soun;
And therfore if that I mysspeke or seye,
Wyte it the ale of Southwerk, I you preye."
     (3136–40)

The sound, then, of his bagpipe that "broghte us out of towne" is like the sound of his voice in that its source is ultimately mysterious, coming from without and within. And it is by way of these sounds issuing from bagpipe and mask that Chaucer sets out to recover, I believe, the original theatrical idea of the human person expressed in the presumed etymology of *persona* as *personare* (or even *per-se-sonare*), "to sound through oneself," which was familiar during the medieval centuries especially because it was cited over and over from Boethius's influential tract *On the Dual Nature and One Person of Christ*:

> Wherefore if Person belongs to substances alone, and these rational, and if every nature is a substance, existing not in universals but in individuals, we have found the definition of Person, viz.: "The individual substance of a rational nature." Now by this definition we Latins have described what the Greeks call *hupostasis*. For the word person seems to be borrowed from a different source, namely from the masks which in comedies and tragedies used to signify the different subjects of representation. Now *persona* "mask" is derived from *personare*, with a circumflex on the penultimate. But if the accent is put on the antepenultimate the word will clearly be seen to come from *sonus* "sound," and for this reason, that the hollow mask necessarily produces a larger sound. The Greeks, too, call these masks *prosôpa* from the fact that they are placed over the face and conceal the countenance from the spectator: *para tou pros tous ôpas tithesthai*. But since, as we have said, it was by the masks they put on that actors played the different characters represented in a tragedy or comedy— Hecuba or Medea or Simon or Chremes,—so also all other men who could be recognized by their several characteristics were designated by the Latins with the term *persona* and by the Greeks with *prosôpa*.[60]

The etymology that Boethius gives is not connected, so far as one can see, with his definition of person as "the individual substance of a rational nature." It seems to be there, rather, to indicate what his philosophical formula eliminates or replaces: a theatrical conception of person as a mysterious matter of masks and sounds that at once conceal and identify the human individual.

Boethius's abstract, essentially Aristotelian definition is itself one climax of a centuries-long discussion of the concept *persona* in the course of which it would seem the theatrical element is progressively pushed aside in favor of the philosophical.[61] We can see this happening in Cicero's influential discussion of the subject in Book I of *De Oficiis*—very likely familiar to Dante and Chaucer—where he distinguishes between two *personae* or "characters" with which, he argues, all of us are endowed (*duabus quasi nos a natura indutos esse personis*):

> One of these is universal, arising from the fact of our being all alike endowed with reason and with that superiority which lifts us above the brute. From this all morality and propriety are derived, and upon it depends the rational method of ascertaining our duty. The other character is the one that is assigned to individuals in particular. In the matter of physical endowment there are great differences: some, we see, excel in speed for the race, others in strength for wrestling: so in point of personal appearance, some have stateliness, others comeliness. Diversities of mental disposition are greater still.[62]

Now, there is no question that for Cicero every human being is constituted by or as the interplay of these two *personae*, the first representing what he calls *universa natura* with its ethical and rational imperatives, the second *propria nostra natura*, our individual bent or genius, be it physical, intellectual, or temperamental. Neither *persona*, in short, exists by itself, and the attempt to give up either one of them is a surrender of our very humanity. But that the idea of the theatrical mask is not far from Cicero's mind is clear from his discussion of the second *persona*. This, he says, is assigned to us by nature, but then he goes on to say that it is also *chosen* by the individual:

> Every one, therefore, should make a proper estimate of his own natural ability and show himself a critical judge of his own merits and defects; in this respect, we should not let actors display more practical wisdom than we have. They select, not the best plays [*fabulas*], but the ones best suited to their talents. Those who rely most upon the quality of their voice take the Epigoni and the Medus; those who place more stress upon the action, choose the Melanippa and the Clytaemnestra; Rupilius, whom I remember, always played in the Antiope, Aesopus rarely in the Ajax. *Shall a player have regard to this in choosing his role upon the stage, and a wise man fail to do so in selecting his part in life?*[63]

Clearly, Cicero's idea of the individual as constituted by the interplay of two *personae* is in many ways still a theatrical one. Indeed, I think it is enormously suggestive for the interplay of the first two tale-tellers in *The Canterbury Tales*, who could be said to stand for or lean toward one and the other of the two *personae* respectively. The Knight tends toward the pole of the *universa natura* that raises man above the beasts and enables him to discover his moral obligations. Contrariwise, the Miller is close indeed to the second, *propria nostra natura*, given us by nature and yet, paradoxically, also chosen, precisely as if it were (what it ultimately is) a mask.

By a happy accident, concerning our idea of epic theater, in Cicero's Latin the word for *play* and *story* is the same, allowing us once more to envision Knight and Miller as actors choosing the *fabula* most suited to them (*sibi accommodatissimas*). The Knight's, as we have seen, perfectly expresses his urge for domination, control, *maistrye*, above all, perhaps, in the intellectual sphere. The Miller's, reminding us, in Yeats's terms, of "the uncontrollable mystery on the bestial floor," allows its characters to act out *their* particular bent, whatever it might be, without passing judgment on them. At this point we also need to remind ourselves, however, that as "plays" the tales are no pure self-expression or self-reflection, but also places, like Dante's three realms, for the encounter of otherness in all its various guises. This means that the pilgrim-performers run the risk, if not of madness and possession, then of a new insight, a change of heart. But these are matters that are left to the reader's intuition. The important point, it seems to me, is that once the interplay between Knight and Miller has been set going, it continues for the rest of the journey.

NOTES

1. Chapter 2 of Michael Lynn-George, Epos: *Word, Narrative, and the "Iliad,"* is entitled "The Epic Theatre: the Language of Achilles" (pp. 50–152), but it deals exclusively with the "theater of language."

2. *Poetics* 60a5–11, trans. Gerald F. Else, *Aristotle's Poetics: The Argument*, pp. 619–20.

3. Unknown to scholarship until the twentieth century. See Guillelmus de Moerbeka, *De Arte Poetica*, Praefatio, pp. 11ff.

4. See Marvin Carlson, *Theories of the Theatre*, p. 26.

5. My translation. See Evanthius, *De Fabula*, pp. 14–15.

6. Else, *Aristotle's Poetics*, p. 620.

7. Eric A. Havelock, *Preface to Plato*, p. 45. Havelock believes that Plato quite consciously developed the term *mimesis* to denote "the basic psychology of the oral-poetic relationship between reciter and listener or between reciter and the material recited, and the corresponding characteristics of the oral-poetic 'statement'" (p. 57, n.22). In origin, *mimesis* referred, not to "copy" or "imitation," but to "theatrical representation," *mimos* meaning "actor," "mime," or the performance by same. For all its differences in emphasis (on which see Else, *Aristotle's Poetics*, pp. 93–95), Aristotle's *mimesis* is in some ways a formalistic version of Plato's.

8. Else, *Poetics*, p. 621. And cf. John Kevin Newman, *The Classical Epic Tradition*: "The distinction made by Brecht ... between his epic drama and Aristotelian drama must not obscure the extraordinary tribute which the very notion of epic drama pays to Aristotle's insight into the dramatic tendencies of the Homeric *epos*" (p. 40).

9. See the chapter "The Norms of Epic" in Thomas Greene, *The Descent from Heaven*.

10. Vincentius Ussani, Jr., ed., *Nicolai Trepeti Expositio Herculis Furentis*, p. 5 (my trans.). For an excellent discussion of the knowledge of Seneca and his theater in the fourteenth century, see Renate Haas, "Chaucer's Monk's Tale."

11. Cf., e.g., *Poetics* 59a17, Else, *Poetics*, pp. 569ff.

12. Keir Elam, *The Semiotics of Theatre and Drama*, pp. 109–10.

13. For a discussion of theater as the *source* of our ideas of selfhood, see Bruce Wilshire, *Role Playing and Identity*.

14. Cf. Singleton's on *Par.* XXX, pp. 502f., and on *Par.* XXXII.116.

15. See Francis Ferguson, *Dante's Drama of the Mind*. In *The Idea of a Theater*, Ferguson singles out the *Purgatorio* as a notable example of narrative that is essentially theatrical: "In this part of the *Divine Comedy*, it is evident that, though Dante was not writing to be acted on a stage, he appeals, like the great dramatists, to the histrionic sensibility, i.e., our direct sense of the changing life of the psyche" (p. 18).

16. "Allegory," pp. 9–10, in *Dante's "Commedia"*; also Gianfranco Contini, "Dante come Personaggio-Poeta della 'Commedia,'" pp. 33–62.

17. This idea of the readerly "supplement" I derive from Wolfgang Iser, "The Play of the Text," in *Languages of the Unsayable*, ed. Sanford Budick and Wolfgang Iser, pp. 325–39. For Iser, this supplement is not just a function of particular textual "gaps" but rather a normal result of the "play of the text," which, he says, "can be acted out individually by each reader, who by playing it in his or her own way produces an individual 'supplement' considered to be the meaning of the text" (p. 336).

18. Michael Goldman, *The Actor's Freedom*, p. 11. Goldman speculates about a special association between primitive drama and the spirits of the dead; e.g., "Drama probably began with ghosts, with prehistoric impersonations intended to transfigure the malice of spirits—to indulge, placate, or wrestle with the dead, to turn Furies into Eumenides" (p. 27).

19. "miserabilis insania"; I am quoting from Augustine's *Confessions*, III.ii, p. 101, in the Loeb ed., trans. William Watts (1951), vol. 1, where he describes his own experience of attending stage plays. On this entire subject, see Jonas Barish, *The Antitheatrical Prejudice*, in which he states that Augustine condemns the theater strictly on the grounds of practical morality because it encourages every form of vice (p. 64); but this is contradicted by his own demonstration that Augustine, following Lactantius, consistently links the theater with demons, and by Augustine's denunciation of actors, his praise of the Romans for "having banished from the number of [their] citizens all actors and players" (*City of God* II.29, p. 73). Tertullian wrote an antitheatrical tract, *De Spectaculis* (ca. 198). On Tertullian, see Barish, p. 63f.

20. In this connection see the comments by Claude Gauvin, "Le théâtre et son public en Angleterre au Moyen-Age et à la Renaissance," especially pp. 58–59 on the "placea" or acting area, frequently on the same level as the spectators and not separated from them by other than a symbolic barrier.

21. Latin *fabula* means both "drama, play" and "tale, story, fable"; I return to this point later.

22. See the comments on Chaucer the pilgrim-poet as "the single evaluating mind placed in the center of the dramatic situation" of *The Canterbury Tales*, by Alfred David, *The*

Strumpet Muse, pp. 70ff., and Donald Howard's discussion of Chaucer the poet-performer in *The Idea of The Canterbury Tales*, p. 194f., and "The Narrative Now," pp. 78ff.

23. For a discussion of this passage from a different perspective, see Lee W. Patterson, "'What Man Artow?'"

24. See various editors' notes to I.164.

25. See Bruce Wilshire, *Role Playing and Identity*.

26. Wilshire, *Role Playing*, passim.

27. "Performance," she writes, "always implies submitting to the gaze and measurement of others"; see Marie Maclean, *Narrative as Performance*, p. xi.

28. On this, see Carl Lindahl, *Earnest Games*. My view of the implications of game and festivity in *The Canterbury Tales* differs radically from Lindahl's.

29. On the rose in *Paradiso* XXXIII as a microcosm of the family of man—the "society" of the *Comedy*—see Joan Ferrante, *The Political Vision*, p. 306f.

30. Venus's tears fall into the lists when she sees that her knight Palamon has been captured (2663–67).

31. Francis P. Pickering, *Augustinus oder Boethius?*

32. Francis P. Pickering, *Literature and Art in the Middle Ages*, p. 174.

33. Ibid., p. 193, speaking of Wolfram van Eschenbach's Grail community; see also Jean Frappier, "Le Graal et la Chevalerie." The religious meaning of "Ful worthy was he in *his lordes* werre" (I.47) thus not only is plausible on historical grounds—the Knight is not connected with any campaigns in France—but would also fit in with his self-interpretation. Certain battles in which the Knight took part were by no means unambiguous; on this see C. Mitchell, "The Worthiness of Chaucer's Knight," and Terry Jones, *Chaucer's Knight*. It could hardly be otherwise, and Chaucer may have expected his knowledgeable readers to be aware of complexities the Knight would not acknowledge.

34. This is a tricky point. Boethius was of course a Christian, and the *Consolation* presumably implies, in the final analysis, something very close to the Augustinian scheme of providential history. Notoriously, however, the *Consolation* also avoids any overtly Christian references, so that it could be used as representing "pagan" philosophy. Pickering cites Konrad's German adaptation (ca. 1170) of the *Chanson de Roland* as an example of a work in which Boethianism is equated with pagan wisdom: "In any well-organized work of Augustinian conception, the philosophy attributed to the heathen may be based on the best *secular* philosophy available, in Boethius"; see "Historical Thought and Moral Codes in Medieval Epic," in H. Scholler, ed., *The Epic in Medieval Society*, p. 15.

35. By way of contrast to the Knight's professed ignorance about the fate of pagans after death, his immediate source, the *Teseida*, describes Arcite's ascent to the eighth sphere (an episode Chaucer had used in his other "pagan" epic, the Troilus [1807ff.; cf. *Tes.* XI.1–3]).

36. Dante's oft-repeated *vidi, vid'io* is of course not unique to the *Inferno*, but in conjunction with the various echoes of that canticle in the entire passage, there can be little doubt that, as he catalogues the imagery of the temples, the Knight imagines himself in a Dantean hell, especially in the temple of Mars; cf., e.g., the forest painted on the wall (1975ff.), clearly inspired by the forest of suicides in *Inferno* XIII. Boccaccio is the intermediary here, of course; Boitani has pointed out various echoes of the *Inferno* in the *Teseida*, especially where the gods are concerned: see *Chaucer and Boccaccio*, pp. 38ff. The Knight's formula replaces *vide(vi)* in the *Teseida* VII (32ff.), where it is used for the personified prayers to Mars and Venus. As epic formula it recalls Aeneas's eyewitness account of the destruction of Troy (*Aen.* II, 499, 501), on which see E. R. Curtius, *European Literature and the Latin Middle Ages*, p. 175.

37. On Tertullian, see n. 19 above. His spirit is alive in Chaucer's time and place, as witness the Lollard attack on mystery plays, "a tretise of miraclis pleyinge," no. 19, in Anne Hudson, ed., *Selections from English Wycliffe Writings*, pp. 97ff. The Knight would have found plenty of hints of such an antitheatrical attitude in his source, the *Teseida*, which, it has been suggested, reflects Boccaccio's antiquarian interests in pre-Christian Rome even as the plot points to a Christian bias against the ancient Roman theater. The gods' intervention leading to Arcite's death has ample precedent in Latin epic, but as James H. McGregor has pointed out, the fact that it takes place, in demonic form, during a ludus in the theater, shows the influence of those who, like Tertullian, saw the theater as dedicated to the worship of demons. See James H. McGregor, "Boccaccio's Athenian Theatre."

38. Barish, *The Antitheatrical Prejudice*, p. 63f.

39. For the source in the *Teseida* of this episode, see McGregor, "Boccaccio's Athenian Theatre."

40. Arcite lacks even the rudimentary tragic stature attributable to most of the protagonists in the Monk's Tale.

41. Cf. 2743–61 (the clinical details of Arcite's fatal illness); 2809–16 (the account of his death): 2820–26, 2835–36 (humorous, flippant comments on grieving women).

42. A parallel ambiguity occurs a little later in the Knight's Tale:

> By processe and by lengthe of certeyn yeres,
> Al stynted is the moornynge and the teres
> Of Grekes, by oon general assent.
> Thanne semed me ther was a parlement
> At Atthenes ...
>   (2967–71)

Some modern editors put a period after "teres," presumably to avoid the obvious implication that all the tears shed for Arcite could be considered theatrical.

43. For a detailed recent discussion of what the Knight—or Chaucer—has done with his Boccaccian source, see Boitani, *Chaucer and Boccaccio*; Boitani also comments on the flatness of the Knight's characters.

44. Most notably at lines 885–92, 1347–54, 1520–24, 1531–39, 1623–26, 1663–72, 2110–16, 2206–8, 2284–88, 2447–49, 2681–82, 2811–14.

45. "The multitude," writes Ortega, "has suddenly become visible, installing itself in the preferential positions in society. Before, if it existed, it passed unnoticed, occupying the background of the social stage; now it has advanced to the footlights and is the principal character" (Ortega y Gasset, *The Revolt of the Masses*, p. 8).

46. There the other demons press their tongues between their teeth "as signal for their leader Barbariccia" (138: "verso lot duca, per cenno"). Singleton's comment is taken from the *Commentary on the Inferno*, p. 377.

47. See the excellent articles by Margery Morgan, "'High Fraud': Paradox and Double-Plot in the English Shepherds' Plays," and Linda E. Marshall, "Sacral Parody in the *Secunda Pastorum*."

48. Is there a special connection between farting and the demonic? The example of Luther would suggest there is. And at the end of the Summoner's Tale the lord calls farmer Thomas a "demonyak" (III.2240) for having thought of the problem of fart-distribution. I assume the lord alleges the inspiration of the devil not just for the problem in "ars-metrik" (2222).

49. As center of attraction, Alison also illustrates the democracy of sexual desire: "She was a prymerole, piggesnye, / For any lord to leggen in his bedde, / Or yet for any good yeman for to wedde" (3268–70).

50. The most outrageous of these is "Allone, withouten any compaignye," l. 2779 in the Knight's Tale, l. 3204 in the Miller's.

51. See l. 3332, "Therto [i.e., to a rubible or fiddle] he song some tyme a loud quynyble." On the figure of Herod, see Roscoe E. Parker, "The Reputation of Herod in Early English Literature."

52. In addition to his use of *occupatio*, there are his numerous addresses to the audience, most notably at lines 885–92, 1347–54, 1520–24, 1531–39, 1623–26, 1663–72, 2110–16, 2284–88, 2447–49, 2681–82, 2811–14.

53. See *Processus Noe cum Filiis*, l. 219 and note, in A. C. Cawley, ed., *The Wakefield Pageants in the Towneley Cycle*.

54. It should be clear that this is not a question of different perspectives on the Miller: for instance, the Miller's sense of himself as member of a despised profession, a virtual outsider in his society, over against the society's view of him as a crude intruder. On the low status of the medieval miller, see G. F. Jones, "Chaucer and the Medieval Miller," p. 11. This point seems to be largely substantiated by the voluminous study of the miller in history by Richard Bennett and John Elton, *History of Corn Milling*. The authors observe that the medieval miller "was little, if at all, raised above the lowly status of the slave who sat behind the mill of Pharaoh" (p. 106f.). For a recent discussion of the social and economic status of Chaucer's Miller, which comes to slightly different conclusions while admitting that given the present state of historical research the matter cannot be resolved, see Lee Patterson, "'No man his reson herde'"; see particularly p. 467 and p. 490, n. 25. Patterson makes, I think, an important point in noting that millers took part in the Peasants' Revolt of 1381 (467ff.). The connection, incidentally, between mystery plays and the Miller and his tale becomes quite ironic if Lydgate's poem "Against Millers and Bakers" (cited by Jones, p. 11) is correct in asserting that millers had no guilds—and thus presumably could not perform in the mysteries. Bennett and Elton, p. 114f., do record an instance of a guild of millers in York in the fourteenth century, but this guild had no hall of its own and seems to have been an exceptional case.

55. V. A. Kolve, The Play Called Corpus Christi, p. 19.

56. K. B. Harder, "Chaucer's Use of the Mystery Plays in the Miller's Tale," p. 194. This is "Robyn the rybadour" with his "rusty words," whom Langland's Truth would expunge from the book of the living along with whores, dice-players, and "folk of that ordre": cf. W. W. Skeat, ed., Piers the Plowman, vol. 1, C. Passus, ll. 73–79. In the Roman de la Rose, ed. E. Langlois, vol. 3 (Paris, 1921), l. 12129, Robin(s) is the name of the traditional conductor of village dances; see note on p. 238 of this edition.

57. See Bernard F. Huppé's interesting analysis of this "remarkable piece of blasphemous wordplay" in A Reading of the Canterbury Tales, p. 78.

58. Cited by G. F. Jones, "Wittenwiler's Becki and the Medieval Bagpipe," p. 213. For further information on medieval bagpipes, see E. A. Block, "Chaucer's Millers and Their Bagpipes"; also D. W. Robertson, Jr., A Preface to Chaucer, index, s.v.; and, finally, the excellent article on bagpipes and music in Shakespeare by L. J. Ross, "Shakespeare's 'Dull Clown' and Symbolic Music."

59. Cf. K. L. Scott, "Sow-and-Bagpipe Imagery in the Miller's Portrait." Scott's view of the Miller is uncharitably moralistic. I share her prejudice against bagpipes but do not hear the Miller's voice as a porcine "squawl" (p. 290). Robert Boenig, "The Miller's Bagpipe," suggests that the bagpipe was a courtly instrument more appropriate to the

Knight than to the Miller; though not altogether convincing, the argument suits my point about the Miller's bagpipe.

60. Trans. H. F. Stewart and E. K. Rand (under the title Contra Eutychen et Nestorium) in the Loeb ed., *Boethius: The Theological Tractates and The Consolation of Philosophy*, pp. 85–87. For the influence during the Middle Ages of Boethius's formulation, see, among others, James H. Hoban, *The Thomistic Concept of Person and Some of Its Social Implications*; Mary H. Marshall, "Boethius' Definition of Persona and Mediaeval Understanding of the Roman Theater."

61. For an account of Latin persona and its semantic evolution, see Hans Rheinfelder, Das Wort "Persona," especially the first chapter. Rheinfelder, p. 31, points out that during the Middle Ages the theatrical meanings disappeared from the Romance equivalents of Latin persona—presumably because of Christian hostility to the theater. (Boethius's tract is written in part to refute Nestorius's contention that Christ had both a twofold nature and a twofold person, divine and human.)

62. Cicero, De Officiis, trans. Walter Miller (London: William Heinemann; New York: Macmillan, 1913), p. 109. In the last sentence I have silently amended Miller's translation, which confusingly renders animis with "character."

63. Italics in the last sentence are mine. Trans. Walter Miller, p. 117. The two additional personae mentioned later by Cicero (p. 116f.) look more like an afterthought than an integral part of his discussion.

MANUEL AGUIRRE

The Riddle of Sovereignty

Chaucer's *The Wife of Bath's Tale* may be said to consist of three sections:

1. An unnamed knight from King Arthur's court rapes a girl and is condemned by the Queen, on pain of his life, to find within a year and a day the answer to the question: "What thyng is it that wommen moost desiren?"[1]

2. The knight meets an ugly hag who offers to give him the answer on condition he should do whatever she asks; he accepts, and is able to inform the Queen that "Wommen desiren to have sovereynetee | As well over hir housbond as hir love." The old crone then demands marriage as her boon.

3. As the knight faces her in dismay on their wedding night, she offers him the choice between having an ugly but faithful wife or a beautiful if faithless one. In despair, he yields the choice to her, at which point, seeing her sovereignty acknowledged, she promises to be both beautiful and faithful.

Three times he is asked a question by a woman; on all three occasions the right answer hinges on acknowledgment of woman's sovereignty; all three are questions demanding an "impossible" answer, an answer which falls, as far as the knight is concerned, outside the realm of the reasonable: first, that women should desire sovereignty over men; second, that a young knight should marry an old hag; third, that the proper choice should reside in surrendering the right to choose. A correlation between woman and the unreasonable is inescapable, but beyond this the present article will inquire

From *The Modern Language Review*, vol. 88, part 2 (April 1993): pp. 273–282. © 1993 by The Modern Humanities Research Association.

into the nature of the unreasonable, the symbolism of woman, and the concept of sovereignty.[2]

To begin with, I shall consider some English analogues of Chaucer's tale. Traditionally, three are mentioned:[3] the ballad "The Marriage of Sir Gawain" (henceforth *The Marriage*); the romance "The Wedding of Sir Gawain and Dame Ragnell" (henceforth *Ragnell*); "The Tale of Florent" (henceforth *Florent*) from John Gower's *Confessio Amantis*.

The Marriage begins in the forest of Inglewood, where Arthur is challenged to a duel by Sir Gromer Somer Joure; Arthur having refused, Sir Gromer binds him to return within a year with the answer to "What thing it is that a woman will most desire." Helped by Gawain, Arthur spends a year collecting answers into a book. At the year's end, Arthur meets a Loathly Lady and spontaneously offers her Gawain's hand if she can help him, an offer which she accepts. The King then returns to Sir Gromer, who contemptuously flings aside his written answers; Arthur then gives him the Loathly Lady's answer: "A woman will haue her will, | And this is all her cheef desire." Sir Gromer reveals that she is his sister, and curses her. Gawain marries the Loathly Lady, and on their wedding night she offers to appear fair either by day or by night. Unable to decide, Gawain replies: "Thou shalt haue all thy will." She then promises to be always fair, and explains that her stepmother had bewitched her.

In the case of *Ragnell*, Arthur is hunting a stag when the mysterious Sir Gromer Somer Joure appears and reproaches him for having given Sir Gromer's lands to Gawain; in reparation he demands to know "Whate women love best in feld and town." Helped by Gawain, Arthur collects answers in a book. Arthur meets the loathly Dame Ragnell, who offers the right answer on condition that Gawain marry her; Gawain agrees, and Arthur (after having his book of answers rejected) is able to inform Sir Gromer that women desire "To haue the souereynte [...] of alle, bothe hyghe and lowe." Gromer curses Ragnell (his sister) and allows Arthur to depart. Ragnell is besought to wed Gawain by night and in private, but she insists on a proper ceremony and thoroughly humiliates him. Once in bed, however, she offers to be fair by day and ugly by night, or vice versa. Gawain yields the choice to her, together with all he owns; she then promises to be beautiful both day and night, and explains that she had been bewitched by her stepmother until the best of England should wed her and give her sovereignty over his body and goods.

In *Florent*, the hero, nephew of the Roman Emperor, is riding around in the borderlands ("marches") when he is attacked by a troop and kills the captain's son before being taken prisoner. Because of his high rank, his captors fear to kill him, until an old woman (grandmother of the slain youth) proposes a ruse to execute him lawfully: he must find out "What alle wommen most desire" within an (unspecified) period of time. In the forest, he meets an ugly hag who offers the answer in exchange for his promise to marry her. He accepts, and she informs him "that alle wommen lievest whoe | Be soverein of mannes love." With this answer he buys his freedom from his captors. Florent marries the loathly hag secretly, at night, and when they meet in bed he finds an eighteen-year-old beauty who offers to be fair by day only, or by night. He asks her to choose for him, she thanks him "that ye have mad me soverein," and reveals herself to be the daughter of the King of Sicily, bewitched by her stepmother until she could gain "the love and sovereignty" of the best of knights.[4]

The picture becomes somewhat more complicated by the existence of an analogue of this tale in Celtic literature, the eleventh-century Irish story known as *Echtra mac n-Echach* ("The Adventure of Eochaid's sons").[5] Here is a summary:

> King Eochaid's three sons and their stepbrother Niall go out hunting (one standard device to discover the true hero and his worth). Having caught, cooked, and eaten a boar, they feel a strong thirst and one of them goes to find some water. He comes across a well, and is about to draw water from it when a revolting old crone bars his way and demands a kiss as her condition for his using the well. The lad then decides to forget the whole thing and goes to tell his brothers he could find no water. One by one they go to the well and balk at the awful condition, but when at last Niall's turn comes he kisses the crone with gusto (in one version he lies with her), after which she is transformed into a beautiful damsel who calls herself Royal Rule or Sovereignty, and proclaims Niall High King of Tara.

The resemblance between the Irish story and the English ones builds on several elements: the hunt as a symbolic prelude to the adventure itself, signifying the entrance into an Otherworldly domain; the young man's encounter with the old hag who demands favours of a sexual nature as an (unreasonable) condition for satisfying his need; the hag's transformation into a young girl; the concept of sovereignty itself. In the Irish story the expression "flaitheas na h-Eirenn" ("the Sovereignty of Ireland") defines the nature of the union as both political and sacred, "the symbolical marriage of an Irish king with the deity representing the land itself."[6] This union is presented as a fulfilment (the goddess becomes herself on meeting the right pretender), and doubtless the image was exploited by different rulers seeking to justify or enhance the righteousness of their kingship. Beyond this, however, the

genuinely mythological character of the image is unquestionable: accession
to the throne was regarded as a hierogamy:

> The idea of the goddess changing her form and her raiment when
> she is without her proper spouse and king is very common in the
> whole of [Irish] literature, and enshrines the ancient belief that
> a land gained or lost fruitfulness and prosperity according as it
> gained or lost its true and rightful king.[7]

The connexion between the Irish and the English stories is nowadays
accepted as a matter of course, but problems arise when one tries to define
it more precisely: here a certain "insularity" tends to be in evidence in both
Celtic and English scholarship; both sides seem to agree that there is a link,
but at the same time they neglect or minimize its value. For an example of the
Celtic position I quote Bromwich who, after stating the relationship, observes
that in the English versions:

> The original significance of the Sovereignty theme has inevitably
> ceased to be recognised and so a fresh explanation for the
> heroine's transformation has been introduced [...]. In two of the
> English versions [*Ragnell* and *Florent*; and in *The Marriage* as
> well] this transformation is explained as due to spells imposed
> by a hostile character, and in addition the riddle-motive "What
> is it that women most desire?" is appended to the story in these
> versions, as it is in the *Wife of Bath's Tale*. (pp. 453–54)

To this Bromwich adds in a footnote:

> Any connection between the *sovereynetee* desired by women
> and *flaithes na k-Eirenn* may be ruled out as entirely fortuitous.
> *Flaitheas* denotes kingship or royal rule, and could not possibly be
> applied to a conception so banal as that intended in the English
> poems. (p. 453)

For a representative statement of the English view I quote F. N. Robinson:

> In the Irish tale, as in Chaucer's, the hag appears to be acting
> independently and is not said to be the victim of enchantment.
> The emphasis, in both stories, on "sovereignty" is also cited as
> evidence that they are closely related. But [...] "sovereignty" in
> the Irish stories means "royal rule," whereas in Chaucer it refers

to domestic supremacy. At this point, then, the parallel is not very significant. (p. 703)

The main differences between the English and Irish versions would seem to be: the presence of the riddle-motif in all the English versions; the presence of a hostile character to explain the transformation of the woman in three of the four English versions (not in Chaucer); the difference between the two concepts of Sovereignty. To these one might add: the appearance of an adversary (Sir Gromer, Florent's captors) who imposes on the knight the riddle and the penalty for not solving it; the fact that Sovereignty is bestowed by the woman in the Irish version, but demanded by her in the English ones; and the presence of a second protagonist, Arthur, who takes up part of the burden of the action in both *The Marriage* and *Ragnell*.

In the rest of this article I propose to show that, first of all, there is a fundamental continuity between the Irish and English versions, and that even their differences are to be accounted for in terms of this continuity. Furthermore, I shall suggest that the changes patent in the English versions with respect to the Irish tale do not have to do with a simple loss of significance but with a subversion of the meaning of the original tale.

THE RIDDLE

As mentioned above, one of the textual functions of the Hunt is to introduce the protagonist into an Otherworldly domain. In traditional thought, Hunt, Voyage, Adventure, and Dream are so many gateways into the realm of the Numinous, a realm which is by definition unknown, where the logic of everyday reality often fails to apply and where, consequently, rational thought or action may be of little avail.[8] On the other hand, Bromwich has studied in detail the connexion between the Hunt and the obtaining of the Lady's (especially the fairy-mistress's) favours; Hunt, Adventure, and Courtship are fundamentally related in traditional myth and folklore. All three are challenges, tests in which the protagonist's abilities are pitted against the logic of the Other, whether this Other manifests itself in the magic of the White Stag, the deceptive road to the Grail, or the mysterious behaviour of Woman. All five tales considered so far in this article are in essence versions of the Test, often presenting it in a variety of parallel symbols; while all five contain the Courtship theme, *Ragnell* and *The Marriage* combine it with the Hunt, while *Florent* places its hero "in the marches," the border territory where the mundane and the Otherworldly meet and which is therefore propitious ground for Adventure.

In addition, a consideration of the threefold division proposed for the English texts shows that each section constitutes a riddle, that each riddle poses a challenge demanding an unreasonable answer, and that the texts therefore simply reinforce the nature of the Challenge, first, by repeating it three times and, secondly, by verbalizing it in the shape of riddles. It may thus be concluded that the Riddle motif has not been merely appended to the English versions but is in actual fact an additional symbol—alongside those of Hunt, Adventure, and Courtship—to give a verbal shape to the test, a test already found in Niall's tale, and central to which stands the loathly hag.

It is the old hag who poses a challenge to the protagonist, whether she gives it a verbal character or not. Her very existence is a contradiction: she is both young and old, both fair and loathly, the *puella senilis*,[9] a numinous being standing outside the categories of human reality. Her ugliness is not simply extreme but unearthly, deliberately designed to revolt the beholder, while her demand requires her "wooer" to act against both instinct and custom, since he must suspend his own inclinations and social conventions for the sake of his brothers (or of his king in *Ragnell* and *The Marriage*). It is a demand which falls, as far as Niall's brothers are concerned, outside the pale of the tolerable, if not of the possible. This basic contradiction which forces the hero to reassess his reality and his options is identical to the test encountered in the English versions, where it is further elaborated in the verbal quandaries faced by the unfortunate knights.

THE HOSTILE STEPMOTHER

Bromwich points out that in *Ragnell* "the role of Arthur has encroached upon that of Gawain, who is the real hero of the tale" (p. 452). Another way of putting this would be to say that Gawain has been relieved of part of the protagonist's function; in effect, this function has been spread over two characters, and therefore Arthur represents simply aspects of Gawain. In a similar way, the hostile stepmother is a projection or "unfolding" of the Loathly Lady herself, a convenient manifestation of her hostile aspect.

In traditional tales, the wicked mother or stepmother opposes the hero's or heroine's fulfilment. She keeps Cinderella covered in rags, thus hiding her true beauty and preventing her from living out her destiny; she tries to kill Snow-White and succeeds in keeping her in a state of suspended life, as she does with Sleeping Beauty;[10] she swears a "destiny" on her rejected son Lleu to keep him from ever receiving a name, being armed, and having a wife in the Welsh tale *Math Son of Mathonwy*; she swears a similar "destiny" on the hero of *Kulhwch ac Olwen*.[11] How the protagonists thwart her curse by finding the "impossible" solution to it shows the wicked mother or stepmother, too, is setting before them what is in essence a riddle, a labyrinthine condition with a non-logical solution.

This is the function she performs in *Ragnell*; but, furthermore, she can be pointed at as the extraneous, disturbing cause for a state of affairs which, but for her intervention, would be very different. Unlike the situation in Niall's tale, the Loathly Lady is not responsible for her transformation and behaviour: another female figure takes the responsibility—and the blame. Change becomes an anomaly wrought by wickedness, while the female figure is split into two clearly distinguished types: the wicked type is wilful, shrewish, prone to wantonness, unpredictable and contradictory, false, whereas the "good" type is submissive, steadfast, unwilling to change. In *Ragnell* she not only renounces her ugly aspect and, hence, her duplicity but also promises to be a meek and obedient wife; in *The Wife of Bath's Tale* she also promises to be faithful. Most important, this good woman is innocent of any participation in the contradiction that confronts the hero: she is as much a victim as he is; riddles and paradoxes, like inconstancy, are as alien to her nature as they are inherent in the wicked woman. The question why this distinction between two types should be found in all the English versions (except Chaucer's) brings me to the third main difference between the Irish and the English tales: the use of the concept of Sovereignty.

SOVEREIGNTY

Sovereignty means royal rule in the one, domestic rule in the others. While this is true, to present the link between these meanings as fortuitous would be to misinterpret the tale. The Sovereignty theme in the Irish story has to do not only with land and kingship but also with woman herself; once we acknowledge this we cannot fail to recognize the essential similarity between the different versions: while only some of them relate to the theme of territorial rule, all of them contain a statement about woman and her symbolic nature.

Woman is the land because in some of the oldest strata of mythological thought the earth is personified as a female figure, the Mother of all life.[12] She is indeed the goddess, the Numen, and as such is endowed with mystery; she moves with the seasons and therefore represents cyclicness and change; she symbolizes fertility and therefore she must periodically take a consort with whom she may renew herself. This symbolism does not vanish with the addition of a political content whereby she becomes not just the land but the territory, her prosperity being dependent on her choice of a rightful king. Because she is the bestower of royal power, to have her hand is to rule the kingdom, and therefore her wooers must be tested and the right king carefully chosen. If the English versions are looked at in the light of this double land-and-woman theme it can be seen that their difference from the Irish tale does not consist only in the presence or absence of territorial symbolism but also in a change in the symbolic status of woman. In fact, there is a direct correlation between the presence or absence of the former and the quality of the latter.

It is usually assumed that the territorial theme is missing in all the English versions, and so the link between the two Sovereignties, the Irish *flaitheas* and the English *sovereynetee*, comes to be reduced to a deceptive coincidence of terms. The link, however, is to be found in one of the English versions, one where the issue of territory is still present but has ceased to be prominent in the general symbolic structure of the tale. At the beginning of *Ragnell*, Sir Gromer Somer joure complains that his lands have been given away to Gawain by Arthur and that Gawain holds them unlawfully. When Gawain agrees to marry Ragnell he obtains the answer to Sir Gromer's riddle, who then withdraws his claim, while calling Ragnell his own sister. In other words, Arthur's bequest to Gawain was not valid; on the other hand, Gromer's lands are effectively taken away from him by his sister Ragnell, and lawfully assigned by her to Gawain as a result of his marriage pledge. In a significantly obscured way, she is indeed Sovereignty, the power that dispenses territorial rule.

Sir Gromer Somer Joure, "The Man of the Summer Day" (his name identifies him with one specific day in the year, the Summer Solstice, a turning-point in the agricultural cycle), is the Yearly King, the earlier holder of Sovereignty over lands he is unwilling to let go, and so, for the space of a year, he opposes Arthur's and Gawain's claim to his domain until they have guessed the riddle of woman—the Riddle of Sovereignty; only then can Gawain assert his right to the land, as to Ragnell's beauty.

In the earlier nature myth, Sir Cromer may have been married to the mysterious lady; he cannot now, however, be represented as Ragnell's consort, since she is to wed Gawain in what is clearly a Christianized version of the tale. The text, therefore, presents him as Ragnell's brother, thereby preserving, in an uncontroversial way, the special "family" relationship between them. But he fulfils another function: ostensibly, the land-issue is now handled entirely between him and Arthur, leaving Gawain and Ragnell free to concentrate on the "wooing" aspect. In other words, in *Ragnell* there is a dissociation between the courtship as such and the matter of territorial rule; put differently, the figure of woman is being taken out of the field of land-symbolism and relegated to the (more literal) domestic sphere: Sovereignty over land is being displaced in favour of Sovereignty in love.

In *The Marriage* and *Florent*, the land issue has disappeared; the Hunt remains in *The Marriage* and *Ragnell*, but is ascribed to Arthur, while in *Florent* it is replaced by the hero's wandering in the marches; in Chaucer the hunt is again absent, while the rape of a young maid by the "lusty bachelor" triggers off the story. If the Hunt is one symbol for the Courtship, then the rape is a literalization of the symbol: it represents the purely sexual aspect of an episode no longer associated with royal rule and territorial issues, just as *sovereynetee* in this tale has ceased to relate to the land and has been narrowed down to sovereignty-in-love. The complex symbol of the Courtship has been split up into sexual domination on the one hand and dominion in love on the other.

In *The Wife of Bath's Tale* there is no stepmother to receive the blame for the lady's transformation. It could be assumed that the text follows, in this respect, an older model than do *Florent* and the Gawain-poems, or that Chaucer dispenses with this character, as he does with that of the male adversary, in the interests of economy. One further possibility, however, must be borne in mind: the stepmother's disappearance from Chaucer, far from keeping the text in line with (or bringing it back to) Celtic models, actually leads it further away from them, because the very wilfulness that could be safely, and hence explicitly, embodied in the marginal figure of the wicked stepmother now reverts, in an equally explicit way, to the central female figure in the tale. She seems to act out of sheer wantonness, but her deliberate behaviour no longer has the sanction of symbolism found in the lady of Niall's tale. What is more, if the Gawain-version and *Florent*-version present her as a more or less grotesque, more or less humorous figure, Chaucer clinches the issue by having her tale narrated by a woman who is herself less than impartial. The Wife of Bath's characterization requires this wantonness in the female protagonist of the story she is telling; less would not befit her high-minded feminism. But one cannot escape the impression that Chaucer is ironically, if lovingly, drawing the picture of what he himself (and his age) considers an eccentric.

There remains the question of why she *demands* sovereignty. The writers of these versions, though aware of a persistent ascription of Sovereignty to woman in their readings, no longer think she is truly entitled to it; not only is territorial sovereignty out of the question for woman, but even her sovereignty in love, still acknowledged by the twelfth-century courtly love conventions, becomes problematic, if not downright preposterous, in the fourteenth and fifteenth centuries. Her vaunted authority becomes merely a claim to authority. As a numinous figure, woman stood for the non-rational; now, deprived of her numinous status, she comes to stand for the unreasonable.

SIR GAWAIN AND THE GREEN KNIGHT

I shall pursue this point in another work, roughly contemporary with Chaucer's and belonging in the Gawain-tradition, *Sir Gawain and the Green Knight*. While acknowledging the complexity of its structure, it yet seems possible to discern in it something like the threefold pattern detected in the other English texts.

First, the Green Knight challenges Arthur's knights to exchange blows with him, himself to receive the first blow and his opponent to submit to the like treatment in the remote Green Chapel within a year and a day. We have the numinous adversary, the one-year-hence deadline, and the challenge itself a straightforward if silly challenge which can be accepted because the Green Knight must surely die; an impossible challenge because he does not die and leaves Gawain with the "riddle" of how to survive a year from now.

Secondly, while biding his time to keep his tryst, Gawain sojourns at Bertilak's castle, where he holds converse with his host's beautiful wife, who appears in the company of a noble crone of great age and ugliness. Then, on three successive mornings he must fend off, firmly yet courteously, the amorous advances of the fair lady while Bertilak is out hunting. Having failed to seduce him, the lady gives him a magic girdle that will protect him from the Green Knight's blow. Here the hero encounters a rationalized version of the *puella senilis*, as represented by two women, one fair and one loathly. As might be expected, the theme of the Hunt is here combined with (indeed, it is presented as simultaneous with) that of the Courtship, but the values assigned to the latter are reversed: the poem's moral sanction is on the knight's rejection of the lady and his preservation of chastity. The "riddle" Gawain faces here hinges on the question how to be both disdainful and friendly towards her, how to obey the dictates of the *fin' amour* convention (of which she takes good care to remind him) in order not to reach but to escape the lady. At the end of his test, he is given a prize, the answer to the first challenge: the magic girdle that will allow him to survive his encounter.[13]

Thirdly, wearing the girdle, Gawain meets the Green Knight and survives his blow, though it slightly wounds his neck. He then learns that the old crone was Morgan le Fay, Arthur's half-sister and Gawain's aunt (a figure embodying aspects of both the Loathly Lady and the hostile stepmother); that she had bewitched Bertilak into the monstrous Green Knight in order to test Gawain's courage; that Bertilak in turn had sent his wife to test Gawain's loyalty; that he received his neck-wound precisely because he was wearing a protection against being wounded. In other words, he erred in his solution to the riddle: he should have heeded the non-rational nature of the challenge and submitted to the unknown instead of accepting advice and help that were meant to foster his weakness.

Curiously, the knight in this tale rejects the lady's amorous advances, and therein, we are told, lies his virtue; curiously, too, the solution given him by the lady is the wrong one; most curiously, he fails the test, if only just, and he returns to Camelot railing bitterly against women, deceivers of mankind. While it is to be acknowledged that *The Green Knight* handles many ingredients and patterns found in *The Marriage*, *Ragnell*, *Florent*, and *The Wife of Bath's Tale*, it appears to have gone further than any other in subverting the traditional meanings. The challenge scene becomes a temptation, the prize is now a bait, and success has turned to failure. The narrative bias is definitely towards chastity, and against woman, her wiles, her wantonness, her almost incomprehensible perversity. If Chaucer pokes gentle fun at woman's sovereignty, the author of *Sir Gawain and the Green Knight* seems to revolt against the very idea.

What reasons may be found for these developments? Undoubtedly the influence of the poetry of courtly love has contributed to this prominence of the love-issue, though I suspect this poetry itself to be but another manifestation of the ongoing separation between land and love matters: in the lyrics of the troubadours woman appears, indeed, as the equivalent of the feudal lord, but the sphere of her dominion has shifted (one might say, contracted) to the emotional or spiritual plane: she rules hearts alone, not kingdoms. In the second place, the *Weltanschauung* imposed by the feudal system has influenced concepts of land-transmission: woman must be left out of them because the social order favours patrilinear inheritance.

In a more general way, there is throughout the Middle Ages a clear trend towards reducing woman's direct participation in the making of society. She is at the same time exalted and degraded, both protected and subjected. She becomes more and more (and precisely because of her rich numinous symbolism) the object of oppression by a mentality which fears the Numinous, stresses linear thinking and rationality, and frowns upon change, cyclicness, and variability as so many signs of faithlessness. Two hundred years later the Wife of Bath will be called Katherine in *The Taming of the Shrew*. In the literary field, the process leads to a restatement of the entire love-issue in the direction of honour, chastity, and woman's subjection. Socially, this process may be seen to reach a height in the fifteenth century when the pact with Satan became, in the view of the intelligentsia of the day, an integral part of the definition of witchcraft and when, in keeping with this view, the Church redefined witchcraft as a heresy, that is, as an act of treason against God.[14] From here on, woman (the wicked woman, the wanton, wilful, inconstant, shrewish, untamed woman, which is to say, the sovereign woman) becomes the great betrayer.

NOTES

1. Quotations are from *The Works of Geoffrey Chaucer*, ed. by F. N. Robinson (Boston, MA: Houghton Mifflin, 1957).

2. This article develops a point made in a short paper entitled "A Link Between *The Wife of Bath's Tale* and its (Disputed) Irish Source," read at the III Conference of the Spanish Society for Medieval English Language and Literature held at the University of Alcalá de Henares (Madrid), 24–28 September 1990.

3. *Sources and Analogues of Chaucer's Canterbury Tales*, ed. by W. F. Bryan and G. Dempster, 2nd edn (Atlantic Highlands, NJ: Humanities Press, 1941).

4. *The Wedding of Sir Gawain and Dame Ragnell, The Marriage of Sir Gawain*, John Gower's *The Tale of Florent*, and *Sir Gawain and the Green Knight*, in *Medieval English Literature*, ed. by Thomas Garbaty (Lexington, MA: Heath, 1984).

5. *Silva Gadelica*, ed. and trans. by Standish O'Grady (London: Williams & Norgate, 1892), pp. 368–73.

6. Rachel Bromwich, "Celtic Dynastic Themes and the Breton Lays," *Études Celtiques*, 9 (1960–61), 419–74 (p. 445).

7. Proinsias MacCana, "Aspects of the Theme of King and Goddess in Irish Literature," *Études Celtiques*, 7 (1955–56), 76–114 (p. 84) and 356–413; 8 (1958–59), 59–65. For examples and reference to various manifestations of this myth, see also R. A. Breatnach, "The Lady and the King: A Theme of Irish Literature," *Studies: An Irish Quarterly Review*, 42 (1953), 321–36.

8. On the symbolism of the Voyage, see my article "The Hero's Voyage in *Immram Curaig Mailduin*," *Études Celtiques*, 27 (1990), 203–20, and sources there given; see also my analysis of the Dream tradition in "The Evolution of Dreams," *Neohelicon*, 17 (1990), 9–26; on Adventure, Labyrinth, and the structure of the excursion into the Otherworld, see my *The Closed Space: Honor Literature and Western Symbolism* (Manchester: Manchester University Press, 1990), especially Chapters 1 and 3.

9. Ernst Robert Curtius, *European Literature and the Latin Middle Ages*, trans. by Willard R. Trask (New York: Harper & Row, 1953); see also Breatnach, "The Lady and the King."

10. Incidentally, Snow-White, Cinderella, Sleeping Beauty are all examples of MacCana's observation that the goddess, of whom these are reduced manifestations, waits for her proper consort to restore her to her true condition. The tale of King Frog or the Frog-Prince concerns the hero's transformation on being acknowledged (in a somewhat aggressive manner) by the young girl. But for this to happen, the girl has had to modify her attitude towards him (Grimm's version suggests a sexual response, even if of a violent nature, in contrast with her previous childish withdrawal). Likewise, an undeniable if submerged theme in *Beauty and the Beast* is the fact that through Beast's own love, patience, and determination, Beauty herself changes, in so far as she learns to accept her own inclinations and, hence, to be herself. It is equally clear that Niall, too, undergoes a transformation as he puts aside conventions and accepts the old hag, and that it is this transformation that is signified by his becoming High King of Tara. Perhaps it should be said, for the sake of generality, that in the universal "monomyth," as Campbell calls it, the encounter between male and female protagonists leads to a double self-realization as *both* become themselves, while specific tales will lay emphasis on this or that aspect of the theme, on this or that transformation: if the man's, then it may be his numinous status that is stressed; if the woman's, then she will be assigned numinous features.

11. *The Mabinogion*, trans. by Gwyn Jones and Thomas Jones (Manchester: Dent, 1978). "A mi a dynghaf dynghet idaw," heb hi, "na chalfo wreic uyth [...]" (*Pedeir Keinc y Mabinogi*, ed. by Ifor Williams (Cardiff: Gwasg Prifysgol Cymru, 1978), p. 83): "And I will swear a destiny on him," said she, "that he shall never have a wife of the race that is now on this earth" (*Math*, p. 68). "I will swear a destiny upon thee, that thy side shall neverstrike

against woman till thou win Olwen daughter of Ysbaddaden Chief Giant" (*Kulhwch*, p. 96). The word "tynged" (Middle Welsh "tyghet," "tynghet") does not seem to have the clearly negative connotations of Modern English "curse;" semantically it is rather related to Old English "wyrd" in its sense of "destiny" or "fate." The Old Icelandic word "Urd" (= Old English "wyrd") is the name of one of the Norns, the Scandinavian Parcae, and carries the same meaning. Curiously, the function of the Norns is not dissimilar to that of the stepmothers of both Kulhwch and Lleu: each embodies a higher, impersonal power which, like Nature, may appear inimical or beneficent but which is, in essence, a manifestation of the eternal, immutable round of things.

12. Joseph Campbell, *The Masks of God: Occidental Mythology* (Harmondsworth: Penguin, 1961).

13. The girdle itself is a symbol of Sovereignty, though in the end it reveals itself a negative one, a symbol of deception. It is given a positive value in, for instance, the *Odyssey*, where Ulysses ties round his waist the veil given him by a nymph, that he may survive the onslaught of the angry Ocean; or in the *Edda*, where Thor borrows a girdle of might from the giantess Grid to fight Geirrod the giant. The multiple and ambivalent manifestations of this symbol in traditional myth are the subject of a study in preparation.

14. In *Europe's Inner Demons* (St Albans: Paladin, 1976), Norman Cohn has exposed as hoaxes a number of widely accepted "documents" which purported to prove that witch-hunts as we understand the term were taking place already in the fourteenth century. As reassessed, the persecution of witches *en masse* began only after the Church had redefined witchcraft as a specifically anti-Christian practice on the part of a sect of people committed to a pact with Satan, in other words, as heresy. Such redefinition was codified for the first time in certain treatises published around the middle of the fifteenth century. See also Russell Hope Robbins, *The Encyclopedia of Witchcraft and Demonology* (London: Hamlyn, 1970).

MICHAEL A. CALABRESE

New Armor for the Amazons:
The Wife of Bath and a Genealogy of Ovidianism

CHAUCER AND HIS OVID

In his imaginary letter of consolation to the exiled Ovid, the bishop-poet Baudry offers this lament: "What we are is crime, if it is a crime to love, / For the God who made me, also made me love."[1] "Alias," says the Wife of Bath some 250 years later, "that evere love was synne," expressing a sentiment inherent to medieval lovers, who are subject to judgment just as Ovid, the servant of the servants of love, was subject to exile and ban. Those in a Christian universe, like the twelfth-century bishop and the fourteenth-century fictional weaver, find themselves confronting forces of authority that are in conflict with their art and their experience.

As a prominent document in the history of this struggle between love and authority, and specifically in the literary history of Ovidian love, the *Wife of Bath's Prologue and Tale* examines the ambitions of a uniquely constructed master of Ovidian art. The Wife is the most deeply embroiled of all Chaucer's characters not only in Ovid's texts themselves but in their medieval manifestations and implications.[2] She is, like Ovid, the master of "experience" (usus).[3] She applies an explicitly Ovidian strategy from both the *Ars Amatoria* III and from Ovid's Old Woman of the *Amores*, and she tells a story from the *Metamorphoses*. In addition, her husband owns a copy of the *Ars Amatoria* in his book of wicked wives. The interplay between these many

From *Chaucer's Ovidian Arts of Love*: pp. 81-111. © 1994 by the Board of Regents of the State of Florida.

"Ovids" constitutes one of Chaucer's most profound dramatizations of sexual and marital power and authority. More than any other poet in Chaucer's library, Ovid was concerned with the power of men and women in the games of love. And so to understand fully the literary historical significance of the Wife and to perceive the full extent of Chaucer's interest in the gendering of authority, we must understand the Wife's Ovid, the Venerean's use of "Venus's clerk."[4]

The Wife's "Ovid," furthermore, is in many respects Jean de Meun's, for the "art of love" that sprawls across thousands of lines of allegory in the *Roman de la Rose* lies behind much of Alison's own art and struggle. This clash of not so ignorant armies helps Chaucer shape the Wife, her many husbands, Jankyn's book, and the battles that ensue. As many scholars have seen, the Wife draws from the advice to lovers offered by her literary "mother," La Vieille. Equally important to our study of the Wife's marital battles is the discourse of Ami, the Ovidian "friend" of Amant whose Jealous Husband's speech is a close analogue and indeed a source for the antifeminist material in the Wife's *Prologue*.[5]

In the entire discourse of Ami we find a "genealogy of Ovidianism" that shows how female greed and male domination caused the end of the Golden Age by creating the need for trickery and fraud—that is, for Ovidian art.[6] This genealogy is explicitly based on Ovid's story of the decline of the Golden Age and the origins of his own love doctrines as described in the *Ars Amatoria* and the *Amores*. As the Wife takes on the antifeminist tradition, she attempts, ultimately, to depict a model for returning to that "golden age" by getting beyond treachery and the claims to authority and power that prevent love. Chaucer's use of Jean's poem not only allows us to comprehend "Chaucer's Ovid" but also illustrates how Chaucer transforms parts of Jean's diffuse allegory into a compressed narrative monologue.[7] As Chaucer reimagines the work of his literary fathers, Ovid and Jean de Meun, he allows the Wife to reimagine the words of her own literary ancestors and to become, finally, his most powerful Ovidian artist.

An artist and a protean rhetorician, the Wife invents reality as both Ovid and her most immediate precursor, Pandarus, do. She enacts various stratagems of Ovidian deceit and basically "holds her husbands on hand" in any way necessary. She "twists" them and extracts, as both Dipsas and La Vieille advise, money and gifts. In return, she offers her husbands what Ovid would call a gift of words, openly lying (ll. 226 ff.) and at times feigning appetite (l. 417). She twice tells the pilgrims that all she says to her husbands "was fals" (ll. 382, 582), and she sums up her art thus: "Atte ende I hadde the bettre in ech degree, / By sleighte, or force, or by som maner thyng" (ll. 404–5), for God gave women the arts of "Deceite, wepyng, [and] spynnyng" (l. 401).[8]

The vital dynamic of the Wife's *Prologue* comes in part because Ovid's love poems are the source, not only of the Wife's craft, but also of much of the conventional antifeminism she embodies. As we will see, her drinking, sexual appetite, trickery, and callousness in looking for a new husband at the last one's funeral are all common antifeminist complaints rooted in Ovid's poems. For the Wife, as for any medieval reader, Ovid was both an ancient *auctor* who knew the wiles of women and also a crafty counselor who knew the "art of love." Ovid is, then, at once her adversary and her benefactor, the founder of the tradition that opposes her and also, ultimately, her own creator.[9] The origins of this duplicity lie in Ovid's own double agency, for in the *Ars Amatoria* he arms both "Greeks" and "Amazons." In the *Troilus* we saw how Chaucer exploits the tension between two Ovidian "moments"—the youthful love poetry and the poetry of change and exile. In the Wife's *Prologue*, Chaucer orchestrates a battle between two opposing Ovidian incarnations—the antifeminist founder and the savior of disempowered women.

In the thick of the battle is Jankyn's book of "wykked wives"—that bound version of the jealous Husband's speech in the *Roman de la Rose*. The false authority it assumes demands that it be surrendered and burned, despite Jankyn's anxieties over losing his source of male power. Throughout her *Prologue and Tale*, the Wife combats the subjection that arises from the definitions of sexual difference generated by antifeminist texts. As she strips Jankyn of the book, she strips him of what he thought was his warrant of wisdom and superiority. As the Wife becomes a new Ovid and composes a new art of love, we can tell that Chaucer's concerns with authority, experience, and textual power create a drama that we did not see in Troy. But we must wonder if "trouthe," which both doomed and ennobled Troilus, will play a part here too.

OVID AND MARRIAGE: "*THEN LET THE BRIDE READ NOTHING*"

To understand better Ovid's diverse role in the Wife's battles, we should examine Ovid's own views on marriage relations—views that contributed to his scandalous reputation and eventually to his exile and ban.[10] He was charged with teaching men to corrupt married women through seduction, and with teaching women to deceive their husbands and commit adultery. The corruption of married women, the *matronae*, is at the heart of each accusation, but the crimes refer to Books I and II of the *Ars* (which arm the Greeks) and to Book III (which arms the Amazons). These teachings were unpopular with Caesar Augustus. Medieval schoolmasters commonly observed that Ovid was exiled in part because "Roman matrons were corrupted" [corruptae fuerant romanae matronae] by his *Ars Amatoria*.[11]

Ovid had tried to preempt controversy by specifying his audience for the *Ars*—high-class courtesans only, the *hetaerae*, and *not* the *matronae*.[12] A letter to Maximus (*Ex Ponto* III, iii) addresses the accusation that men armed with the *Ars Amatoria*—were nonetheless seducing the higher class of women. Ovid contends that he has "not disturbed lawful wedlock," and he asks the God of Love: "Have you at any time, by following my law, learned to deceive brides and to make descent uncertain?" (III, iii, 53–54). Nevertheless, to Rome his games were serious matters, shifting marital power relations and endangering the future of the patriarchal social order.

Ovid was aware that some might think his guidance in *Ars Amatoria* III would dangerously empower the *matronae* to seek secret love for themselves. He tried again to specify his audience while teaching the newly freed slaves to deceive their men and guardians. So that no one will think he intends these arts for the *matronae*, he pointedly announces a politically correct Roman marital doctrine: "Let the bride fear the husband" [nupta uirum timeat], "for this is what law, right, and modesty command" (III, 613–14). As Wilkinson observes, "Ovid is at pains to emphasize that his poem has nothing to do with married or 'respectable' women."[13] Augustus felt, however, that "respectable" women were learning from Ovid how to deceive their husbands anyway. The emperor did not believe Ovid's claim that Roman fathers "need not fear the legitimacy of their children," and he may even have felt that Ovid's games led his own granddaughter Julia into disgraceful adultery.[14]

In the *Tristia*, Ovid addresses these charges by distinguishing his poetry from the popular mime plays that "show" women how to deceive men (*Tristia* II, 497ff.). He repeats his claim to an unmarried audience (II, 253ff.), and states explicitly that "no brides learned deception" from him as teacher (II, 347). In response to Augustus's statement that *matronae* might learn adultery despite Ovid's innocent intentions (II, 253), Ovid issues the bold, even Miltonic challenge, "Then let the bride read nothing" [Nil igitur matrona legat] (II, 255). If poetry translates immediately into behavior, then almost any poem ever written could prove dangerous. The only way to protect the public, if individuals cannot choose for themselves, is to ban all poetry. As Ovid says elsewhere, "Any text can corrupt" (see *Tristia* II, 255–56, 264).

In this entire controversy, we learn something about Ovid's teachings that will prepare us to consider the literary historical context of the Wife's encounter with authority. In banishing Ovid, Augustus was trying to protect Roman law and mores; the issue of antifeminism does not arise. Despite his place in medieval antifeminist texts, Ovid never wrote explicitly about the evils of women, not even in the *Remedia Amoris*, where Amor, not femina, provides the opposition. If a pupil gets too deeply embroiled in love and flirts with suicide, then Ovid can liberate him from this self-destructive passion.[15] Indeed, part of the *Remedia*'s advice is to find another woman, and Ovid explicitly states that though he addresses the *Remedia* to men, his words will help women as well.[16] Ovid has no committed agenda or antifeminist burden. Unlike church fathers and medieval clerks, he does not argue an ecclesiastical position exhorting celibacy. Rather, he plays—and plays so as to *join* lovers, not keep them apart. It is the manner of "joining" that brought on Roman wrath.

Even though Ovid is not essentially an antifeminist author,[17] medieval intellectual and literary history saw the *Ars* and the *Remedia* as antifeminist texts. Christine de Pizan makes this clear in her treatment of Ovid in the *Book of the City of Ladies*, which she wrote specifically to counter the excesses of antifeminism. Christine asks the character Reason why Ovid (a renowned poet, though inferior to Virgil) would write such foul things about women in these two poems.[18] Later, Rectitude responds to a similar question, saying that since Ovid and other antifeminist writers armed men against deceitful women, these writers ought to have done the same for women—arming them against the wiles of deceitful men (II, 54, 1).[19] These passages tell us that the love poems, though not initially designed, of course, as misogynist or misogamist texts, were appropriated as such by the medieval authorities whom Christine battles. Accordingly we find Ovid's works included in antifeminist anthologies, as Chaucer's index to Jankyn's book of wicked wives indicates. The Wife's and Christine's specific references to Ovid's status provide our best evidence that Ovid, despite his intentions and despite the rhetorical complexities of his gendered voices, was a founding father of the medieval antifeminist tradition.

A survey of the works in Jankyn's book further indicates Ovid's role in the antifeminist tradition and shows precisely what the Wife of Bath must confront.[20] The book contains, among many others, "Valerie," "Theofraste," and "Saint Jerome." Valerius, the fictional name of Walter Map, refers to his *Discourse to Ruffinus the Philosopher Lest He Take a Wife*. Theophrastus wrote a tract against marriage, known only because it is preserved by Saint Jerome, whose *Epistola Adversus Jovinianum* is one of the founding texts of medieval antimarital literature. And, of course, the anthology includes "Ovides Art" (Wife's *Prologue*, I. 680). Ovid appears here (and is the focus of Christine's attack) because the antifeminist texts draw from Ovid's love poems and make them, like the *Metamorphoses*, sources for sordid details about mythic women such as the incestuous Myrrha and Pasiphaë, the bride of a bull. Ovid's poems, furthermore, sometimes describe woman as greedy, vain, and given to "that fierce female lust" [ista feminea libidine) (*Ars* I, 341). Despite Ovid's supposed fairness in arming both Greek and Amazon, many of his comments on sex, however playful, rhetorical, and, indeed, contradictory, lend themselves easily to antifeminist use.[21]

Jankyn's book offers us a definitive example: the wife lists for us the characters her husband has studied, including Pasiphaë, who is grouped with Eve, Delilah, and Clytemnestra—women who brought their men to disaster. Jankyn reads to the Wife:

> Of Phasipha, that was the queene of Crete,
> For shrewednesse, hym thoughte the tale swete;
> Fy! Spek namoore—it is a grisly thyng—
> Of hire horrible lust and hir likyng.
>   (ll. 733–36)

In the margins of a *Canterbury Tales* manuscript, we find a gloss on this passage from one of the actual texts in Jankyn's book—Jerome's own catalog of wicked wives:

> Why should I refer to Pasiphaë, Clytemnestra, and
> Eriphyle, the first of whom, the wife of a king and
> swimming in pleasure, is said to have lusted for a
> bull, the second to have killed her husband for the
> sake of an adulterer, the third to have preferred a
> gold necklace to the welfare of her husband, etc.,
> thus Metellius Marrio according to Valerius.[22]

In its manifestations as Jankyn's reading and as an actual gloss to a fifteenth-century manuscript of Chaucer, Jerome's short catalog indicates that women's lusts bring their husbands to disaster.

Ovid alludes to the story in the *Metamorphoses* but tells it in full in *Ars* I, among a series of catastrophes brought on by "female lust." Ovid offers here not a vote for celibacy but proof that women can be had: "Come, then," he encourages his students, "do not doubt that all women can be won" [Ergo age, ne dubita cunctas sperare puellas] (*Ars* I, 343). Ovid is playing—*sperare* may also mean "to fear"—but the context is winning women, not rejecting them, as an antifeminist text would. Ovid says that women are lustful and therefore all the more *available* to the eager seeker. Jerome converts Ovid's advice into a misogamist argument: Women are lustful and therefore *dangerous*, so stay away. Jankyn has not only the original story of Pasiphaë in his copy of the *Ars Amatoria* but also Jerome's comments, giving him both text and gloss and allowing him access to the details that Jerome omits.

The Wife's refusal to tell the "tale" in any detail—a tale Jankyn thinks "swete"—hints that she knows the full, "grisly" version of the story found in the *Ars Amatoria*. Furthermore, her phrase "horrible lust" may be an echo of Ovid's "ista feminea libidine," for it accurately translates the scornful Latin intensifier "ista." In this episode, then, Ovid's hopeful, albeit rather bestial, assertion of a man's chances of sexual conquest becomes a frightening argument against marriage and a fitting inclusion in Jankyn's antifeminist book. We see here why the Wife has to do battle with glossators and clerks in this complex combat of words and authorities, a medieval battle of the books that seriously studies gender and power.[23] We also see here the power inherent in collections like Jankyn's that include both primary Ovidian material and patristic glosses; the book's diversity and cross-referencing make it a dynamic, elastic force.

As we move through the *Prologue* and look at the Wife's defenses against this book, we have to try to determine which antifeminist texts lie behind her words. Displaying rhetorical genius and sound scholarship, the Wife uses Ovid against the antifeminist texts that themselves, as in the case of Pasiphaë, form another part of the medieval Ovidian tradition. Ovid provides power to whomever can use him well, and as the Wife herself says, the first one at the mill is the first to grind the wheat (l. 389).

ARS AND THE WOMAN

To begin to understand the intertextual complexity of these Ovidian battles, we must examine in detail the Wife's use of Ovid to see just how comprehensively Chaucer has shaped the *Prologue* into a neo-Ovidian art of love. By embodying details from the antifeminist tradition and incarnating the sterile bits of academic detail from Jankyn's book, the Wife becomes what men fear most, the fully armed, nimble Amazon, wise through experience yet still skilled at the "olde daunce." She reclaims parts of Ovid's *Ars Amatoria* III and employs its stratagems against men. However, when Ovid's arts are insufficient or counterproductive, the Wife bends them to suit her own needs. Her protean flexibility in this regard does not surprise us, for it is itself an Ovidian hallmark.

I would like to look at five primary instances of the Wife's use of Ovid in her *Prologue*. In the first, she renders some Ovidian verses on the function of the woman's body in sexual economics. In the next four, I will first, if possible, consider the Wife's words in the context of antifeminist ideology, and then examine the original Ovidian verses behind what she says. Tracking down both text and gloss reveals the ideological assumptions and conventional imperatives of the Wife's play and illustrates that she knows how to set Ovid and the antifeminist conventions against each other. Prominent in some of these instances is the Wife's use of the body: Although she is a "text," she is also a "body," powerfully asserting her physicality in sexual politics. As

Hélène Cixous says of women writers, "A woman without a body ... can't possibly be a good fighter."[24]

1. After her long disquisition on Scripture and virginity and after the interruption of the Pardoner, the Wife offers the pilgrims a sample discourse on how to control a husband, in the course of which she takes on and refutes a long series of antifeminist accusations. One issue is woman's freedom—as the Wife attacks her theoretical husband for wanting to "Be maister of my body and of my good" (ll. 308ff.). "We love no man," says the Wife, "that taketh kep or charge / Wher that we goon; we wol ben at oure large" (ll. 321–22). He cannot control both her body and her goods; if he locks up her goods, he must be ready to say, "Wyf, go whet thee liste; / Taak youre disport, I wol nat leve no talys" (ll. 318–19). At the end of this assertion of independence, the Wife tells her husband that as long as she continues to please him, he should not worry about what she does with her body on her own time: "Have thou ynogh, what that thee recche or care / How myrily that othere folkes fare?" (ll. 329–30). She continues:

> For, certeyn, olde dotard, by youre leve,
> Ye shul have queynte right ynogh at eve.
> He is to greet a nygard that wolde werne
> A man to lighte a candle at his lanterne;
> He shal have never the lasse light, pardee.
> Have thou ynogh, thee that nat pleyne thee.
>   (ll. 331–36)

Editors are fond of citing Cicero's *De Oficiis* and the *Roman de la Rose* for this passage.[25] The version in the *Roman* is a difficult one in which Ami criticizes jealousy and says that she is so greedy that if she had to share anything, she would still want to retain the whole of her initial portion, the way a lantern retains its entire flame. There is no concrete sexual application here, and the Wife's use of the passage must be based on Ovid, who like the Wife discusses sexual relations.

Ovid's words come in the context of advice to women in *Ars Amatoria* III: "Do not refrain from giving your "joys of Venus' to men," Ovid says, "and if they deceive you, what did you lose? It's all still there" [Gaudia nee cupidis uestra negate uiris. / ut iam decipiant, quid perditis? omnia constant] (III, 88–89). And then he offers the image "quis uetet adposito lumen de lumine sumi" (III, 93), further encouraging his pupils not to be shy or "dangerous" but to seek pleasure and forget about the instability of men. "I am not prostituting you," says Ovid tellingly, "just stopping you from fearing false loss" (III, 97–98).

Ovid's masculine persona here seems to "care" but speaks an oppressive sexuality. However, Ovid's verses also imply that women are compelled to use their bodies as sexual tender. This "false loss," the generous rendering of the *gaudia*, allows men to fulfill their desires without feeling they are taking anything from the woman. Ovid assures women that they will continue to be taken, that they will not lose their ability to please. Men never tarry, of course, but women will always have the means to draw men to them. Behind this "comfort" we must see woman's fear of rejection and isolation, for if the vagina were actually to be depleted, what would a woman do next? The *gaudia veneris* indicates female dependence on male desire; it has no value until man begins to partake of it. In Ovid's verses, we see that "what women want most" is of no value or interest; all they are allowed to be are bodies that serve male pleasure.

The Wife's use of the image reveals that she will be no victim of male deceit but will do the deceiving herself. She uses her "instrument" as part of her plan for control over her husbands—part of her argument that they should *leave her alone*, let her do what she wants, stop being so suspicious: "Have thou ynogh, thee thar nat pleyne thee." She does not care if men never tarry, because she will not tarry either. Not waiting to be "taken" by men, she reclaims the body as her own, not as the tender that cedes the precious *gaudia*—the only coinage left to a woman deceived—but as her own source of freedom. The Wife effectively silences men by giving them what they want most, because it is this silencing, this abdication of male power, that gives the Wife what *she* wants most—to control her own body and use it as she wishes. She needs no assurances, fears no loss, and turns her *gaudia veneris* into her own gain.

2. Farther on in her sample discourse, the Wife explains another technique by which she keeps her husbands under control. She accuses them of flirting with other women ("Of wenches wolde I beren hem on honde") and tells them that her own nighttime wanderings are "for t'espye wenches that [they] dighte" (ll. 393, 398). The Wife admits that these techniques are a bit harsh, acknowledging the "peyne" and the "wo / Ful giltelees" that she put the men through. However, she contends ultimately that "Whoso that first to mille comth, first grynt" (l. 389)—it is best to be in control by striking first.

Looking at the ideological context here, we see that Chaucer's immediate source is Deschamps's *Miroir de Mariage*, and Deschamps's source is, in turn, Theophrastus, included, not surprisingly, in Jankyn's (as yet unintroduced) book. In the *Miroir*, which seeks to dissuade its readers from marriage, women's whining accusations prove that they cause too much trouble to be of any positive value. They complain all night about where the man has been, his being late, and his flirting with the maid:

> Vous regardez, quant elle vient,
> No voisine, bien m'en pergoy,
> Car vous n'avez cure de moy;
> Vous jouez a no chamberiere:
> Quant de marchié venis arriere,
> L'autre jour, que li apportas?
> Las! de dure heure m'espousas!
> Je n'ay mari ne compaignon.
> Certes se vous me fuissiez bon,
> Et vous n'amissiez autre part,
> Vous ne venissiez pas si tart
> Comme vous faictes a l'ostel.
>   (*Miroir*, ll. 1600–11)

> [You look at our neighbor when she comes—I can
> see this easily—since you have no concern for me.
> You toy with our maid. When you returned from
> the market the other day, what did you bring her?
> Alas, the sad hour that we wed; I have neither a
> husband nor a companion. Certainly if you were
> good to me and if you didn't love others, you
> wouldn't come home so late, as you do.][26]

But if we look to Ovid, and to the *Roman de la Rose*, we see the Wife's strategy *as* strategy, not as antifeminist warnings. Ovid says that a sure way to control a man is to make him feel loved:

> efficite (et facile est) ut nos credamus amari:
> prona uenit cupidis in sua uota fides.
> spectet amabilius iuuenem et suspiret ab imo
> femina, tam sero cur ueniatque roget;
> accedant lacrimae, dolor et de paelice fictus,
> et laniet digitis illius ora suis.
>   (*Ars* III, 673–78)

> [Make it, and this is easy, so that we think ourselves loved. Desire
> makes a man gullible. Let the woman look at him kindly and sigh
> deeply. Then let her ask why he comes late; let her shed tears as

well, feign sorrow over a rival, and scratch his cheeks with her nails.]

La Vieille adds vehemence to the advice and says that the woman should feign anger (*semblant aïrer*), run at the man and say she knows that he is not late without a reason (*Roman*, ll. 13823 ff.). In both passages these actions are ruses, ways of "getting to the mill first," as the Wife would say.

The relations between the several texts are immediately apparent. Neither of the canonical antifeminist sources—Theophrastus or Deschamps—reports that women do such complaining as strategy; it is, rather, "nagging." As Theophrastus says, they go on "all night long with babbling complaints" [deinde per noctes totas garrulae conquestiones].[27] Thus, by harassing her husbands, the Wife does not simply fulfill a female stereotype but employs an Ovidian *strategy*, filtered through La Vieille's added violence. She tells the pilgrims she *pretends* to nag, that she knows "al was fals." Chaucer certainly knew and used the *Miroir de Mariage* here, but the specific power and function of the Wife's actions come through Ovid and Jean de Meun. She knows that the male claims against women are constructs, as her scornful "thou saist" indicates. She knows there is no "real" authority here, but rather a fabricated force, and so she plays a game herself—summoning her own authorities, Ovid and La Vieille, who empower women. We begin to see, really, that the *Prologue* recounts a medieval battle of the books, with the Wife marshaling texts designed for women (of course still written by men) against the texts in the antifeminist arsenal.

3. After her long discourse, the Wife turns specifically to her fourth husband, who was a "revelour." This leads her to reminisce a bit about her salad days when she was "yong and ful of ragerye" (see ll. 453ff.). Here, in words rooted in Ovid's *Ars Amatoria* III, the Wife freely admits that she likes to drink and that when she drinks, she must think on love:

> And after wyn on Venus moste I thynke,
> For al so siker as cold engendreth hayl,
> A likerous mouth moste han a likerous tayl.
> In wommen vinolent is no defence—
> This knowen lecchours by experience.
>   (ll. 464–68)

Again, let us consider the ideological and textual contexts of the Wife's allusions.

MS Egerton 2864, Add. 5140, contains a gloss on the passage: "A drunken woman is filled with great anger and pride, and has no defense against sin."[28] The gloss moralizes the Wife's drinking and, indeed, like the gloss from Jerome, can probably be found in Jankyn's book, since it is derived from Ecclesiasticus, the following chapter of which Jankyn himself quotes. The text is biblical, but its application here constitutes a medieval gloss in itself that betrays the same attitude toward women as the book of wicked wives does. The Wife is right when she says that men gloss "up and doun," but little did she know that her own text would be glossed—behind her back as it were.

Turning once again to Ovid, we see that (as in the case of the advice to feign distress at a rival) Ovid directs his words to women, as part of a passage on self-presentation, with a caution that excessive drink is unbecoming and, like sleep, makes a woman vulnerable to all sorts of unexpected sexual encounters (*Ars* III, 761ff.). The advice parallels Ovid's telling men to go to banquets where they "might find something more than wine" [est aliquid praeter uina, quod inde petas] (*Ars* I, 230). Ovid here praises wine as a giver of strength and relaxation, but warns that drunken men cannot judge beauty and are vulnerable to wanton women who can at this time "snatch their spirits" (I, 243).

Both men and women who drink are vulnerable, and so the warnings seem parallel—except that Ovid says women *deserve* whatever happens to them while drunk, but says no such thing about men: "Digna est concubitus quoslibet illa pati" (*Ars* III, 766). The object in each case is optimum union of the sexes, not celibacy and rejection. But it is the optimum for the man only. Taken together, the two passages say that men do not want either ugly or drunk women, and so neither sex should drink. As often happens, when we look closely at Ovid's "fair" distribution of power, it disappears. But the notions of pride, anger, and sin—the focus of the gloss—are absent from Ovid's and indeed from La Vieille's advice (see *Roman*, ll. 13452ff.), which warns against excessive drink but makes no Bacchus-Venus connection. In that the Wife, like Ovid, refers specifically to Venus, her passage shows a direct link to the *Ars*. Chaucer read the *Roman*, must have liked its use of Ovid, as he liked Boccaccio's in the *Filostrato*, and went back to Ovid to exploit fully the implications of the passage in light of the Wife's struggle with authority.

She drinks, despite her husband's restrictions, and she turns to love—one of her weapons of control against men. In that she refuses to be disciplined by her husband, she converts Ovid's decorous warning into a source of power and freedom, overcoming not only her husband's control but also the gloss's accusations of "sin." The gloss has turned "love" into "sin," simply substituting one word for the other. But they are not the same. Who knows this better than the Wife, whose famous lament, "Alias that evere love was synne," exposes the false conclusions of the gloss.

One medieval commentary on the *Ars*—exhibiting the scholastic tendency to disarm the work by classifying it as ethics—says that the purpose of Ovid's discussion of feminine *mores* is that women can learn "how to be retained" [quibus modus retineri valeant], reflecting Ovid's own comment that he is going to teach women how to love so that men will not leave them.[29] The Wife does not worry about how to be "retained"; she has her own agenda and her own desire to "win." Thus, when she asserts her knowledge of both Bacchus and Venus, she converts what to Ovid is an embarrassing faux pas, what to the antifeminist mind is "sin," and what to a school commentator are "mores," into an expression of freedom and an assertion of the body, which is, for her, not simply something a woman grooms to please men.

4. The Wife's next discussion, which extends to the end of the *Prologue*, concerns Jankyn the clerk, husband number five. One of her early meetings with him occurs during Lent, when her husband "was at Londoun," and in the course of discussing her freedom that spring, the Wife tells us that she "hadde the bettre leyser for to pleye, / And for to se, and eek for to be seye" (ll. 551–52). The detail has its immediate source in the Jealous Husband's speech and also appears in Deschamps's *Miroir de Mariage*. In the *Roman*, the Jaloux complains that women, "vont traçant par mi les rues / Pour voeir, pour estre veües" (ll. 9029ff.), and Deschamps entitles a chapter "Comment femmes procurent aler aux pardons, non pas pour devocion qu'elles aient, mais pour veoir et estre veues" [how women seek pardons (at church), not because of their devotion, but in order to see and to be seen).[30] Both of these antifeminist diatribes use this detail as evidence of female pride.

But the ultimate source for these writers (Deschamps refers to Ovid by name) and for Chaucer is *Ars* I, 99, where Ovid tells men to go to public shows because women go there "to see and to be seen" [spectatum ueniunt, ueniunt spectentur ut ipsae]. Ovid, far from warning men of female vanity and inciting them to celibacy, is trying to tell them where to find lovers. Female vanity reliably starts the whole hunting process. If Ovid were reading Chaucer, he would want to argue that Criseyde went to that temple that day for the same reason.

Ovid does not condemn women, but we can see how easily his "essentialist" generalization could become an antifeminist comment, and so it seems the Wife is just playing her part as the vain female of the antifeminist texts. But she makes Ovid's advice to men part of her own art of love, freely venturing out while her husband is away. Although she is not, as she speaks to the pilgrims, married, her presence on the Canterbury pilgrimage also displays her freedom, for she tells them that her trips include "these pilgrimages."[31] The Wife has taken a shred of attack and stereotype from the male tradition and converted it from "they do" to "I do," affirming craft and will. In relation to Ovid's text, she becomes much more than merely a reliable prey that makes itself present so that male hunting season can begin. She does the hunting herself, clearly emphasizing the "seeing" over the being seen.

5. After describing this secret meeting with Jankyn, the Wife then explains how at her husband's funeral her eye was again on Jankyn, whom we know she later marries:

> To chirche was myn housbonde born a-morwe
> With neighebores, that for hym maden sorwe;
> And Jankyn, oure clerk, was oon of tho.
> As help me God, whan that I saugh hym go
> After the beere, me thoughte he hadde a paire
> Of legges and of feet so clene and faire
> That al myn herte I yaf unto his hoold.
>   (ll. 593–99)

Deschamps's *Miroir* seems to be the direct source for these lines. It explains that women will take a dead husband's possessions, offer only a short service [*courte messe*], and look for another husband among the crowd of mourners: "Et regardera en le presse / A parter le deffenct en terre, / Quel mari elle pourra querre / Et avoir après ceste cy" (ll. 1974–77).[32] Frightened antifeminists, like the persona of this text, see these actions as evidence of woman's insensitivity and evil.

But when we turn to Ovid's handbook, we find a quite different context. In *Ars* III, he explains to his widow-pupils that "Often a man is found at a man's funeral; it is best to go in tears, with your hair tousled" [Funere, saepe uiri uir quaeritur; ire solutis / crinibus et fletus non tenuisse decet] (ll. 431–32). The Wife takes this tip and eyes Jankyn at her fourth husband's funeral, *restoring* its Ovidian function and status as advice to women. One of the great ironies of the whole situation is that the husband she finds at the funeral is the clerk who has all this material in his book and, perhaps, has already read about the Wife's strategy in his version of the *Ars Amatoria*. On one level, he and the Wife are both victims and products of inherited texts, scripts in which each must play a role. The drama comes in the Wife's simultaneous fulfillment of and restlessness with that role.

In the various dramatic instances I have analyzed, the Wife creates herself out of antifeminist fragments of fear and ignorance, those things that men say women are made up of—lechery, trickery, garrulousness, and pride. When she displays these "wicked" features, she illustrates that she herself is a product of a male literary tradition. But by manipulating the texts in this tradition and by "spoiling" Ovid's armaments, she empowers herself to shape her own art of love in the tradition of *Ars Amatoria* III and La Vieille. In this way she takes control of both man and text, or, rather, of man *through* her control of texts and of her own body. Most important, perhaps, her arts reveal that Chaucer is aware of at least two Ovids, one a founder of antifeminism, the other a father of an opposing tradition that is born within the *Ars Amatoria* and advanced by La Vieille. It is not altogether clear that we should call this tradition "feminist," which in this case would be a hopelessly anachronistic term. But Chaucer has intricately reimagined his *auctores* to create a voice that reimagines woman's power and speaks woman's language as it has never been spoken before.

AMI'S GENEALOGY

With the Wife's "arts," Chaucer establishes a new vision of love within the context of the "genealogies of Ovidianism" offered by both Ovid and Jean de Meun. Throughout her *Prologue*, the Wife battles not just the texts of Jankyn's book but also the role that sacred history has assigned to her, based on the actions of her other mother, Eve, who, significantly, heads the catalog of "wicked wives." Jankyn reads to her:

> Of Eva first, that for hir wikkednesse
> Was al mankynde broght to wrecchednesse,
> For which that Jhesu Crist hymself was slayn,
> That boghte us with his herte blood agayn.
> Lo, heere expres of womman may ye fynde
> That womman was the los of al mankynde.
> (ll. 715–20)

Here we have a brief, but entirely typical, view of women's role in sacred history. Redemption itself is subordinated to woman's "wickedness" which brings on all humankind's "wretchedness." Chaucer does not try to rewrite that history, nor does he offer a heterodox revision of Scripture. Rather, he uses the pagan Golden Age mythology from Jean (who borrows from Ovid) to set forth an analysis of woman's "wickedness" different from and more complex than that in Jankyn's book.

In the *Roman de la Rose*, Ami explicitly bases his history of gender conflict on Ovid's story of the decline of the Golden Age and the origins of "Ovidian" love doctrines, as the Roman poet describes them in the *Ars Amatoria* and the *Amores*. Ovid makes clear in *Ars* II that his art is for the poor and not the rich, whose wealth makes "art" unnecessary:

Non ego diuitibus uenio praeceptor amandi;
nil opus est illi, qui dabit, arte mea.
secum habet ingenium qui, cum libet, "accipe" dicit;
cedimus, inuentis plus placet ille meis.
pauperibus uates ego sum, quia pauper amaui;
cum dare non possem munera, uerba dabam.
    (*Ars* II, 161–66)

[I have not come as the teacher of love for the rich. My art is nothing
to anyone who can "give." Whoever can say, when he wants, "Please
accept this gift," has his own arts. I concede; he pleases more than
my techniques. I am the prophet of the poor, because, poor myself,
I loved. I couldn't give gifts, so I gave words.]

Later he continues the theme of feminine greed, saying that women do not
now value poems as gifts:

Carmina laudantur sed munera magna petuntur:
dummodo sit diues, barbarus ipse placet.
aurea sunt uere nunc saecula: plurimus auro
uenit honos, auro conciliatur amor.
    (II, 275–78)

[Songs are praised, but great gifts are sought. As long as he is
rich, the barbarian can please. We are certainly living in a "golden
age." With gold comes great honor, with gold comes love.]

We find a related discussion in *Amores* III, viii, where Ovid gives a tour
de force expose on girls, gifts, and the Golden Age. Ovid makes no pun on
"golden" here, but laments that in the real Golden Age, before the economic
expansion of the empire, there was no moneyed military class able to win
women's hearts by spreading wealth around. Now women scorn poetry
and want only gifts that the nouveaux riches can bring.[33] If we put Ovid's
comments from the *Ars* and the *Amores* together into one larger narrative, we
see that his love doctrines result directly from this fall from a Golden Age.
The fall brings an end to the power of poets, and thus, to "conciliate love,"
poor men, whose poetry is now scorned, need to give a new gift—a gift of
verba since the rich and powerful have their own form of *ingenium* in their
money. As friend of the poor and friend of the poet, Ovid helpfully supplies
the craft that will allow poor men to compete with the wealthy, though
artless, lovers who control the market. Ovidian art, then, fits into a grand

economic, historical scheme, and, as is customary in Ovid's world of love, verba compensate for a lack, creating some kind of Ovidian justice, balancing the economic inequality that prevents crafty but poor poets from fulfilling their desires.

Turning to the *Roman de la Rose*, we see that Ami, borrowing Ovid's phrases, also describes an age in which "honey flowed from the oak and no one furrowed the earth."[34] Love was free, equal, in a pure and simple state women craved no gifts, and men craved no dominance. Now the world is changing, Ami tells us, and women have become greedy monsters: "If a woman were to see a heavy purse ... she would run to it with open arms.... Everything is going into decline" (ll. 8347ff.). And so Ami, like Ovid, knows that wealth, or, in the allegorical language of the poem, taking the road of "give too much," can get Amant into the castle and win him the rose with ease: "Its walls will shake and the towers waver and the gates will open by themselves" (ll. 7915ff.). One can take this shorter way "without my art or teaching," says Ami, who thus makes clear that he directs his strategy—a long discourse directly from the *Ars Amatoria*—to the poor man, just as Ovid had. The poor man did not have to compete in this way in the Golden Age, when, as Ami says, "loves were loyal and pure, without greed and rapine." So now, in lieu of "gold," men need Ovidian art to soften the gatekeepers, appease Fair Welcoming, and get into the castle. Ami knows that Ovid provides an answer to the question of how to play the game of love, and he describes the fall into a desperate state that demands deceit and, therefore, demands Ovid.[35] This Ovidian ethic dominates much of the poem, since even Reason recommends, or at least condones, deceit: "It is always better ... to deceive than to be deceived, particularly in this battle when one never knows where to seek the mean" (ll. 4399ff.).[36]

Ami has shown how women's greed forces men to become Ovidian artists. In the Jaloux's speech that follows, Ami shows the other side of the issue, demonstrating how male desire for domination forces women also to become Ovidians, employing fraud and trickery. Male possessiveness, like female greed for gold and gifts, has helped bring an end to the age of free and simple love. These two crimes explain, we might say, the origins of *Ars Amatoria* I and III. However, we must realize that Jean de Meun does not base the Jealous Husband's speech and the commentary that follows on Ovid. Jean offers them as part of his own contribution to the "art of love."

Ami delivers the Husband's diatribe to expose the evils of male possessiveness, as had Reason before him in her long discourse on lust and mercantile greed. In this portrayal of the Jaloux as a mad boor who should be "fed to wolves," we hear an awareness that antifeminism, as thoroughly represented here as anywhere, is based on an excessive desire for power that "violates the law of love." The Jaloux, Ami says, "makes himself lord over his wife, who, in turn, should not be his lady but his equal and his companion, as the law joins them together." Ami continues, "For his part, he should be her companion without making himself her lord or master" (ll. 9421ff.). The result of such a claim to *maistrie* is that "love" will fail, for "love must die when lovers want lordship; [it] cannot endure or live if it is not free and active in the heart."

Jean de Meun has given the traditional antifeminist texts a voice, embodying what in the source texts is disembodied and distanced, as if fallen from heaven as knowledge.[37] He demystifies the texts of Theophrastus et al., so stolid and so "anthologized" in books like Jankyn's, and attributes them to a brute. Jean de Meun knows, as the Wife of Bath does, and as Christine de Pizan will later claim in her *Book of the City of Ladies*, that the accusations against women are arbitrary and unauthoritative. Historically, the antifeminist texts are designed to guide clergy away from marriage, and their effect on "romantic" love is never at issue.[38] Significantly, then, Ami has looked beyond the antifeminist tirades to see what effect they have on love, holding them responsible for poisoning it.

After the Jaloux's raving catalog of female evils, Ami explains that women will certainly respond to men's abusive quest for domination with scorn and trickery in order "to defend and protect themselves" (ll. 9383ff.). Female fraud does not cause men's suspicion and hatred; they are, rather, its source. The "cause and effect" implied here reveals Jean's insight into the workings of authority, power, and love. By seeing antifeminism as a cause of this "fall," Jean de Meun reverses the assumptions at the heart of the antifeminist texts—that the Christian "fall" is the result of female carnality, as the Wife's first excerpt from Jankyn's book makes clear.[39]

Jean de Meun's treatment of the Jaloux and his depiction of woman's deceit as the result of man's violating the law of love constitute a new chapter in the gender/power relations described by Ovid—a chapter that paves the way for the Wife of Bath and her battles with "Foul Mouthed" and "Jealous" husbands. Chaucer saw in the *Roman de la Rose* not just an anthology of Ovidian quotes and images but a genealogy of Ovidian craft—the reasons why men and women employ treachery. In view of this genealogy, the Wife of Bath has no choice but to respond to male power with fraud and manipulation. It is a fallen world, and Ovidian art is the lot of fallen (wo)man.

"LIKE MY MOTHER TAUGHT ME": LA VIEILLE

Using *Ars Amatoria* I and II, Ami arms Amant against Fair Welcoming, Foul Mouth, and the gatekeepers, teaching him how to pursue and win his love. La Vieille, expanding *Ars Amatoria* III, arms the *women*, fulfilling Ami's prediction that women must use fraud to do combat with men. She does not just lift material from Ovid; she synthesizes Ovidian strategy from the *Ars* and from her own literary mother, Dipsas. And though her discourse is heavily indebted to *Ars* III, particularly its dicta on cosmetics and hygiene, La Vieille does not try to make women more appealing to men, as Ovid does. She seeks to make them better equipped to *deceive* men. Accordingly, we find throughout La Vieille's discourse an increased interest in deceit.

As Ovid arms the Amazons he attacks men, like "false Jason" (fallax Iaso), for being treacherous and deceitful to their women. Later (in what he calls a mad rush of insanity) he tells freed female slaves how to deceive their men and guardians (*Ars* III, 29ff., 667ff.). Thus it appears that Ovid fairly balances his aid to the Greeks, but in many ways this third book does not parallel the first two. In Book III, Ovid proposes to teach women "how to love"; men already know how, because they have read his books. At the outset he gives a catalog of deceived women, and then tells us: "Quid uos perdiderit, dicam: nescitis amare: / defuit ars uobis; arte perennat amor" [What destroyed you I say? You did not know how to love. You had no art, and art preserves love] (III, 41–42). Men deceive women, so women must know how to prepare against this deceit and sustain love. Ovid then suggests grooming—a woman should make herself attractive, clean under her fingernails, and avoid bad breath. But he makes no statement that would balance his advice to men in *Ars Amatoria* I to "deceive the deceivers" (the women) who actually inflicted the first wound (l. 645).[40] In *Ars* III, Ovid never says that women, in turn, should deceive men. Instead he tells them to respond to men's deceit with *knowing how to love* so as to avoid rejection.

Ultimately, then, Ovid's guide for women tells them how to remain appealing and be chosen. In the *Roman de la Rose*, La Vieille's "art of love" displays an increased directness and vehemence; she takes Ovid's idea that men are dangerous deceivers and concludes—unlike Ovid—that *women* should now do the deceiving. For example, Ovid says that women should dress so as to accentuate the positive because whenever he sees a snowy shoulder, he would gladly kiss it (III, 307ff.). La Vieille adds emphasis (ll. 13313ff.): a woman with white skin should have her dressmaker design a low-cut outfit, not to invite kisses, but so that she may "deceive more easily." Ovidian counsel takes on a new status when a woman, the new Dipsas, does the teaching, turning *Ars* III into an effective response to the craft and low cunning taught to men in Books I and II.[41]

Not only does La Vieille provide a woman's voice for *Ars* III, she borrows some material from Ovid's enemy (and her own "mother") Dipsas, the old counselor from the *Amores*. Forget poems and get money, says La Vieille

(l. 13617) as she sends Homer packing and repeats Dipsas's advice to reject poets and their worthless gifts.[42] Ovid, evidently aware of Dipsas's words, tells his pupils to make their poetry a "type of gift" by cleverly writing verse praising their women (*Ars* II, 281–86). La Vieille is not so easily deceived, for she adds Ovid's own name to Homer's as she banishes the cheap poets—a direct attack on the *magister* himself, implying that his evolving, shifting "gift of words" fools no one.

Ovid playfully confounded himself—a bit—by writing *Ars Amatoria* III. La Vieille confounds him more fully, teaching the scorn and trickery Ami says must erupt from the mistreatment of women in a fallen world. Jean's dramatic reworking of Ovid provides a major step toward the Wife of Bath. Chaucer saw that Jean, using Ovid, defended the Amazons and "historically" justified their strategies through Ami's genealogy. Chaucer also saw in La Vieille a powerful rewriting of *Ars Amatoria* III. He allows his Wife of Bath to adopt Ami's advice to trick slanderers and also to adapt La Vieille's arts of profit and control. Omitting Ovid's hygienic hints about pimples and bad breath, the Wife represents Chaucer's own dynamic contribution to the tradition of writing an "art" to arm the Amazons. In the Wife's use of her ancestral texts, Chaucer offers his own vision of Ovidian love in a post-Golden Age world of sexual combat and competition. The literary historical evolution behind Chaucer's poem is here primarily pagan. But the Wife's world is, of course, Christian, so we must examine Ovidian language and female behavior in relation to the Christian Fall, a mythology equally pertinent to Chaucer's depiction of human language and society throughout the *Canterbury Tales*.

AN ENEMY POISED

Ovid's and Jean de Meun's depictions of the fall from the Golden Age both place Ovidian deceit in a large historical scheme. In contrast to these genealogies, some medieval Latin evaluations of Ovid depict his art not as the solution to the problems of the fall but as a reflection of the fallen state of men and women, sinners trapped in falseness and carnality. Ovid may have playfully seen himself as the enlightened voice of the disenfranchised, but these authors see him as the sinful enemy of truth.

William of St. Thierry describes the fall away from God and from the natural love of the spirit as just such a fall into the flesh. "Love," he says, "was placed in the human spirit by the author of nature." But "after man let God's law slip," "love had to be taught *by men*" (italics added). It should have been taught as pure and solidified, but carnal love "had its own teachers"—such as the "doctor artis amatoriae" who "wrote of the fire of carnal love." William's attitude toward Ovid wavers; he attempts, as Leclercq puts it, to "excuse Ovid" but cannot avoid condemning him. William grants that Ovid was creating a system to control passion and tried in the *Remedia* to cure the ills he had caused earlier: "Indeed he did not aim to excite the rise of carnal desire that burns with a natural fire, without [maintaining] a proper mixture of reason." Despite Ovid's efforts to rule love, however, he led his disciples "into all kinds of misbehavior and useless foment of desire, pressing on toward some kind of insanity."[43] For William, finally, Ovidian love represents the explosive state of desire in a fallen world, an earthly perversion of God's love. By comparison, in the *Roman de la Rose*, Ami offers Ovidian strategy as the necessary response to the possessiveness and greed that in themselves constitute the initial "violation of the law of love."

The *Antiovidianus*, in its feisty condemnation of Ovid's corpus, provides an equally fascinating version of Ovid and the fall:

> Nasonem mea musa ferit, quia stercora sumens
> Auravit musa tam rutilante sua
> Effecit suis decorosis versibus, vt sit
> Fel mel, nox lux, mors vita laborque quies.
> Inde sathan, draco callidus, hostis iniquus et audax,
> Insidians iuuenum mollia corda capit.
> Subuerterunt mala verba fidem, sanctos quoque mores
> Corrumpunt sepe. Sit michi prima parens
> Hinc testis, sathane pravis seducta loquelis.
> Heu patimur verbis omnia dampna malis!
> Hoc opus oro vide, visum diffundere cura.
> Quondam Nasonis, sis rogo preco dei.
>   (Kienast, ed., ll. 3–14)

[My muse strikes Ovid, because taking up dung, with his shining muse he made it gold, and in his pleasing verses made gall into honey, night into light, death into life, and labor into rest. From whence comes Satan, the subtle dragon, bold and base enemy; poised, he snatches the soft hearts of the young. Evil words subvert faith and often corrupt sacred mores. Let our first parent be witness to me of this, for she was seduced by the depraved speech of Satan. Lo! all our sorrows we suffer because of evil words. I beg you, behold this work, which, having been seen, seek to spread. You who. were once a herald of Ovid, be, I pray, a herald of God.]

These are strong words, but the poet offers nothing maverick or heterodox in his portrayal of Ovid's deceitful rhetoric as the source from which

Satan will come to snatch "the soft hearts of the young." The poet, like the theologian William, locates Ovid's poems in a scheme of Christian sacred history by linking Ovid to the Fall. Eve, he tells us, was tricked by the depraved speech of Satan, whom we must imagine to have been quite the Ovidian. Here and in William's tract, we see that Ovid can be source, result, or symptom of the Fall. In Ami's genealogy, by contrast, he is an expedient tool, and in his own writings, of course, he is benevolent savior.

These theological evaluations of Ovidian love could lead us to see a stern critique of Ovidian rhetoric in the Wife of Bath. After all, if Ovid is a great Satan, then "Ovid" and "woman" are both at the heart of the Christian story of the Fall. As Saint Bernard laconically puts it, "Eve spoke only once and threw the world into disorder."[44] A playful but strident thirteenth-century French *dit* warns its readers that woman's appearance belies the poison within:

> Femme par sa douce parole,
> Atret li home e puis l'afole;
> Femme est dehors religiouse,
> Dedanz poignaunt e venimose.
> (Le Blasme des Fames, ll. 47–50)

[Woman, with her sweet words, attracts man and then drives him crazy. Outwardly she is nun-like, but inwardly she is prickly and venomous.]

Woman is a "hell mouth," she "shuns fidelity," and is "more artful than the devil."[45] Just as Christian moralists link Ovid to the Fall, this dit links "woman" to the deceitful language of carnal, fallen man. An "Ovidian woman," then, would either be redundant or pose a double threat.

As we have seen, Petrarch offers the fascinating complaint that Ovid showed a "womanly spirit" not only about his exile but in his love of poetry too. And Boccaccio says that Ovid's love poems show him as "an effeminate and lascivious man." It is easy to look at Ovid's love strategy and think of him as a "sexist" poet, but we must be aware of the morally gendered vocabulary leveled against him by Christian writers. To Ovid's medieval opponents and critics, both "woman," as the first sinner, and Ovid, as the ribald poet of falseness, display foul weakness and depravity.

How, then, should we read the Wife's arts? Which "medieval Ovid" should we use to gloss her? Alison's craft displays much more than simple carnality or Satanic evil. Chaucer gives the Wife an Ovidian power not in order to condemn her but to equip her for an important confrontation. Her actions more closely follow the history of gender conflict described by Ami than they do the moral schemes traced by William of St. Thierry and by the *Antiovidianus* poet. The Wife's *Prologue*, then, not only illustrates Chaucer's "translation" of Ami's Ovidian genealogy but also goes far beyond any simple moralization of Ovid as it attempts to forge a way back to the Golden Age, when love was fair and balanced. As a recent study of medieval tracts on "marital affection" shows, Jean de Meun, in composing Ami's discourse, may have been influenced by contemporary debate on love and fairness between married people.[46] Chaucer's poem also works toward a code of marital affection that is beyond treachery and beyond claims to inherited power. As we will now see, the Wife attempts to overcome these conventions most dramatically when she teaches Jankyn that he does not need that book of wicked wives. If he burns it, she will drop all the fearsome qualities it attributes to her and will leave off her practice of Ovidian craft. In this way the Wife's "art of love," ultimately, will look toward a marriage and a romantic world that are free of art and game.

The Book

Jankyn's book defines the Wife as a "wicked" source of human "wrecchednesse," and so it must be surrendered before the couple can attempt to restore any kind of Golden Age. Unlike the old rich stooges the Wife has controlled before, Jankyn seems immune to her Ovidiana, creating a dire emotional situation that leaves the Ovidian mistress craving what she cannot have. Part of Jankyn's power must derive from the texts in his book of wicked wives, including "Ovides Art," where he may have read that women seek new lovers at their husbands' funerals. Jankyn's control over the Wife comes from his careful hesitancy—he is "daungerous" with his love, making the Wife desire him more:

> We wommen han, if that I shal nat lye,
> In this matere a queynte fantasye:
> Wayte what thyng we may nat lightly have,
> Therafter wol we crie al day and crave.
> Forbede us thyng, and that desiren we;
> Preesse on us faste, and thanne wol we fle.
> With daunger oute we al oure chaffare;
> Greet prees at market maketh deere ware,
> And to greet cheep is holde at litel prys.
>   (III, 515–23)

She loves a man who needs to be bought, despising one who is a bargain.

"Every wise woman knows this," says the Wife, and the advice comes from no less an authority than La Vieille herself. La Vieille explains that since men scorn what they can get for nothing, a woman should not give a man her love without first making him deliver some goods (*Roman*, ll. 13695ff.). The Wife works just such a scheme on husbands one through four. But Jankyn flips the gender roles; though the *Roman de la Rose* is not in his book, unless it is one of the "many others mo," Chaucer has it in his library, and he uses it to make Jankyn a good match for the Wife.[47] Jankyn has read and appropriated one of her texts—indeed, her "mother's" advice—and thus has almost neutralized her power. In this conflict we see that Jankyn and the Wife wage a literary battle that eventually drives them into physical conflict.

As they reach an accord, the Wife takes the "bridel" so that she can have "governance of hous and lond" and of Jankyn's "tonge" and "hond" (ll. 812ff.). To solidify this *maistrie*, the Wife must act the censor: "[I] made hym brenne his book anon right tho" (l. 816). This forced destruction burns away not only Jankyn's power but also the very details of the Wife's own identity and art. What is possibly left of the Wife when the book is gone, and what could be left of Jankyn the clerk when his fathers' text is lost? The irony, as Pratt long ago pointed out, is that he has never actually followed the main thrust of the book—to avoid marriage.[48] His bitterness must come from this tension: he reads the tales and thinks them "swete"; he tries, too, to inflict them on the Wife, but he himself cannot obey them. In burning the book, the Wife liberates them both from this tension, from the literary imperatives that define them. The book's the thing, she knows, that prevents love.

The Wife's exposure of the antifeminist tradition finds powerful support, just a few years after Chaucer created her, in the work of an actual woman writer, Christine de Pizan. As she builds the City of Ladies, an extended refutation of antifeminist "authority," Christine has the character Reason explain why men write about the evils of women. The causes include the men's own vices and the defects of their bodies; jealousy or the pleasure they get from committing slander, and "to show they have read many authors." Those in this last group "base their own writings on what they have found in books and repeat what others have said and cite different authors."[49] "They believe they cannot go wrong," Reason continues, "since others have written in books what they take the situation to be, or rather, *mis*-take the situation" (I, 8, 10).[50] Later in discussing antimatrimonial literature, Reason's sister Righteousness makes a similar point: "Without my having to say any more to you, you can easily see that such foolishness spoken and written against women was and is an arbitrary fabrication which flies in the face of truth" (II, 13, 1).[51]

The very existence of Christine's work arises from her desire to demystify this magical, male creation of authority. At the outset of her story, Christine is near despair, finding herself believing everything she has heard about the evils of women. After thinking about the antifeminist corpus, including Mathéolus and, we must assume, the *Roman de la Rose*, Christine reports: "I finally decided that God formed a vile creature when He made woman.... As I was thinking this, a great unhappiness and sadness welled up in my heart, for I detested myself and the entire feminine sex, as though we were monstrosities in nature" (I, 1, 1).[52] Both Christine and the Wife know the power of books of wicked wives, in any manifestation, and they try in their own ways to discredit them.[53]

Strangely enough, Walter Map, Valerius in Jankyn's collection, provides some insight into this problem of authority. In his *De Nugis Curialium*, which includes the previously circulated antimatrimonial tract *Ad Rufinum* (his contribution to Jankyn's book), Map wonders why the epistle has been "greedily seized upon, eagerly copied, and read with vast amusement" (313). He complains that many have tried to deny that he wrote the work, attributing it to the ancient Valerius, a name Map invented. "My fault," he says, "is in this only—that I live. I am not inclined, however, to amend this by dying" (312). Map knows that he has created authority by giving his text apparently classical origins. He fears that when he, a living man, is fully acknowledged as the author, the excitement will end and his work will "fall out of the blanket into the mud." Therefore, he can only look forward to his death and bodily decay, for then, he predicts, the "book will begin to receive favor," and "for the remotest posterity, antiquity will make me an authority" (212).[54] Map knows that authorities are made, not born, and though he never challenges antifeminist doctrines, he exposes the whole process by which a text becomes an authority, just as Christine does in her attack on authors who blindly rehearse bits of antifeminist jargon and lore.

Jankyn's book, then, full of works by white males who were dead even in Chaucer's time, carries this same sort of pseudo-authority and pretends to give its owner wisdom and power. Jankyn has something the Wife does not have, and possession of this text provides the clout that creates a sexual and marital hierarchy. This power comes not from "truth," but from the weight of ancient doctrine built up in the anthology, doctrine that Christine de Pizan calls "arbitrary and false." "Men" are those empowered by such a tradition of texts, and "women" are not only the object of these texts but are those who lack such texts of their own. "By God," the Wife cries, if only "wommen hadde writen stories, / As clerkes han withinne hire oratories," then we would hear of more male "wikkednesse / Than al the mark of Adam may redresse" (ll. 693–96).

The Wife of Bath does all she can to arm herself against the power that the male tradition has amassed. By reviving *Ars Amatoria* III and importing the French theorist La Vieille, she seeks both to topple male authority and to show that she herself has a textual history—a history that knows something of male "wikkednesse" and male violations of the law of love. In the process she creates herself as a "text," that of woman as trickery, garrulousness, and greed. These fabricated identities, both the Wife's and Jankyn's, arise from the same literary conventions, and both ultimately must fail. But the Greeks are more powerful than the Amazons, traditionally better armed and able to supplement their power with physical dominance, as we see when Jankyn hits the Wife. And so, before the couple can find peace, and before the Wife will deliver kindness and fidelity, the book has to go. Giving up the book is easier said than done, and Jankyn's aggressive reaction to having a few pages torn out reflects a distinct anxiety over the potential loss of privilege and power.

Is Jankyn still a "man" without the book? And what is left of the Wife if her genealogy, as men have imagined it, is burned up? The Wife offers us a glimpse of at least one version of this post-Ovidian, post-antifeminist world. Liberated from their conventional identities, Alison and Jankyn cease their respective pursuit of domination, and a "golden age" ensues. We may suspect that their unity, wrought by deceit and violence, is no real unity at all. But the text only tells us that they lived together happily and faithfully. If they faltered before Jankyn's untimely death, the poem tells us nothing about it.

We might also object that the "golden age" the Wife forges includes her own *maistrie* and control. We cannot determine just how much "maistrie" the Wife maintains after Jankyn submits to her will. But perhaps the power she wields does not represent an unfair swing, since Ovid's Golden Age simply meant that one could seduce a woman without digging into his pocket. And since Jankyn is not rich, by loving him the Wife tacitly surrenders the materialistic desire that guided her in the past. Right after their marriage, she gave him her own "lond and fee" (l. 630), and now, at the end of the battle of authorities, as the Wife finally receives *maistrie*, she continues to give, pledging to Jankyn her kindness and fidelity. This giving, this putting off the "old woman," leaving the strategy of Dipsas, *Ars* III, and La Vieille, balances Jankyn's surrender of his elders' book of wisdom. We may be witnessing not so much a mythic Golden Age, but the best relations possible in a world of conflicting authorities and inherited demands on identity.[55]

But after the qualified resolutions of her *Prologue*, the Wife reimagines her experiences in fictive form, creating a text in place of the one she just burned. To do this she trades the role of Ovidian *magister* for that of Ovidian narrator. The Wife's *Tale* includes her self—indicting version of Ovid's tale of Midas. As storyteller, the Wife transforms the account into a criticism of women, making a basically neutral Ovidian text into an antifeminist depiction of women as hopeless gossips, as overflowing mouths in search of an audience. The Wife revises the tale intentionally, not to tease bad male listeners, but to illustrate the co-opting and glossing behind the creation of texts like those in Jankyn's book.[56] She writes a new chapter in this abusive volume to flaunt power over the production of truth. Men gloss up and down, and this is how they do it.

A surge of the same rhetorical power allows Socrates to argue any given side of an argument in Plato's *Phaedrus* and allows Ovid to make utterly contradictory statements in arming all sides in the arts of love. The Wife shows what rhetoric can do, shows how an author can manipulate words to create a new version of history and truth. But she does not let the narrative rest here, for she applies her art to another old but more local story. In her Arthurian tale, she again plays with the women's roles, not, this time, parodying the inanities of antifeminist lore but depicting a feminine wisdom and power that go beyond Ovidian deceit. The story of the Old Hag and her young pupil, the knight-rapist, redefines, or indeed abolishes, the gender/power struggles the Wife found in Ovid's love poems, in the *artes* of love in the *Roman de la Rose*, and in her own *Prologue*.

The central "metamorphosis" rejuvenates the Old Hag, whose control over the hapless knight reflects the Wife's own power and constitutes a cameo appearance by Ovid's Dipsas or La Vieille. Through the Old Hag, the Wife implicitly acknowledges and honors her own literary heritage. Without them, she would not have made it. Yet the Old Hag differs from her elders and from the others in the *Tale*'s analogues who are trying to overcome enchantment.[57] Her unique speech on true "gentilesse" exposes the same type of arbitrary assignments of value that inform the antifeminist tradition. In no analogue to the story would such a distinction be meaningful, for it refers back to the textual battle fought in the *Prologue*. The Old Hag does in miniature what the Wife does in her assault on her husbands—reveals the conventionality of social and sexual hierarchies and the corresponding myths of male superiority.

It seems that the Wife and the Old Hag have both achieved ultimate success by transforming their respective men into humble, gentle, obedient husbands. And so the Hag herself, like the Wife at the end of the *Prologue*, "puts off the old woman" and becomes young and beautiful. Chaucer gives the Wife the power of imaginative creation, which seems to have worked in what one critic, in another context, calls "the 'wish-world' of metamorphosis."[58] She has reversed the "great [Ovidian] inconstancy of things" in the triumph of art over experience.

She has also transferred her chaotic marital experiences into the authority of art, offering in her *Tale* a "literary" version of the story of Jankyn concluding that his wife should rule him. The knight-rapist's final submission recalls Jankyn's pledge of obedience. Jankyn tells Alison, "Myn owene trewe wyf, / Do as thee lust the terme of al thy lyf" (ll. 819–20); the knight's words to his new wife sound the same gracious note of affectionate marital calm: "My lady and my love, and wyf so deere, / I put me in youre wise governance ... For as yow liketh, it suffiseth me" (ll. 1230–31, 1235). In this parallel, the rape itself corresponds to the objectification of women inherent in the production and use of antifeminist texts. Although rape of a virgin and disdain for marriage seem separate methods of dominance, both express the male power that is central to the universe of the poem.[59]

The Wife knows that the story in her *Prologue* is not enough, that it has no authority. Like Walter Map, she knows that antiquity creates authority, and so she tells a story from the "days of old." As Map creates an ancient Roman aura around his epistle, so the Wife reaches back to old Briton. Both know that authority must come from a distance, either fictive or chronological. Map's authority was weak because he was alive, the Wife's because she is a woman, a situation that she, like Map, no doubt, has no desire to remedy. She will not become a man, but she will assume the role of story-teller—she will write a story of rape and the powerful women of authority who have the knight at their mercy. Implied here is a little bit of the "wikkednesse" that women would tell of if they had literary position and power, which for this moment the Wife has. Her old tale, she hopes, will provide some corrective to the equally and indeed more ancient tradition against her.

Ovid plays many roles in the *Wife of Bath's Prologue and Tale*, throwing many complicated voices into the narratives and love languages that Chaucer weaves together in this, his most ambitious study of love and power. The Ovidian Wife, though herself a created voice, becomes an expert in these Ovidian voices, this rhetoric of craft and control, as she combats the antifeminist rhetoric of fear and scorn. In the *Troilus* we traced the opposition between Ovidian words and the divine Word. Why does Chaucer here provide no comparable anti-Ovidian critique, allowing Ovid to serve, rather, as the triumphant doctor who supplies arms to the disempowered?

The *Troilus* critiques a worldview that restricts itself to game and to secret, lusty rapture. Troilus, an innocent, puts his faith in this world, one of manifest Ovidian game, and makes it into "ernest." The Ovidian bound aries reflect those of the pagan world—to be pagan is to read Ovid literally, to invoke his doctrines as the only source of identity and discourse. The Wife's *Prologue and Tale* also looks to a world beyond Ovidian craft. Ovid serves the Wife well in the fallen world, the world of the Jaloux and the book of wicked wives. As Ami's genealogy makes clear, Ovidian fraud and trickery are her only recourse against the gendered hierarchies constructed by antifeminism. Women are not born Ovidians; they have Ovidianism thrust upon them.

The question the *Prologue and Tale* raises, then, is this: How can men and women both get beyond inherited, bookish identity and get out of the fallen world of Ovidian language, games, and strategy? The Wife's *Prologue and Tale*, like the end of the *Troilus*, looks beyond this imprisoning cycle of Ovidian words. The Wife will drop all her Ovidian arts if Jankyn will surrender the pseudo-Ovidian antifeminist power he has marshaled. The Old Hag will be faithful and beautiful if the knight-rapist surrenders his claims to authority and shows that he has wisdom enough to follow his wife's will.

I earlier proposed that the skepticism surrounding Ovidian art in the *Troilus* becomes celebration in the Wife's *Prologue and Tale*. We see now that this celebration is not an end in itself, it brings about another kind of celebration, that of marital affection and unity. Surprisingly, then, Chaucer's view of Ovidian art here is not so drastically opposed to what he offered in the *Troilus*. Rather, the Wife represents an evolution in his treatment of Ovid. The issues are more complex, the Ovidian voices more varied and intertwined, and mastery over them so much more empowering and crucial to one's identity and fate. Chaucer has worked hard in the story of the Wife to express the literary, textual, and social conflicts in terms of Ovid, just as he had in the *Troilus*. But in this second art of love we see a more intricate account of Ovidian game, as a character struggles for her own identity and for a share of marital affection in a world of gritty human experience and abstract clerkish authority.

As she addresses modern women writers, Hélène Cixous, a more recent French theorist than La Vieille, exhorts her readers to "kill the false woman who is preventing the live one from breathing."[60] Looking back at the Wife's *Prologue and Tale*, we are tempted to report that the Wife kills the false woman by incarnating herself according to antifeminist tradition and then by exposing the arbitrary origins of her identity and burning the book of accumulated misreadings that prevents the real woman from living. This would be quite a neat coda to our study of the Wife's Ovidian power and poise. But to what extent has the Wife done this? To what degree has she overcome her identity as "text," that is, the false text written by and for men? To what degree does celebration of Ovidian art actually give way to a "golden age" beyond convention and beyond game?

Our study of Ovid has shown several features of the Wife's struggles and art: she takes on and routs the antifeminist tradition; she parodically retells the tale of Midas; and she reinvents the education of the knight rapist. In all cases she reimagines the discourses and identities she has inherited. Through her creative power, Chaucer himself reimagines the works of his clerkly fathers,

Ovid and Jean de Meun. But the Wife's ultimate "liberation" as a woman is hard, indeed impossible, to gauge. Tracing the Wife's movement toward freedom from the conventions of identity, I have neglected to address that what we know of the Wife comes, obviously, from her current report—what she tells the pilgrims, in the only moment in which we hear her voice. Does she show any signs of liberation, of having preserved any of the "golden age" luster she enjoyed with Jankyn? Or is she hopelessly bound to a series of inescapable conventions and voices? In a word, what would she do with the sixth? Would she court him in textbook Ovidian fashion, as Diomede does Criseyde, using her "tonge large" to lay out hook and line?

Ultimately, the Wife has given us a glimpse of marital affection, of the peace and equality she once worked toward and achieved. But the "golden age" is over; she is there no longer. Nor is she up in the eighth sphere, looking down on the wretched world as Troilus does. She is on horseback, an ageless Ovid, still teaching the "olde daunce" and ready for a whirl or two if the price is right. Still a "wife," she must live in language and artistry in an eternal Ovidian "gift of words."

NOTES

1. "Quod sumus, est crimen, si crimen sit, quod amamus / Qui dedit esse, deus prestat amare michi" (Hilbert, ed., *Baldricus Burgulianus Carmina*, no. 97, ll. 55–56).

2. Critical discourse on the Wife has always been vital, and her relations to Ovid have by no means been neglected. Her debt to Dipsas, for instance, is noted by Robertson, who links the two in the course of framing his famous definition of the Wife as "a literary personification of rampant 'femininity'" (*A Preface to Chaucer*, 321). These connections were most firmly made by Richard Hoffman, who sees the Wife's use of Ovidian doctrine from the *Ars* as powerful evidence of her carnality. Concerning her use of Ovid's comparison between the vagina and a light-giving lantern, Hoffman concludes: "The Wife's defense of adultery on the grounds that her 'lantern' will not be diminished ... illustrates her lecherous and literal-minded devotion to the precepts of the *Ars Amatoria*." The Wife's "carnal appreciation of the Ovidian image accords well with her reliance upon the letter of the Old Law rather than the spirit of the New" (*Ovid*, 129, 130). Beyond this, unfortunately, the work done on Ovid's "arts of love" and the Wife of Bath is rather sparse. Part of the reason for this neglect is that when critics refer to the Wife's Ovidianism, they are usually discussing, not her role as doctor of love, but her mistelling of Ovid's tale of Midas. For example, see Patterson, "'For the Wyves Love of Bath,'" who surveys several critical views of the Wife's Ovidian narrative.

3. She is the only character, save Chaucer, actually referred to in the Tales as an authority. See the *Merchant's Tale* IV, 1685ff., where her text has become codified as a handbook on love.

4. On the issue of female power in medieval texts, see Sheila Fisher and Janet E. Haley, *Seeking the Woman*, who rightly point out, in part quoting Marshall Leicester, that "there is no Wife of Bath, no 'she' no 'her,'" for characters like the Wife and Milton's Eve "do not refer to real women" (5). On the issue of the Wife's referentiality, see Leicester,

"Of a Fire in the Dark"; and Hansen, *Chaucer and the Fictions of Gender* and "The Wife of Bath." For a more "referential" reading see Amsler, who argues that the Wife's *Prologue* offers a "bourgeois, urban critique of woman's sexual, textual, and political economy in the fourteenth century" ("The Wife of Bath," 68).

5. On the Wife and La Vieille, see Muscatine, *Chaucer and the French Tradition*, 204ff. P. M. Kean, who, like Muscatine, does not address Ovid, offers a detailed study of the Wife, La Vieille, and female dominance (*Chaucer and the Making of English Poetry*, 148ff.). Patterson, "'For the Wyves Love of Bath,'" offers an elaborate comparison, tracing their respective arts of sexual "delay" and even charting and diagraming their rhetorical rhythms.

6. In discussing marriage relations in several of the *Tales*, Kean cites this passage as a locus classicus on the issue of dominance, but she does not link it to Ovid or apply it directly to the Wife and her husbands. See Kean, *Chaucer and the Making of English Poetry*, 140–42.

7. The exegetical readings of the Wife by Hoffman and Robertson have been powerfully challenged as Chaucerians seek to illuminate various ideological aspects of the Wife's struggle with the texts and institutions of male authority. The new awareness of the Wife's status is evident, for example, in that Derek Pearsall, in his handbook overview of the *Prologue*, can now say casually that the Wife uses her powers "to win a measure of independence in a world that is unfair to her sex" (*The Canterbury Tales*, 73). In an important essay, "The Wife of Bath," Mary Carruthers explains the Wife's quest for *maistrie* in terms of her socioeconomic status, responsibility, and good sense, which provide her the independence and the freedom to love that "auctoritee" deny her. A number of critics (including Sheila Delany, Peggy Knapp, and Carolyn Dinshaw) have furthered the cause of the Wife by addressing her "sexual poetics." In "Strategies of Silence," Delany redefines the question "what do women want most" as "what do men think women want most," which translates, she says, into "what do men want women to want" and "what do men want" or "what do I want." It does not matter that "in the tale the original question is both set and answered by women, because only a man could ask this question, and it can only be asked on behalf of men" (65). Knapp, examining the complex "fabric" of the Wife's discourse and identity, explores the Wife not only as "exegete and commentator" on Scripture but as "entrepreneur, feminist, temptress, and sociopath" (*Chaucer and the Social Contest*, 114). In *Chaucer's Sexual Poetics*, Dinshaw approaches an area in which the Wife has traditionally suffered attack, her glossing of texts, which is as unjustified and opportunistic as that done by men. Dinshaw is most interested in how the Wife, "as the literal text," the "devalorized feminine letter in the discourses of patriarchal hermeneutics," insists on "the positive, significant value of the carnal letter as opposed to the spiritual gloss" (120). Reading the Wife's Ovid is essential to our apprehension of these textual/sexual issues.

8. Ovid tells men to use tears (*Ars* I, 659), Ami tells Amant the same, and we also find this advice in medieval versions of the *Ars*, such as the *Key to Love*. Use a wet hand to apply fake tears, says Ovid, for "they do not always come in time"; the author of the *Key* says use an onion (see Shapiro, ed. and trans., *Comedy of Eros*, 35–36).

9. There is no specific study of Ovid and the antifeminist tradition. Wilson and Makowski, *Wykked Wyves*, make occasional references to the debt owed Ovid by various scholastic writers, such as Andreas and Walter Map, who draw from Ovidian poems in the course of their larger projects. Manuscript evidence suggests that Ovid did appear in collections like Jankyn's. British Lib. Add. MS 34749, for example, contains the tracts of Map and of Theophrastus, along with part of the *Ars Amatoria*. Pratt (who unfortunately

gives no bibliographic details) testifies to Ovid's appearance in such collections in "Jankyn's Book of Wikked Wives"; his is the best, though limited, study of the topic.

10. For an excellent survey of Roman legislation concerning marriage and sexual relations, see Brundage, *Law, Sex, and Christian Society*, 22. Brundage does not discuss Ovid but does examine the Lex Julia de adulteriis of 18 B.C., providing a clear context in which to see Ovid's supposedly corruptive influence.

11. See Huygens, *Accessus ad Auctores*, 35. The text is an *accessus* to the *Ex Ponto*.

12. *Ars* I, 31 ff., and *Ars* III, 57–58, contain these audience specifications.

13. Wilkinson, *Ovid Recalled*, 121.

14. As Brundage notes, "Roman marriage, at least among the upper classes, was concerned with property, politics, and power.... *Paterfamiliae* (male heads of households) had intercourse with their wives in order to produce heirs for their property who would continue the existence of their families" (*Law, Sex, and Christian Society*, 22). According to the Lex Julia, then, "upper-class women were forbidden to have sexual intercourse with anyone at all, save for their husbands" (30).

15. Medieval commentaries on the *Remedia*, working from the opening of the text itself, repeat that youths were suicidal or overwhelmed by passion. See Ghisalberti, "Medieval Biographies of Ovid," 45, appendix D.

16. "Sed, quaecumque uiris, uobis quoque dicta, puella, / credite: diuersis pattibus arma damus" (ll. 49–50).

17. In Ovid's letter to his stepdaughter, a young woman poet whom he calls Perilla (*Tristia* III, vii), we find a sensitivity, encouragement, respect, and recognition for the woman artist whom he compares to Sappho.

18. Chapter references are to the translation by Earl Jeffrey Richards. For the French, see the edition done by Maureen Curnow, 647–49.

19. See Christine de Pizan, "Le Livre de la Cité de Dames," ed. Curnow, 926ff., esp. 928–29.

20. See Pratt, "Jankyn's Book of Wikked Wives"; and the annotations in the *Riverside Chaucer*, ed. Benson (871), for fuller descriptions of the contents of Jankyn's book. Here I have identified the three major works of the tradition that figure most significantly in the Wife's *Prologue*. On the Wife's play with authority, see Leicester, *The Disenchanted Self*, 114–39. Dinshaw notes that the gynecological treatises attributed to the woman Trotula (mentioned as part of Jankyn's book) were actually written by men, which testifies to the "correlation between the masculine silencing of women's writing ... and the masculine control of their bodies" (*Chaucer's Sexual Poetics*, 20).

21. It is sometimes difficult to specify medieval sources, especially if stories are included in both the *Metamorphoses* and the love poems. For example, when Walter Map discusses the modesty of Penelope and the Sabine women and the vice of Scylla and Myrrha, he may be working from the *Ars Amatoria* or from the "book of bodies changed." See *De Nugis Curialium*, 295. The *Ars* fits well into Jankyn's book because it focuses on "female lust" and offers examples, some, such as the story of Pasiphaë, recounted in greater detail than in the *Metamorphoses*.

22. Jerome, *Epistola Adversus Jovinianum* 1, 48, quoted in *Riverside Chaucer*, 872. The editors indicate that quoted Latin glosses are taken from "the Ellesmere and related manuscripts" (865). See Silvia, "Glosses on the *Canterbury Tales*."

23. For a lively, recent discussion of the Wife's struggles with texts, authority, and "glossing," see Hanning, "'I Shal Finde It in a Mener Glose,'" who explores glossing as a "metaphor for all kinds of language manipulation, even what might be called textual harassment" (27).

24. Hélène Cixous, "The Laugh of the Medusa," 284. In saying that the Wife is both text and body I mean to indicate that she is both a compilation of scholastic antifeminist features and an expressive figure aware of her distinctly female sexuality as she pursues her own sexual politics. Dinshaw explores the medieval metaphorical relations between the physical body and the "body" of a text, arguing that in the Wife's assertion of the carnal, she depicts herself as "the truth of the text." Dinshaw combines various medieval interpretive theories to explore the Wife's assertion of the bodily as it stands in opposition to the Pauline interpretive model that would "discard the female when the male spirit has been uncovered." See *Chaucer's Sexual Poetics*, 113–31.

25. The Riverside Chaucer edits out Robinson's correct citation of *Ars* III, giving the impression that the Wife is just manipulating proverbs.

26. Bryan and Dempster, eds., *Sources and Analogues*, 217.

27. Ibid., 211.

28. See *Riverside Chaucer*, 869. This glosse cannot be taken as an "authoritative, historical" interpretation of Chaucer's meaning; rather, it is accidental evidence of what the Wife is up against.

29. See Huygens, *Accesses ad Auctores*, 33. This comment is to be distinguished from the common evaluation of *Ars* II as a book about how to retain the woman who has been sought and seduced, for the schoolmaster here is clearly referring to the guide to the women themselves, *Ars* III.

30. Deschamps, *Miroir* rubric to chapter XVIII. Deschamps at this point discusses the dangers of allowing a woman to venture about freely, particularly at church, where she may flirt with other men. See *Miroir* XLIII, ll. 4102ff.

31. Christine de Pizan warns women against exercising this type of freedom: "Neither should she use pilgrimages as an excuse to get away from town in order to go somewhere to play about or kick up her heels in some merry company. This is merely sin and wickedness in whoever does it, for it is offensive to God and a sad shame" (*Treasure*, 152). The Wife, who says quite explicitly that she seeks to "pleye" in the company of "lusty folk," is thus in many ways alone in her assertion of freedom if even a soul mate like Christine, the author of stories of great women and a combatant in the war with male authority, issues restrictions.

32. Also quoted in Bryan and Dempster, eds., *Sources and Analogues*, 220.

33. See *Amores* III, viii, 1–4, 9–10.

34. *Roman*, 8355ff.; and compare *Amores* III, viii, 39–40.

35. See *Roman*, ll. 7231ff., and Langlois's notes for the many Ovidian borrowings in Ami's discourse—including the famous advice to brush dust from your lover's dress. If there is no dust, "brush off what's not there."

36. "Car adès vient il meauz, beau maistre, / Deceveir que deceüz estre; / Meïsmement en cete guerre, / Quant le meien n'i sevent querre."

37. See Leicester, *The Disenchanted Self*, 114ff., where the author discusses the assumed authority of the antifeminist texts.

38. On the antifeminist textual tradition, particularly the uses and abuses it was put to, see Wilson and Makowski, *Wykked Wyves*, 1–11.

39. Dinshaw, *Chaucer's Sexual Poetics*, gives a convenient survey of this medieval reading of "woman" and cites scriptural commentaries on Genesis. See her introduction and its notes. On early patristic views of women (esp. Origen and Tertullian), see Brundage, *Law, Sex, and Christian Society*, 64ff.; on views from the High Middle Ages, including comments by Nicholas of Lyra, Aquinas, and Hortiensis, ibid., 425ff. On medieval conceptions of

women's nature, see Bloch, "Early Christianity and the Estheticization of Gender," in his *Medieval Misogyny*, 37–63.

40. Later, from exile, Ovid will give his "straight" evaluation of marriage: "wives" should respect and obey husbands according to right and law. Brundage notes that "the amused tone of Roman authors faded ... when they talked about marriage" (*Law, Sex, and Christian Society*, 22).

41. La Vieille not only balances Ovid's call for men to deceive women but combats the generalized notion that the *Ars Amatoria* is all about the evils of women. Even 200 years later, Christine de Pizan lamented in the *Book of the City of Ladies* that Ovid wrote that women were deceptive and false, expressing no awareness, strangely, that Ovid was a double agent and later armed the Amazons. It is unclear why Christine does not mention the third book; she was likely responding to the generalized reputation of the *Ars Amatoria* as an antifeminist text. Perhaps our best evidence for this reputation is its inclusion in Jankyn's book. Lucia Rosa mentions a copy of Arnulf's commentary on the *Ars* that stops somewhere in Book II for no apparent reason (see Rosa, "Su alcuni commenti inedite," 202), indicating perhaps that the neglect of Book III was part of actual practice. As we have seen, *Ars* III was glossed as ethics, focusing on the cosmetic, not the combative, strategy.

42. *Ars* II similarly advises women to accumulate, in the section on the Golden Age (discussed above), and also reports that without gold, Homer himself is scorned.

43. *PL* 184, 381aff. See also Huygens, *Accessus as Auctores*, 17–18. I have consulted the French translation in Jean Dechanét, *Oeuvres Choisie de Guillaume de St. Thierry*, 151–73. See also Minnis's mention of the passage (*Medieval Theory of Authorship*, 51); and Leclercq's translation and discussion in *Monks and Love in Twelfth-Century France*, 66–69.

44. Vance, surveying some of the relations between language and social order, quotes Saint Bernard and also John of Garland's assessment that "in death's eternal kingdom Woman is enthroned forever, from her mouth flows gall that is taken for nectar and kills [*necat*] body and soul" (Vance, *Mervelous Signals*, 259). The image is strikingly similar to the description in the *Antiovidianus* of the form/content rift in Ovid that creates, among other paradoxes, gall/honey [fel mel] (Kienast, ed., l. 6).

45. "Femme est enfer qe tut receit, / Tut tens ad seif e tuit tens beit. / Femme ne set estre fel.... Femme ad un art plus qu deable" (*Le Blasme des Fames*, ll. 95–97, 101, in Fiero, Pfeffer, and Allain, eds., *Three Medieval Views of Women*, 127). For help with the Old French throughout this chapter, I thank Robyn Holman. Translations from the *Book of the City of Ladies* are those of Earl Jeffery Richards.

46. See Kooper, "Loving the Unequal Equal," where the author discusses the theological texts on marital affection that may be behind Ami's call for equality at *Roman*, ll. 9391–9400.

47. Although Chaucer does not name the *Roman de la Rose* or Deschamps's *Miroir* in Jankyn's book, these poems provide the Wife a pool of antifeminist doctrine to embody as well as refute. Chaucer only omits them because they do not have classical, "auctorial" status and because Chaucer at times does not like to be too explicit about his sources. Consider, for example, his refusal to mention. Boccaccio as the source of the *Troilus*.

48. Pratt, "Jankyn's Book of Wikked Wives," 27.

49. "Autres, pour monstrer que ilz ont biaucoup veu / d'escriptures, se fondent sur ce qu'ilz ont trouvé en livres et dient après les autres et aleguent les autteurs" (Curnow, 643).

50. "Et leur semble que ilz ne pueent mesprendre, puisque autres ont dit en livres ce que ilz veullent dire, et come ce medire" (ibid., 646–47).

51. "Et sans que plus t'en dye, to puez bien sçavoir que ces babuises dittes et escriptes contre les femmes furent et sont choses trouvees et dittes a voulenté et contre verité" (ibid., 818–19).

52. "Et in conclusion de tout, je determinoye que ville chose fist Dieux quant il fourma femme.... Adonc moy estant en ceste penssee, me sourdi une grant desplaisance et tristesce de couraige en desprisant moy meismes et tout le sexe feminin, si somme ce ce fust monstre en nature" (ibid., 619–20).

53. Priscilla Martin quotes a longer version of this passage, commenting that "Christine's *persona* has internalized the material which Jankyn uses against the Wife." Her argument is that "through Jankyn and Chaunticleer Chaucer mocks the pompous and prejudiced uses men can make of books" (13) and that "Chaucer is well aware of the effects of man-made language" (12). See pp. 231–33, for citations on reading and women. See also her discussion of the Wife (90–102).

54. "In remotissima posteritate michi faciet auctoritatem antiquitas."

55. Hanning, "'I Shal Finde It in a Maner Glose,'" toward the end of his discussion of how Alison "has been fighting books more than people" (46), concludes by emphasizing the Wife's complex and seemingly inevitable entrapment by acts of "textual harassment": "The Wife is thus an ironic representation of Chaucer's awareness of how, by imposing identity on others by means of transmitted authorities, we let them choose only between conforming to stereotypes and being attacked—and in the latter case, conforming to counterstereotypes" (49). Hansen has argued that the Wife represents "not the full and remarkable presence we have normally invested her with, but a dramatic and important instance of women's silence and suppression in history and in language" ("The Wife of Bath," 400). "The Wife," she says, "turns out to be a reflection of 'categorizing principles' rather than a speaking subject" (413) and "ineffectively and only superficially rebels against the patriarchal authority that has produced her" (407). See also Hansen's longer discussion of the Wife, in *Chaucer and the Fictions of Gender*, 26–57.

56. Patterson, "'For the Wyves Love of Bath,'" is right that the retelling involves the "self-gratification" of antifeminism, but I do not agree with his convoluted argument about the Wife's rhetorical art of "delay," which intentionally lures the male audience away from the "full story." There is a parallel, Patterson says, between Midas (a bad, carnal listener who prefers the song of Pan to Apollo), and the male antifeminist audience of the Wife's *Tale*—both neglect the reading that leads to "self-knowledge" (658).

57. The others thus have more tangible "self-interest" than the Old Hag of the Wife's *Tale*. See Bryan and Dempster, eds., *Sources and Analogues*, 223ff.

58. Wetherbee, *Chaucer and the Poets*, 93.

59. We may even see the rape as an extreme type of patristic "glossing." Dinshaw, *Chaucer's Sexual Poetics*, 127ff.

60. Cixous, "The Laugh of the Medusa," 284.

EILEEN JANKOWSKI

Chaucer's Second Nun's Tale *and the Apocalyptic Imagination*

Chaucer's *Second Nun's Tale* presents a particularly intriguing challenge for critics: how to analyze a tale described by one critic as "a saint's life 'Englished,' no more, no less,"[1] that proposes a particularly narrow view of religious belief and behavior, but which is placed among the rich variety of *Canterbury Tales*, many of which either question or explode generic expectations. Historically, critics have expressed a wish for something "other"—perhaps a Protestant Chaucer, a more womanly Saint Cecilia, a more affective display of Christian piety, or a less disturbing array of miraculous improbabilities.[2] More recently, critics explore Cecilia's "subversive actions and speeches" in relation to medieval feminine challenges to patriarchal authority,[3] or her "strategies of dissent" against an "increasingly secularized and impersonal Church."[4] As David Raybin states, "By refiguring the parameters that govern the reception of a saint's life, Chaucer invites one to see such matters as gender relations and spiritual values in a more problematic context. In doing so he reconstructs both the story and the human life which it presents. He recreates the saint's life as something else."[5]

I would suggest that this "something else" lies in the "medieval apocalyptic imagination" apparent in the *Second Nun's Tale*, evident in specific narrative techniques, including Chaucer's focus on eschatology, renovation, and the collapse of time as the next world pulls against the current age.[6]

From *The Chaucer Review*, vol. 36, no. 2 (2001): pp. 128–148. © 2001 by The Pennsylvania State University.

Richard K. Emmerson and Ronald B. Herzman explore the development of the apocalyptic imagination in several medieval texts, focusing on four "keys" drawn from the writings of Joachim of Fiore, the best known twelfth-century exegete.[7] Briefly, these are that apocalyptic texts often include: 1) references and imagery that suggest a generalized body of evil, universal and timeless, often linking the cosmic, universal, and allegorical to the personal, individual, and historical; 2) agents of evil that are inversions of agents of good, frequently pairing symbols to indicate this inverse relationship; 3) parallels between these linked figures or agents and their careers; and 4) many symbolic numerical patterns as they relate to actual historical figures or events. While the authors do not suggest a specific direct or even indirect Joachimist influence on later medieval authors, they very persuasively argue that "later authors share with Joachim ... an imaginative manipulation of the tradition" of apocalyptic thought and imagery.[8]

For example, the authors argue for an overall connection to Christian eschatology in the *Canterbury Tales* in its very frame motif of pilgrimage, which always displays both a personal and a universal dimension. The earthly journey to Canterbury undertaken by a specific group of Chaucerian characters symbolizes the heavenly direction all Christians must follow to reach the New Jerusalem.[9] Extending their paradigm to the *Second Nun's Tale*, I would argue that the legend of St. Cecilia similarly combines the personal and the universal in an intense moment of apocalyptic illumination as the pilgrims near the end of their earthly journey. To date the tale has not been examined in light of its representation of an apocalyptic imagination, but its blend of church beginnings and endings (eschatology) and the apocalyptic narrative form in which this message is conveyed remain crucial to an understanding of the tale's function as part of Chaucer's "sense of an ending" for the *Canterbury Tales*.[10]

That the *Second Nun's Tale* is the beginning of the end is generally agreed upon by critics. Larry D. Benson has forcefully restated the argument for the Ellesmere order which places Fragment VIII near the end of the *Canterbury Tales*.[11] From a thematic standpoint, the highest ideal of conduct "happens at the end" of the Tales, according to Donald Howard, when St. Cecilia's noble life is held up to view.[12] James Dean claims that "beginning with the Second Nun's Tale," the final four tales close down the Canterbury project by offering particular ending themes.[13] Stephen Knight argues that the last four tales finish Chaucer's process of steadily "closing down ... the historical imagination" that is explored more fully in earlier tales.[14]

Perhaps the most useful way to assess this "closing down" is to consider the apocalyptic imagination that operates both historically and structurally in the *Second Nun's Tale*.[15] In terms of Church history, Cecilia historically stands at the very beginning, her story highlighting the moment when Christians struggle to establish what is to become an extremely powerful institution. Paradoxically, the *Second Nun's Tale* concurrently highlights the very end of the salvation story—judgment day when apocalyptic prophecies are fulfilled, earthly institutions and concerns fall away, and the vision of heaven predominates.[16] The tale moves effortlessly between these two historical moments, one personal and one universal, linking them through the use of a specific apocalyptic narrative technique.

Structurally, within the *Canterbury Tales* the legend of St. Cecilia also reflects the apocalyptic imagination at work. "This mayden bright Cecilie"[17] is placed between two negative apocalyptic figures, the Pardoner and the Canon. As Emmerson and Herzman point out, the Pardoner stands as "a contemporary version of Simon Magus ... the first great spiritual challenger of the early Church."[18] The Pardoner's hypocritical and sacrilegious pollution of grace with monetary gain stands in stark opposition to Cecilia's steadfast purity and commitment to the highest religious principles. Just as St. Peter and St. Paul literally and figuratively invert Simon's challenge to Church authority by causing him to plummet from the heights to his death, St. Cecilia successfully inverts the Roman challenge to Christianity by actually increasing the number of converts in the face of Almachius' persecution. She "answers" the Pardoner's claim that "I am wont to preche for to wynne" (VI 461), specifically to win money for the dispensation of false grace, by "ful bisily" (VIII 342) preaching of Christ's passion and death to "doon mankynde pleyn remissioun" (346).

Fittingly, both historically and structurally, the deceitful Canon makes his appearance directly following the story of St. Cecilia. Many critics have pointed out the thematic and imagistic contrasts between the Canon's Yeoman's and Second Nun's tales,[19] noting particularly that while Cecilia's "werke" results in eternal light and salvation, the Yeoman makes clear that all of the Canon's "werkyng nas but fraude and deceite" (VIII 1367). Even the Pardoner's attempts to dupe his congregation pale in comparison with the Canon's "magical" tricks and direct dealings with the "feend" (VIII 1159), characteristics that suggest the latter's association with the Antichrist, incarnation of the devil who, in the final days, will dazzle unwary humans with false wonders. The *Second Nun's Tale* explicitly warns readers of the deadly consequences of such failure to see the truth clearly and resist the tricks of the arch-deceiver, holding Cecilia up as an example of one who is "wantynge of blyndnesse" (VIII 100), able to defy worldly temptations and focus her, and our, eyes on a heavenly vision.

These historic and structural connections to apocalyptic imagery are complemented by a narrative structure in the *Second Nun's Tale* that relentlessly insists on such a vision. One critic defines such an apocalyptic narrative form as embodying a "revelatory shift," or "that point of radical differencing in any narrative at which 'what is' gives way so that 'what ought to be' may reveal itself."[20] In this moment of revelation, the personal, individual time frame is inevitably linked with the universal, cosmic time frame of the apocalyptic. Frank Kermode also defines apocalyptic narrative temporality, employing the terms *kairos*, a "moment of crisis," "the fate of time," or "God's time," and *chronos*, or "passing time," "waiting time," those successive moments during which all events march inexorably towards some expected end that will "bestow upon the whole duration and meaning."[21] In the story of St. Cecilia, the persecution of individual early Christians swiftly gives way to the universal, heavenly reward accorded to faithful followers of God's word. The tale accomplishes quick transitions from earthly to heavenly realms in order to capture the urgency of this apocalyptic moment.

Thus unlike many of the *Canterbury Tales* that tease out various themes and motifs, the *Second Nun's Tale* offers a saint's life stripped to essentials. Old men and angels appear to deliver their messages, then vanish when their task is done; conversions follow swiftly upon one another without exploration of the process involved; and even the trial scene, the "high point" of the narrative,[22] moves so swiftly that logical gaps in argumentation occur. Some readers account for the fast pace by claiming that Chaucer tries to heighten the tale's drama by avoiding repetition or to sharpen the focus on Cecilia.[23] Such explanations are entirely plausible, but I would offer another—Chaucer, by choosing this particular saint's life that stresses the urgency of immediate "assent," momentarily shifts the *Canterbury Tales* into an apocalyptic narrative mode where marvels and wonders increase, ordinary human experience takes on new meaning, and plodding, digressive earthly time is replaced by a vision of a heaven that "is swift and round and eek brennynge" (114).

For example, Cecilia's guardian angel rewards Valerian's decisions to embrace the Christian faith and to abide by her demand for a chaste marriage by handing him a crown of lilies, symbolizing Valerian's "body clene and ... unwemmed thought" (225). The purifying rite of baptism seals Valerian in his new faith, but the white crown is not his only reward. After the angel explains the crown's power to unmask the unworthy, he offers to make one wish of Valerian's come true:

> And thow, Valerian, for thow so soone
> Assentedest to good conseil also,
> Sey what thee list, and thou shalt han thy boone
> (232–34)

Valerian is granted a "boone" not as a further reward for rejecting pagan ways and embracing Christ's, but precisely because his decision is made with such dispatch. Valerian's conversion thus illustrates both through narrative and thematic structure the urgency of the apocalyptic moment. Doubt and hesitation, briefly represented in Valerian's questioning of Cecilia's story of her guardian angel, make way for clear, "soone" acceptance of "good conseil," constituting a model of what ought to be in an ideal, God-centered world.

In this scene, apocalyptic imagery complements the force of time manipulation. In terms of Joachim of Fiore's second "key," the figure of the angel, as an obvious agent of good, will be inverted by the agent of evil in the text, the Roman Prefect Almachius, when he deprives Valerian and Tiburce of their "crowned" heads. But just as Simon Magus fails to turn the essence of the Holy Spirit sent by Christ to the apostles into an evil commodity, so Almachius will fail to stem the tide of Christianity by eliminating the noble, faithful brothers.

This abrupt juxtaposition of events serves as an example of the often radical manipulation of time in apocalyptic narratives. These texts fail to do the expected: connect, diversify, explain, make concords, facilitate extrapolation. Certainly such texts display "no temporality, no successiveness."[24] The reader must make sense out of the confusion, suspending traditional desires for ordered discourse and fulfilled expectations.

This disorientation is evident narratively in conjunction with suggestive imagery from the Book of Revelations. The Apostle John describes a visionary moment when he beheld "one like the son of man," white-haired and white-robed (Rev. 1:13–14), and "fell at his feet as though dead" (1:17).[25] Similarly, an "oold man, clad in white clothes cleere" (201) suddenly appears before Valerian, whereupon he "as deed fil doun for drede / Whan he hym saugh, and he up hent hym tho" (204–5). Narratively, the neutral word "and" serves as the only link between Valerian's total collapse and quick recovery. In the space of a half line Valerian is back on his feet, ready to read the words in the book the old man holds (analogous to the book of life).[26] How has dread been transformed so quickly into eager curiosity? The reader must supply the missing element that connects the description of Valerian's fear with the actual outcome of this *exemplum*: Valerian's paramount desire to know more about God.

The narrative, in failing to provide reasons for Valerian's quick recovery, focuses attention on the act of recovery itself rather than dwelling on explanations for it, introducing the message repeated throughout the tale: the time for reflection is past, the time for immediate action is now. This urgent call is promptly reinforced in the next lines of the tale. After reading a sentence from the golden book, Valerian is peremptorily asked, "Leevestow this thyng or no? Sey ye or nay" (212). The text offers no explanation of how Valerian reaches his decision, but apparently without a moment's thought he answers "I leeve al this thyng" (213), thus abandoning paganism and embracing the totality of Christian thought and belief. Again, the action itself is brought into high relief by the omission of either biblical exegesis or the questioning one might expect from a pagan so abruptly introduced to an entirely new belief system. Following the first "key" to the apocalyptic imagination, the tale thus links a very personal, individual moment to the universal in that God's word here very effectively preempts human concern for explanation. Valerian's choice is immediate acceptance or rejection, "ye or nay," just as God will judge each soul at the end of time, "ye or nay."

On the heels of Valerian's conversion comes his baptism ("And Pope Urban hym cristned right there" (217)), the official purgation from sin that Cecilia requires of her husband before he is allowed to see her guardian angel.[27] This section of the text seems to belie an apocalyptic lack of successiveness in the sense that, albeit swift and without elaboration, events do follow in some kind of logical order: Valerian is exposed to the Word, accepts it, and is baptized as a result. Yet the crowding of event upon event also serves to disorient the reader who has become used to Chaucer's teasing out of themes and exploration of situations. Valerian's conversion is reduced to a speedy "yes" and the imposition of a rite whose terms and conditions one must assume Valerian either understands or has no need to understand. Here again a specific, individual action is immediately linked to the cosmic implications of the salvation story, reinforcing the message that the time for rhetoric, debate, and/or elaborate thought has passed.

Sherry Reames addresses this tendency of the text to omit searching reflection and/or didacticism, arguing that Augustine's proposal that the whole of Christian life provides an opportunity for a series of conversions, gradually moving the soul toward final illumination and purification, is replaced in this tale by a system of quick conversions imposed from without. Human capability to direct at least part of the conversion process is affirmed by Augustine, resulting in our ability finally to come "face to face" with our maker. Reames claims that in the *Second Nun's Tale* this ability is denied to those who must wait passively for the bestowal of cleansing grace. However, her conclusion, that Chaucer's retelling of the *Second Nun's Tale* reflects his "increasing theological pessimism,"[28] seems unsupported by the tale itself.

First, Chaucer may well be attempting to focus on the results of conversion rather than on the process itself, his interest lying not in presenting a particular conversion model, Augustinian or otherwise, but in holding up to view the heavenly reward available to faithful Christians on judgment day. In the *Second Nun's Tale* the promised reward is release from this life so that one's place at God's banquet may be taken, but after their baptisms the more immediate reward conferred on both brothers is a glimpse, in the angel's face, of God's coming glory. Again and again the tale shifts from the changeable possibilities of earthly human existence to the "changeless, spaceless, timeless" eschatological possibilities offered through acceptance of God's promise of redemption.[29] The parallel with promised reward as described in Revelations is particularly clear in the many references to eating at God's table: "Here I stand knocking at the door; if anyone hears my voice and opens the door, I will come in and sit down to supper with him and he with me" (Rev. 3:20); "Happy are those who are invited to the wedding-supper of the Lamb!" (Rev. 19:9); "Come and gather for God's great supper" (Rev. 19:18). In addition, there are frequent references to the great splendor of many of the angelic messengers who award John a glimpse of the glorious New Jerusalem to come.

Second, after Augustine's long, agonizing struggle to unite his divided will and accept God, there remains, finally, a moment—that particular instant in the garden when he says "yes" to God's will and relinquishes his own. At this apocalyptic point in Augustine's text, *chronos* cedes its narrational prerogative to *kairos*. Reames would prefer that Chaucer follow Augustine and privilege the process, but in the story of St. Cecilia Chaucer seems clearly more interested in the aftermath of that crucial moment of conversion.

For example, as in Valerian's conversion, Tiburce is confronted with a miraculous occurrence that sparks an intense transformation. He begins by wondering about the odor of roses and lilies "this tyme of the yeer" (246), but instead of an extended meditation on the meaning of this strange occurrence, Tiburce proclaims at the end of the stanza that the "sweete smel" has "chaunged me al in another kynde" (251–52). This alteration of "kynde," of the deepest part of Tiburce's psyche, constitutes the profound change required for true acceptance of God's word. In Valerian's situation, a visual experience reading the word of God precipitates conversion; Tiburce needs only the smell of sanctity to reshape himself. Once again, the nature of his change is not made clear, but his readiness to adopt a new outlook is unmistakable and sufficient.

Yet when told to seek Urban, the fugitive lurking in the catacombs, Tiburce checks his eagerness with common sense, reasoning that since the Romans will surely burn Urban "[a]nd we also, to bere hym compaignye" (315), it is a "wonder dede" (308) that Valerian should suggest such an action. Obviously Tiburce's change to "another kynde" has not been as complete as Valerian's; perhaps the slight slowing down of the tale at this point is required as a concession to this weaker, more fearful faith that necessitates a more extended and, in a certain way, more sensual description of God's reward.

Tiburce's common sense assessment of the dangers of association with Urban is promptly overcome by what might be termed a "divine sense" assessment of the real danger inherent in rejection of God's saving grace. Cecilia boldly exhorts him to look beyond this life to a better one to come, again stressing the apocalyptic priority to shift to heavenly rather than earthly concerns. Cecilia calms Tiburce's fear of being "ybrend in this world" (318) by reminding him of the "oother place" God has promised:

> Men myghten dreden wel and skilfully
> This lyf to lese, myn owene deere brother,
> If this were lyvynge oonly and noon other.
> But ther is bettre lif in oother place,
> That never shal be lost, ne drede thee noght,
> Which Goddes Sone us tolde thurgh his grace.
>   (320–25)

Here Cecilia lifts Tiburce's eyes away from man's earthly fate of lurking "in halkes alwey to and fro" (311), never daring to "putte forth his heed" (312), to a vision of a better, fuller life that can never be lost once gained through God's saving grace. John in Revelations describes "a new heaven and a new earth" (21.1) to come after all are judged, as the voice from the throne proclaims, "I am making all things new!" (21.5). The process by which this "bettre," new life is won is not detailed in the tale, the revelatory vision of glorious reward providing sufficient incentive to seek it, indicating that the reticence of the tale is part of its meaning.[30]

Yet while Cecilia's role is to teach, her preaching on Christ's passion is summarized in five lines in the tale (342–47), not quoted in full. A version of the Cecilia legend available to Chaucer, the *Passio*, includes two very long passages expounding the central beliefs of Christianity, but Voragine, and, following him, Chaucer, replace those passages with the preface to Saint Ambrose's mass and Cecilia's brief discourse on idols.[31] One might argue that at this point the narrative does slip from an apocalyptic mode into predictable "earthly" debate or exhortation, much as readers find in the *Tale of Melibee* when Prudence argues for right action and wise counsel.

However, although the *Second Nun's Tale* does include brief instruction by Valerian and Cecilia, their teaching touches on but one Christian belief: the commandment against false idols. There is no time for the searching examination of one's soul the Parson recommends for those preparing to confess and repent; recognizing false gods and worshipping only the one, true God assume the highest priority for those about to face final judgment. Valerian promises Tiburce his own crown of lilies "if that thou wolt reneye / The ydoles and be clene, and elles naught" (268–69), and Cecilia continues the lesson by showing him "al open and pleyn / That alle ydoles nys but a thyng in veyn / … And charged hym his ydoles for to leve" (284–87). This single lesson prefigures the issue in Cecilia's trial and her debate with Almachius, but, more importantly, serves to reduce the whole of Christian thought to one essential question—does Tiburce believe in "O Lord, o feith, o God, withouten mo" (207) or not?

The claim that apocalyptic stories fail to diversify and explain seems particularly applicable at this point when the opportunity for the exploration of Christian belief is replaced by a concentration on the kind of question that conceivably might be put to all at the final judgment. Again, the universal implications of the particular question asked of Tiburce highlight an insistence on the link between the cosmic and the personal typical of apocalyptic texts. Understanding Christ's crucifixion and the promise of his resurrection helps only those who must remain bound in an earthly struggle; Valerian, Tiburce, and Cecilia are bound in another direction altogether.

The real reward for unquestioning faith in God's Word lies beyond flowered crowns and angelic favors granted. Derek Pearsall, referring to the *Monk's Tale*, proposes an explanation for the litany of those who have fallen from high estate that also perfectly fits the overall pattern found in the *Second Nun's Tale*. Pearsall states that "man's chief cause of concern is not that he is doomed to die, but that he is doomed to live."[32] This same concern is apparent in St. Cecilia's tale as the three main characters move quickly to escape the cares and persecution of earthly time and embrace the life-in-death that union with God in heaven promises. The vision the Second Nun provides always pulls away from earthly rationales or rewards in order to stress the place in heaven God has reserved for the faithful.

For example, the angel conveys God's pleasure in Valerian's request that Tiburce "may han grace / To knowe the trouthe" (237–8) not only by granting Valerian's wish, but also by extending the dimensions of God's pleasure, promising "And bothe with the palm of martirdom / Ye shullen come unto his blisful feste" (240–41). This promise of martyrdom as reward is confirmed again in the preface to the mass of St. Ambrose that connects the "myracle of thise corones tweye" (270) with

> The palm of martirdom for to receyve,
> Seinte Cecile, fufild of Goddes yifte,
> The world and eek hire chambre gan she weyve
>   (274–76)

God's ultimate gift to humankind is a collapse of earthly, historical time to permit a quick death and subsequent release from earthly trials; only by abandoning ("weyve") life can one realize life in paradise. Others may be doomed to live in the troubled, pagan world of the tale, but those who wholeheartedly and quickly "assent" to God's offer of that "oother place" find a better life.

Appropriately in an apocalyptic narrative, this cosmic vision of life in death is never allowed to fade into the background, but remains the impetus for the urgency of action in the story. Valerian recognizes and even welcomes their imminent fate and so presses Tiburce to "withouten slouthe \ Bileve aright" (258–9). When Tiburce asks if all he has heard has been a dream, Valerian answers, interestingly enough, in terms of time:

> "In dremes," quod Valerian, "han we be
> Unto this tyme, brother myn, ywis.
> But now at erst in trouthe oure dwellyng is."
>   (262–64)

Valerian pinpoints a specific moment when their lives change from dream to truth, the crossroad between *chronos* and *kairos*, but the usual categories of experience are reversed in Valerian's explanation. Humans generally view earthly "tyme" as real and true in the sense that events actually happen, but Valerian characterizes this kind of perceived reality as a dreamstate, false and unreal. On the other hand, heavenly "tyme" is the only reality and truth one can strive to experience. Until this moment when both brothers recognize, accept, and act upon the truth that has been revealed to them, they have only been imagining life; for the first time ("at erst") they are in touch with the reality represented by God's truth and find their new "dwellyng" in it. But the place promised them by the angel is at God's "blisful feste" (241) and, indeed, in the tale the brothers soon "losten bothe hir hevedes" (398) because of their devotion to the Christian faith, escaping the doom of living any longer in an imperfect and hostile world.

Only when past, present, and future fuse "into a point in time filled with significance" does one experience *kairos*, a time charged with meaning precisely because of its intimate relation to and effect on the end. Humans, poised "in the middest" between origin and end, desire these moments of significance that "harmonize" these two unknowable concepts. Chaucer's story of St. Cecilia concentrates on these moments of crisis, these individual moments in time, since all that is past becomes insignificant when compared to the present moment of decision. Valerian's pagan past is inconsequential in the tale; any deeds he may have done, for good or ill, have no bearing on his immediate worthiness or ability to answer the question, "Leevestow this thyng or no?" (212). As a soul facing God, thus linked to universal time, his fate will be decided by his immediate answer. Once he replies affirmatively, his "ye" becomes part of his past, and in fact, stands as the only significant moment in that past.

This verbal "crossing over" from personal events to cosmic significance clearly displays the apocalyptic imagination at work in the *Second Nun's Tale*. Subsequent events move swiftly towards the "end" that lies embedded in Valerian's acceptance of Christian faith. His baptism qualifies him for the victor's palm of martyrdom and a place at God's table; past, present and future fuse in the present moment as waiting is replaced by fulfillment. In *Paradise Lost* the archangel's words characterize this moment:

> How soon hath thy prediction, Seer blest,
> Measur'd this transient World, the race of Time,
> Till time stands fix'd.[33]

During the brief interval the *Second Nun's Tale* provides in the *Canterbury Tales*, a beam of light focuses on these moments when "time stands fix'd," when secular, and even many religious, concerns are laughed away in the face of an apocalyptic vision that, instead of producing untold terror and bloodshed, actually clarifies the problems of belief, right action, and meaning.

While Tiburce and, to a lesser degree, Valerian struggle with the decision to accept God's challenge, for Cecilia such problems never even exist. She is as suggested, a substance "fixed" so perfectly that she can endure the heat of any physical or mental "fire" without alteration.[34] But she is "fixed," in the sense of being able both to withstand earthly torments and to comprehend perfectly heavenly visions, precisely because she "exists," textually at least, as both an individual and as an apocalyptic type, a character perfectly poised "in the middest." Cecilia wholeheartedly understands and accepts the vision of heaven promised to the faithful at the final judgment and thus stands in the realm of God's time, yet while trapped in the "contagioun" (72) of her body she must at the same time endure present, historical circumstances. The Prologue introduces many of these conditions of imperfect, earthly time and Cecilia's corresponding perfection: spiritual blindness vs. spiritual insight, idleness vs. busyness, darkness vs. light. Most significantly, however, the etymologizing characterization of her as "the hevene of peple" (104) lifts her out of the realm of ordinary mortals struggling with questions regarding the proper form of busyness, the development of spiritual insight, and ways to preserve some form of purity in a corrupt world.

Metadramatically the tale itself performs the same function within the *Canterbury Tales*, providing the continuum between early church images of the Pardoner as a type of Simon Magus and end of time images of the Canon as a type of the Antichrist. As a type of the perfect, faithful champion of the Church, St. Cecilia represents the highest form of Christian life—perfect, unselfish devotion to God, even to the point of welcoming martyrdom. The final image evoked in the etymology of her name explicitly connects Cecilia with a vision similar to that of John's, when he describes the New Jerusalem as a city "of pure gold, bright as clear glass" (Rev. 21:18):

> And right so as thise philosopres write
> That hevene is swift and round and eek brennynge,
> Right so was faire Cecilie the white
> Ful swift and bisy evere in good werkynge,
> And round and hool in good perseverynge,
> And brennynge evere in charite ful brighte.
>   (113–118)

In heaven light shines eternally because of God's presence ("And the city had no need of sun or moon to shine upon it; for the glory of God gave it light, and its lamp was the lamb" (Rev. 21.23–24)). Cecilia, then, comes to stand for the closest approximation to heaven possible here on earth, the Church Militant, which carries the flame of God's love by "brennynge evere in charitie ful brighte," gathering the "hool" of believers into its circle of souls seeking salvation, and busying itself "ful swift" in good works. Cecilia engages in "bisynesse" that is "leveful" (5) because her work is sanctioned by the institution of the Church itself as the best way to withstand the devil who preys on idleness.[35]

This connection between the devil and idleness is cleverly played out in the tale during Cecilia's trial when she scoffs at the "ydoles" to which Almachius insists she sacrifice. She points out the "idleness" of worship offered to what is and always will remain a lifeless stone:

> And thise ymages, wel thou mayst espye,
> To thee ne to hemself mowen noght profite,
> For in effect they been nat worth a myte.
>   (509–11)

The economic terms Cecilia uses reflect the stress placed on God's power and willingness to reward generously those who offer homage to Him; "leveful bisynesse" is "profitable" to one's eternal soul both in keeping the devil at bay and in reaping the benefits of faithful "reverence / To Crist" (434–35). Thus the maneuvers of the Pardoner and Canon to profit from false relics and alchemical tricks appear particularly deadening to the soul compared to Cecilia's wise use of resources. In fact, John reveals that such "liars" and "sorcerers" are condemned to "a second death, in the lake that burns with sulphurous flames" (Rev. 21.8), rather than basking in the glory of "myghty God … in his hevenes hye" (508).

Cecilia's joust with Almachius over useless images and idle threats (his stone idols have no power to harm faithful Christians) reflects the upset and turmoil of an apocalyptic age. Even Cecilia, steadfast and pure, a tireless worker, is beset with trials and confrontations while on earth, just as historically the Church she represents is plagued by persecution. "Transition" is one stage in the apocalyptic process, that time when the old order "narrows to its apex" as it nears the end and the new "broadens toward its base" as it thrives and grows. In this process "the old and new interpenetrate … [and] where apex and base come together you have an age of very rapid transition."[36] This particular saint's life is set in just such a time, when Christians are establishing their presence and broadening their base of influence and when pagans have lost so much ground that a woman can laugh in open court at the prefect's commands. The voice of the prophet announces in Revelations that once God begins to dwell among men, the "old order" will have "passed away," and the new order will come to pass: "Behold! I am making all things new!" (21:4–5). Chaucer thus emphasizes both the particular historical moment when events are stirring as well as the general movement towards an apocalyptic end when those found wanting are to be "leyd ful lowe" (441).

This time of transition and struggle between Rome's institutionalized (but weakening) authority and the Church's unorganized (yet strengthening) power base is particularly evident in the text in the interplay of secrecy and openness on the part of the Christians and the Romans.[37] Urban must hide in the suburbs and Cecilia must come at night with priests to baptize Maximus and his people; more strikingly still, she is compelled to bury the three martyrs' bodies "softely" (408), under a stone. "Softely" can mean "gently" or "tenderly," but also can mean "quietly,"[38] this latter definition especially appropriate considering Urban's handling of Cecilia's body after her death, burying it "by nyghte" (548). Such secrecy is associated with night and underground activities outside the city, yet the Christians (and the poem itself) move steadily towards a new openness and light, above ground and in the center of Rome, suggesting the angel's biblical promise that "[t]here shall be no more delay; but when the time comes for the seventh angel to sound his trumpet, the hidden purpose of God will have been fulfilled" (Rev. 10:6–7).

The description of the burials of Valerian, Tiburce and Maximus is noteworthy in that it also contrasts the secrecy with which the Christians must act with the openness of the Romans:

> Cecile hym took and buryed hyn anon
> By Tiburce and Valerian softely
> Withinne hire buriyng place, under the stoon;
> And after this, Almachius hastily
> Bad his ministres fecchen openly
> Cecile, so that she myghte in his presence
> Doon sacrifice and Juppiter encense.
>   (407–13)

The visibility or "presence" of the Romans is realized in their physical numbers and their occupation of seats of authority that allow Almachius to summon Cecilia to court "openly" and arrogantly, but this power does not extend beyond checkerboard moves of pawns into the "presence," or vicinity of the prefect's manifest power. Almachius senses that any real authority he once had to control his subject's beliefs, to require sacrifice to the Roman gods, is badly eroded, tellingly indicated by his "hastily" issued command. Maximus' defection from pagan ranks, his conversion "of many a wight" (404), and subsequent martyrdom have alerted Almachius to the growing "presence" of the Christians, their power and influence felt on his own doorstep. Time becomes an important factor in squelching this increasingly visible and threatening sect.

But, to put it tritely, time has run out for Almachius. His arrogant openness in summoning Cecilia backfires when she uses the occasion for a public attack on his authority and beliefs, in daylight and in Rome itself. Paul Beichner's excellent analysis of the trial scene points out Cecilia's contentiousness and Almachius' stupidity which do, I think, focus attention on this confrontation rather than on Cecilia's martyrdom that is highlighted in most other versions of her life.[39] But the debate is inconclusive, in the sense that by the end of their exchange neither Almachius' or Cecilia's stance has altered; the prefect remains unconvinced and unconverted, while Cecilia persists in her determination and devotion to God. Hence, the historical moment contrasts starkly with the implications of the apocalyptic moment in this scene, highlighting once again the apocalyptic narrative form of the text.

However, since the debate was intended "to produce not a convert but a martyr,"[40] Cecilia's bold words of challenge that end the discussion focus attention on the changing nature of power and authority as the old order reaches its term and is "interpenetrated" by the new order's insistent challenges. The *Second Nun's Tale* captures this period of apocalyptic transition; although Almachius does "win" the debate by silencing Cecilia's voice, her faith triumphs both in the church of St. Cecilia and in the family of converts who "into this day" (552) serve Christ and not a Roman ruler.

Cecilia is thus literally and figuratively the guiding light through this time of trial, boldly and confidently marching to a martyr's death once she has fulfilled her duty of broadening the base of Christ's soldiers through the family of converts she produces from her chaste marriage. V. A. Kolve and others have treated Cecilia's procreative chastity very thoroughly elsewhere,[41] but I would like briefly to consider the function of the "fruyt" (193) of her seed of chastity in apocalyptic terms. The term "renovation" characterizes the hope that out of the terrors and upheaval of moments of crisis some sort of renewal might emerge.[42] At several points in Church history, writers, philosophers, and thinkers expressed the urgent need for *renovatio* to reform or rebuild the Church.[43] Never was the necessity for growth more crucial than in the early years when the small Christian sect faced much work ahead before ascending as a body to heaven, indicating that earthly time is not yet over.

The chain of conversions springing from Cecilia's wedding night increases almost exponentially, her preaching and the example of the two brothers bravely marching to death so moving Maximus and each of his relatives that they throw off their pagan beliefs and are baptized. Maximus "with his word converts many a wight" (404) before being beaten to death. Almachius' ministers are "converted at hir [Cecilia's] wise loore" (414), martyrdom paradoxically serving to thin the ranks of the pagans surrounding the prefect rather than ridding Rome of Christians. Cecilia plans to continue her work of renewal even after death by dedicating her house "perpetuelly" (546) as a church, implying that until the final apocalypse, the faithful will proliferate, such renovation serving to ease the suffering of those "doomed to live" until this final moment arrives. Hence the tale manages to manipulate time, both *kairos* and *chronos*, by showing on the one hand how Christians must be prepared to respond quickly and boldly to God's ultimatum in the moment of supreme crisis (Judgment Day), and on the other hand how they must fill the waiting time with "leveful bisynesse" and charity.

One further aspect of "Judgment Day" thinking bears notice—the prophecy that as man's final reckoning approaches signs and wonders will increase. The nature of these portents in the *Second Nun's Tale* differs significantly from those described by John in Revelations, who warns humans to prepare for "hail and fire mingled with blood" (8:7), plagues of locusts, "a great red dragon" (12.3:6), and violent thunder and lightening. Rather, Cecilia's matter-of-factly announces that "I have an angel which that loveth me" (152), perhaps symbolic of the many angelic prophets in Revelations who relay God's warnings to the world. Cecilia's ready acceptance of this remarkable visitor occasions little surprise since her devotion to God is previously outlined in the tale. However, Valerian's calm reception of the news, merely requesting visual proof, reinforces the movement in the text from "normal" discourse to the apocalyptic imaginings that begin to accumulate as the tale progresses. The startling appearance of an old man in white holding a book occasions a quick recovery. The comfortable tone of "Valerian gooth hoom and fynt Cecilie / Withinne his chambre" (218–19) is disrupted by the next half line that points out that the two are not alone—an angel stands beside her. At the angel's "word" (242) Tiburce suddenly and conveniently appears on the scene; no one voices wonder that Tiburce only smells the flowers, but cannot see them. Maximus watches the brothers' souls "glyde" to heaven escorted by angels (412), but instead of pausing to marvel at the sight immediately begins to preach the new faith he has learned.

Of course, these wonders as well as the many miracles "Jhesus for hem wroghte" (359) are considered signs of spiritual sight awarded to those who accept the Christian faith or are visual symbols of God's grace at work, but they also highlight the apocalyptic tone of the tale. Since past and future are conflated in present moments of conversion, these promised visualizations of God's activity in the world form an integral part of such moments, occasioning little comment or amazement from the converts. John's dire warnings concerning the signals Christians must expect prior to the final coming of Christ arm the faithful with the knowledge to recognize the approaching day of judgment and to stand prepared.

According to James Dean the *Second Nun's Tale* posits an "incredible" view of reality, commenting as others have done on the "intellectual challenge" it presents.[44] Reames misses the exploration of doctrine and human motivation in a text where conversion is presented as the immediate and complete acceptance of God's teaching.[45] These concerns seem to bear out the claim that apocalyptic narratives are "always *not* doing things which we unreasonably assume [they] ought to do: connect, diversify, explain, make concords, facilitate extrapolations."[46] But by categorizing the tale as a purely intellectual view of reality, a saint's life wholly concerned with ideal notions of human thought and action, such critics fail to account for the representations of human emotions that surface periodically. Pearsall flatly states there is "little or no human feeling in the Second Nun's Tale, and no sense of pain or fear."[47] Yet Pope Urban, Maximus, and Almachius' ministers weep, Tiburce expresses great fear of being burned with Urban, Cecilia welcomes Tiburce into the fold with a kiss, and at the end she lives in torment for three days before dying.

While I would grant that clear-eyed stoicism informs most of the text, this stern outlook is tempered by moments of real human love and affection. These instances function as counterweights to the agonizing personal moments in the text; rather than impeding the apocalyptic narrative structure, their example of simple human affection offers an earthly approximation of the "heighe place" (68) full of "cleernesse and of light" (403) where the faithful are rewarded with God's eternal love.

For example, in the Prologue, just as the main themes of busyness and idleness, light and dark, chastity and increase are prefigured, so the concept of charity is introduced. Heaven is described as "eek brennynge" (114), but Cecilia as "hevene" (96) is "brennynge evere in charity ful brighte" (118). Since her name has just been so emphatically associated with work and busyness, the definition of charity as "good deed, act of charity" seems appropriate, but the word is also defined as the "Christian virtue of love" or "fondness, affection."[48] This more personal aspect of the tale emerges several times, most notably when Cecilia addresses Valerian on their wedding night as "sweete and wel biloved spouse deere" (144), or when she kisses Tiburce's breast and declares him her kinsman, symbolically enfolding him in both an earthly and heavenly family.

Valerian, Urban, and Maximus also display moments of touching emotion. When granted a boon by the angel, Valerian's first thought is for his brother: "'I have a brother,' quod Valerian tho, / 'That in this world I love no man so'" (235–6). Urban responds with tears of joy at Valerian's conversion ("The teeris from his eyen leet he falle" [190]) and "with glad herte and light" (351) at Tiburce's. Maximus is moved to tears at the plight of the brothers condemned to death, but he weeps "for pitee" (371) rather than for joy. This moment of grief not only reflects Maximus' as yet imperfect grasp of Cecilia's teaching, but also introduces a poignancy that is repeated when he "with pitous teeris" (401) tells others of the brothers' beheading. Maximus is still of this earth, but after seeing their souls glide to heaven, begins to convert many people with his newly-acquired vision.

Through the interjection of relatively brief moments of pathos, love, and joy into an otherwise intellectual account of an ideal saint, the *Second Nun's Tale* not only more effectively highlights Cecilia's perfection, but also reminds readers that while "feithful bisynesse" (24) directed towards the transcendental goal of union with God is required while here on earth, this holy work also includes "charitie" towards fellow strugglers. Love and affection, pity and tears, are uniquely human emotions that temper the despair of those "doomed to live" until God's final summons. But by alluding to these emotions almost in passing, the tale succeeds in focusing attention on those moments when spiritual insight counters human emotions, lighting the way to God's message of salvation and bliss.

Chaucer, then, fixes time in the *Canterbury Tales* by choosing this particular saint's life for the "beginning of the end" of his project. As Howard claims, all previous discussions of moral, secular, or religious values are called into question by the Second Nun, who issues an implicit warning in her Prologue to those who would waste time in "ydelnesse" (7).[49] Previous tales are suddenly cast as vain speculations on earthly life, marriage, morality, and literature, opening the way for the "feend" (13) to "so lightly cache" (11) unwary pilgrims in his trap. The game of tale-telling is drawing to a close and the tales that follow the Second Nun's even more insistently question the value of such speculations, particularly the role of the poet engaged in "muchel speche" which "synne wanteth naught" (MancT 338). Speech is kept to a minimum in the *Second Nun's Tale*, much to the consternation of those critics who chafe at the lack of development in the story. The only sin to receive much attention is sloth; Chaucer reserves the exploration of "muchel spekyng" (MancT 335) to the Manciple and the sermon on sin and repentance to the Parson. If the *Manciple's Tale* graphically demonstrates the follies to which false speaking can lead, the *Second Nun's Tale* graphically demonstrates the proper end of speech, to affirm one's faith in God's truth.

In his discussion of Fragment VIII as Chaucer's attempt to dismantle his Canterbury book, James Dean only goes so far in his analysis of the place of the *Second Nun's Tale* in this dismantling scheme to say that the tale is idealistic and serves "to point directly toward the final story," the *Parson's Tale*.[50] I would suggest that the *Second Nun's Tale*, while ostensibly retelling the life of a Christian saint in a pagan past, points well beyond the Parson's contemporary world of sin and repentance and attempts to characterize that moment when earthly, historical time ends and deliberations about the state of one's soul are replaced by unquestioning faith in cosmic, universal time, that time beyond time; an end beyond the end; an end which is really a beginning without end. The *Second Nun's Tale*, then, stands as more than a prefatory occasion for something better[51] or merely as an exemplum of chaste sainthood, but lifts the *Canterbury Tales* briefly and abruptly beyond the world of pilgrimage and folk longing for spiritual healing on earth to a time when "men dradden nevere for to dye" (15) in answer to God's final call for their souls.

Interestingly, however, Chaucer did not place this tale of perfection and high vision at the very end of the *Canterbury Tales*, preferring to bow out of the tale-telling game with the Parson's lengthy sermon on sin, confession, and repentance. Perhaps this choice reflects Chaucer's practical awareness that while humans must be aware of the approaching apocalypse and ready with a bold "ye" to the inevitable question God will put on Judgment Day, this earthly pilgrimage to the celestial city is far from over and the best "armure of brightnesse" (385) available to such travelers is, finally, the knowledge of human limitations and the hope that through personal effort and God's grace these obstacles may be overcome.

NOTES

1. V. A. Kolve, "Chaucer's *Second Nun's Tale* and the Iconography of Saint Cecilia," in *New Perspectives in Chaucer Criticism*, ed. Donald H. Rose (Norman, Oklahoma, 1981), 139.

2. For an excellent discussion of the movement beginning in the nineteenth century to create a Protestant Chaucer, see Linda Georgianna's "The Protestant Chaucer," in *Chaucer's Religious Tales*, ed. C. D. Benson and Elizabeth Robertson (Rochester, NY, 1990), 55–69. V. A. Kolve asks, "Where are we to find the woman in Cecile?" in "Chaucer's *Second Nun's Tale* and the Iconography of Saint Cecilia," (cited above), 51. The "puzzling" lack of affective piety in the tale is discussed by R. K. Root in *The Poetry of Chaucer* (Gloucester, Mass., 1957), 277–80. Both Thomas R. Lounsbury and David Aers, critics writing in different centuries and for different purposes, discuss the religious improbabilities in the tale; see Thomas R. Lounsbury, *Studies in Chaucer: His Life and Writings*, 3 vols. (New York, 1892; repr. 1962) and David Aers, *Chaucer* (Atlantic Highlands, N.J., 1986).

3. Karen Arthur, "Equivocal Subjectivity in Chaucer's *Second Nun's Prologue* and *Tale*," *Chaucer Review* 32, no. 3 (1998): 217–231.

4. Lynn Staley Johnson, "Chaucer's Tale of the Second Nun and the Strategies of Dissent," *Studies in Philology* 89, no. 3 (Summer, 1992): 314–333.

5. David Raybin, "Chaucer's Creation and Recreation of the *Lyf of Seynt Cecile*," *Chaucer Review* 32, no. 2 (1997): 198.

6. The term "apocalyptic imagination" is introduced and thoroughly discussed in Richard K. Emmerson's and Ronald B. Herzman's book *The Apocalyptic Imagination in Medieval Literature* (Philadelphia, 1992). The authors, in discussing the apocalyptic imagination within "a general pattern of movement in *The Canterbury Tales*" (159), focus on the comic tales as "in some ways Chaucer's most appropriate vehicles for embodying apocalyptic concerns" (162). Their discussion also includes a thorough analysis of the Pardoner as a type of Simon Magus, as well as the Canon as an "Antichrist-like deceiver" (170).

7. Ibid., 1–35.

8. Ibid., 23.

9. Ibid., 149.

10. Frank Kermode, *The Sense of an Ending* (London, 1966).

11. See Larry D. Benson, "The Order of the *Canterbury Tales*," *Studies in the Age of Chaucer* 3 (1981): 77–120, for both a summary of the criticism and an excellent argument for the Ellesmere order.

12. Donald R. Howard. *The Idea of the* Canterbury Tales (Berkeley, 1976), 288–306.

13. James Dean, "Dismantling the Canterbury Book," *PMLA* 100 (1984): 746.

14. Stephen Knight, "Chaucer's Religious Canterbury Tales," in *Medieval English Religious and Ethical Literature: Essays in Honour of G. H. Russell*, ed. Gregory Kratzmann and James Simpson (Cambridge, Engl., 1986), 158.

15. I am indebted to Richard K. Emmerson for suggesting this historical and structural position of the *Second Nun's Tale*, details of which are developed within this essay.

16. Barbara Nolan argues for a focus on transcendent spirituality in the four rhyme-royal tales in "Chaucer's Tales of Transcendence: Rhyme Royal and Christian Prayer in the *Canterbury Tales*," in *Chaucer's Religious Tales*.

17. Geoffrey Chaucer, *The Riverside Chaucer*, ed. Larry D. Benson, et al. (Boston, 1987), VIII.119. All quotations from *The Canterbury Tales* are from this edition and will be indicated by line numbers in parentheses in the text.

18. Emmerson and Herzman, 172. For a full discussion of the Pardoner as a type of the biblical Simon Magus figure, see pp. 170–81.

19. See Bruce Kent Cowgill, "Sweetness and Sweat: The Extraordinary Emanations in Fragment Eight of the *Canterbury Tales*," *Philological Quarterly* 74 (1995): 343–57; Glending Olson, "Chaucer, Dante, and the Structure of Fragment VIII (G) of the *Canterbury Tales*," *Chaucer Review* 16 (1982): 222–23; Joseph E. Grennen, "Saint Cecilia's 'Chemical Wedding': The Unity of the *Canterbury Tales*, Fragment VIII," *Journal of English and Germanic Philology* 65 (1966): 466–481; Bruce A. Rosenberg, "The Contrary Tales of the Second Nun and the Canon's Yeoman," *Chaucer Review* 2 (1968): 278–91.

20. Howard V. Hendrix, *The Ecstasy of Catastrophe: A Study of Apocalyptic Narrative from Langland to Milton* (New York, 1990), 3.

21. Kermode, 46–47.

22. Paul E. Beichner, "Confrontation, Contempt of Court, and Chaucer's Cecilia," *Chaucer Review* 8 (1974): 204.

23. Beichner, 199, where he discusses the elimination of repetitious words and phrases. The sharpened focus in the Tale is discussed by Roger Ellis, "Saint's Tales: The Second Nun's Tale," *Patterns of Religious Narrative in the* Canterbury Tales (London and Sydney, 1986): 95; John C. Hirsh, "The Politics of Spirituality: The Second Nun and the Manciple," *Chaucer Review* 12 (1977): 136; and Sherry L. Reames, "The Cecilia Legend as Chaucer Inherited It and Retold It: The Disappearance of an Augustinian Ideal," *Speculum* 55 (1980): 57.

24. Kermode, 21.

25. Biblical citations are from *The New English Bible*, Oxford Study Edition, Samuel Sandmel, gen. ed. (New York, 1976), and are indicated in parentheses in the text. Traditionally, the old man in white has been identified with St. Paul, but Emmerson suggests that the figure symbolizes the "ancient of days" found in Rev. 5 and 6. The old man's white robes also represent a recurring apocalyptic image in John; see Richard K. Emmerson, "Introduction: The Apocalypse in Medieval Culture," in *The Apocalypse in the Middle Ages*, ed. Richard K. Emmerson and Bernard McGinn (Ithaca and London, 1992), 322.

26. As a further example of the suggestive apocalyptic imagery that runs throughout the tale, the book from which Valerian is urged to read figures prominently as an object in John's Apocalypse; see Emmerson's, "Introduction: The Apocalypse in Medieval Culture," 301 and note.

27. See Bernard McGinn, "John's Apocalypse and the Apocalyptic Mentality," in *The Apocalypse in the Middle Ages*, p. 6 (full citation above). McGinn points out two broad types of the genre apocalypse, both of which include the mediation or agency of an angel or other celestial figure to convey the heavenly message.

28. Reames, "The Cecilia Legend," 45–46.

29. Hendrix, 13.

30. In the last chapter of John's Apocalypse, after the vision of New Jerusalem has been detailed, the reader/listener is told, "These words are trustworthy and true. The Lord God who inspires the prophets has sent his angel to show his servants what must shortly happen. And, remember, I am coming soon!" (Rev. 22:6–7).

31. Sherry Reames argues in her article, "A Recent Discovery concerning the Sources of Chaucer's *Second Nun's Tale*," *Modern Philology* (May 1990): 337–61, that Chaucer compiled the tale from two sources: Jacobus Voragine's *Legenda Aurea* (closely translated from lines 85–344, summarized in lines 345–48), and a manuscript of the Franciscan abridgement (translated closely from line 349 on). However, if Chaucer in fact chose not to translate the *Passio* version of the St. Cecilia legend for this tale, despite the evidence that the *Passio* was readily available and that the tale seems still to reflect certain of its elements, his decision to use the shorter versions supports my theory that he preferred an already "apocalyptic" narrative form to include at the end of the *Canterbury Tales*. Please note that I am not arguing achronistically that Chaucer knew the term or deliberately searched for this particular narrative form; I believe he may have been attracted to its theme and style (and perhaps brevity, since it is an early work of translation) as appropriate for the beginning of the end.

32. Derek Pearsall, *The Canterbury Tales* (London, 1985), 283.

33. Cited in Kermode, p. 31, and found in *John Milton, Complete Poems and Major Prose*, ed. Merrit Y. Hughes (Indianapolis, 1957), 466–467.

34. Grennen, 471.

35. John's words in Revelations are addressed specifically to the seven churches existing in Asia during John's time (Rev. 1:11, 22:16), indicating the responsibility of the institution both to heed and proclaim these revelations of the end. For a fuller discussion of "the apocalypse as an ecclesiological text," see Emmerson, "Introduction to the Apocalypse in Medieval Culture," 392–95.

36. Kermode, *The Sense of an Ending*, 100. It is beyond the scope of this article to explore the influence of Joachim of Fiore on medieval conceptions of the apocalypse, but as Kermode and others point out, "Joachim formalized the idea of transition," followed by renovation. See Frank Kermode, "Waiting for the End," in *Apocalypse Theory and the Ends of the World*, ed. Malcolm Bull (Oxford, 1995), 255 et. passim. For comprehensive studies, see Bernard McGinn, *The Calabrian Abbot: Joachim of Fiore in the History of Western Thought* (New York, 1985) and Marjorie Reeves, *The Influence of Prophecy in the Later Middle Ages: A Study in Joachimism* (Oxford, 1969), as well as "The Apocalypse and Joachim of Fiore" in Emmerson's and Herzman's *The Apocalyptic Imagination in Medieval Literature*.

37. In *The Apocalypse in the Middle Ages*, 10–11, Bernard McGinn discusses the problem early Christians faced by the delay of the return of the risen Christ, a delay traditionally interpreted as *the* central event in the growth of the Church.

38. *Riverside Chaucer*, ed. Larry Benson (Boston, 1988), 1291.

39. Beichner, 349.

40. Ellis, 89.

41. Kolve, 137–74.

42. Kermode, *Sense of an Ending*, 98.

43. See Emmerson and Herzman, *The Apocalyptic Imagination in Medieval Literature*, who trace *renovatio* as one of the "keys" to the apocalyptic imagination through Joachim of Fiore, Bonaventure, and others.

44. Dean, 749.

45. Reames, "The Cecilia Legend," 55.

46. Kermode, 21.

47. Pearsall, 255.

48. *Riverside Chaucer*, 1228.

49. Howard, 176–77.

50. Dean, 747 *passim*.

51. Both Grennen, 466–81, and Rosenberg, 278–91, propose this view of the *Tale*.

BARRIE RUTH STRAUS

Reframing the Violence of the Father: Reverse Oedipal Fantasies in Chaucer's Clerk's, Man of Law's, and Prioress's Tales

Modern readers of medieval saints' lives are often surprised by the amount of physical violence those stories contain. My focus in this essay[1] is not on the physical but on the psychic violence inherent in the symbolic structure of the family, the unit on which Western culture claims to be based.[2] Freud articulates the notion of the family romance—idealization of the father and of a "happy" family unit—created for the good of all as a reaction to, and defense against, the violent actuality that *necessarily* constitutes the family. Inherent in the child's experience of the family are such sexual and generational conflicts as the child's incestuous feelings *for* Oedipal parents, as well as hostility *from* and disappointment *in* them. Freud explains how the child attempts to alleviate these feelings by means of a fantasy formation that represses the mutual hostility through self-aggrandizing idealizations of an Oedipal parent, especially the father—whose paternity Freud reminds us is always uncertain.[3] According to psychoanalytic theory, cross-generational relations are necessarily conflictual, for the notion of fatherhood implies not only the extension of the father's lineage but also the necessity of the father's death and replacement by the child—a situation that arouses murderous paternal rage against the child as replacement, and an equal rage against the necessity of the mother, without whose ability to give birth that replacement

From *Domestic Violence in Medieval Texts*: pp. 122–138. © 2002 by Eve Salisbury, Georgiana Donavin, and Merrall Llewely Price.

cannot take place.[4] Motherhood from this point of view entails the violence of sacrifice in the name of the father of all other aspects of womanhood.

The concept of the family romance, then, provides us with a structure of defense against psychic realities whose violence seems too difficult for us to face directly in our lives. From the way the violence of the structure of the family is presented in three of Chaucer's saints' lives, the Clerk's, Man of Law's, and Prioress's Prologues and Tales, these truths seem too difficult to face directly in some literature as well. In each tale the transmission of culture from one generation to another is problematic in a way that can be understood behaviorally and symbolically in terms of the violence of the father, and psychodynamically in terms of the father's reverse Oedipal fantasies. I am especially concerned to articulate the way the tales' presentation of the violence of the family re-creates the structure of the fantasy formation of the family romance. In each tale the violence of the father is revealed during the unfolding of the plot, only to be denied, repressed, and concealed. The process is effected by structural and narrative devices that present the father's desires as fictions, by "happy endings" in which families are reunited without harm, and by a series of fictional frames that defend the characters in the drama and its readers/listeners from having to confront the violence of the family.

The pattern is clearly outlined in the Clerk's Prologue and Tale. The prologue frames the violence of the family that Walter enacts in the tale with the violent masculine rivalry between the Host and the Clerk. The Host's opening attack on the Clerk's manhood—"Ye ryde as coy and stille as dooth a mayde / Were newe spoused, sittynge at the bord" (IV.2–3)— announces an anxiety about masculinity inherent in the violence of the father.[5] The Host strives for recognition as "more of a man" (a plea for greater recognition from the symbolic father, the idealized father identified with the phallus)[6] by asserting that the Clerk is not just a lesser man but a castrated man, that is, a woman.

Rhetorically, then, the tale that follows can be seen as the Clerk's witty, multileveled exploration of what it is to be a man. The Host enacts his model of manhood, the denigrating bully. He follows his opening aspersions with taunts about the scholar's (maidenly) silence and his studies: "This day ne herde I of youre tonge a word. / I trowe ye studie aboute som sophyme" (IV.4–5). He asserts his control over the Clerk's attitude and his story by commanding the Clerk to change to a more pleasant mood—"beth of bettre cheere" (IV.7)—and by insisting twice that the Clerk tell a "myrie tale" (IV.9, 15). When he chides that the Clerk must necessarily submit to him since the Clerk has already entered into his "pley," saying, "For what man that is entred in a pley, / He nedes moot unto the pley assente" (IV.10–11), the Host turns the Clerk's act of assent into a sexual and denigrating act of submission. The Clerk's response to being placed in the submissive position traditionally ascribed to woman, on the other hand, enacts the scholar's different model of manhood, one that only ostensibly assumes that submissive position.[7]

In the prologue, the Clerk deflects the Host's attempts to control both the kind of tale the Clerk should tell—"Telle us som myrie tale, by youre fey! ... / But precheth nat, as freres doon in Lente, / To make us for oure olde synnes wepe, / Ne that thy tale make us nat to slepe. / Telle us som murie thyng of aventures" (IV.9–15)—and the way he should tell it: "Youre termes, youre colours, and youre figures, / Keepe hem in stoor til so be ye endite / Heigh style, as whan that men to kynges write. / Speketh so pleyn at this tyme, we yow preye / That we may understonde what ye seye" (IV.16–20). Even as the Clerk "graciously" agrees to obey the Host, however, the Clerk adds the caveat "as fer as resoun axeth" [as far as reason demands] (IV.25). Adhering to a spirit of play different from what the Host might understand, the Clerk's caveat immediately undoes the obedience he has averred, by opening up a space for disobeying any demands that could be considered unreasonable. At the same time, the Clerk violates the Host's command to "speak plainly" without the rhetorical terms of a high style.[8]

As the Clerk continues, he also violates the Host's command to tell some "myrie tale." Tracing the lineage of the story of domestic violence he is about to tell—to the poet Petrarch, who wrote in the high style in another time and language and place, and who is dead—the Clerk dwells on the brevity of life and the inevitability of death: "But Deeth, that wol nat suffre us dwellen heer, / But as it were a twynklyng of an ye, / Hem bothe hath slayn, and alle shul we dye" (IV.36–38). The double imperative of death that is part of the violence of the family—the recognition that since men must die, they must replace themselves by heirs to continue their lineage—is both asserted and denied when the Clerk refers to it in terms of the transmission of fictions, a history of writing that the Host specifically told him not to tell. Moreover, the Clerk's excessive zeal in declaring Petrarch, the father of his story, "nayled in his cheste" (IV.29), and then in simultaneously proclaiming Petrarch's proheme irrelevant while covertly inserting its crucial details into his own prologue, enacts the violence of parricide against the text and the Host.[9]

The prologue then marks as "literary" that is, as fictional, highfaluting, irrelevant, and irreverent, the relationship between, on the one hand, cross-generational transmission and translation of fictions and, on the other, the fictions of lineage that mark cross-generational transmission of culture and the violence of the family. In these ways the prologue establishes a concern with the violence of the father—with issues about masculinity, sexuality, domination and submission, death, and transmission of culture. Yet at the same time it allows and encourages members of its audience (s)—both the characters in the drama and its listeners/readers—to distance themselves from that violence by attributing it to the dynamics of a fiction told in the context of sexual and class rivalry between two men, and of stories of the transmission of literature.

The Clerk's Tale, however, by extending this discourse through time and space, establishes it as more widespread and enduring than the mere rivalry of two middle-class English men. The tale quickly relates the transmission of fictions with human lineage through its setting, characterization; and plot. The landscape contains fertile plains with towers and towns still standing though built "in tyme of fadres olde" (IV.61). The Clerk emphasizes Walter's lordship and lineage, describing him as "lord ... of that lond, / As were his worthy eldres hym bifore" (IV.64–65) and, "to speke as of lynage, / The gentilleste yborn of Lumbardye" (IV.71–72). Walter's subjects enjoin their reluctant lord to give up his freedom and marry, because the spectre of death is a constant "deeth manaceth every age, and smyt / In ech estaat, for ther escapeth noon; / And al so certein as we knowe echoon / That we shul deye, as uncerteyn we alle / Been of that day whan deeth shal on us falle" (IV.122–26)—and necessitates ensuring heirs: "Delivere us out of al this bisy drede, / And taak a wyf for hye Goddes sake! / For if it so bifelle, as God forbede, / That thurgh youre deeth youre lyne sholde slake, / And that a straunge successour sholde take / Youre heritage, O wo were us alyve!" (IV.134–39). Walter accedes to his subjects' plea; he agrees to marry, to give up his freedom of his own free will, in order to protect his lineage—but with a condition: that *he* and not his subjects will choose his wife. Walter acknowledges that his paternity, and the way his lineage will turn out, is not in his control: "For God it woot, that children ofte been / Unlyk hir worthy eldres hem bifore" (IV.155–56). For this reason, he states, he will trust in God's bounty. In other words, in agreeing to take on the role of paterfamilias by establishing a social family, Walter acknowledges something that patriarchal culture often keeps confused and suppressed: that the actual father is not the symbolic father. By acknowledging that he is not the symbolic father (named God in this case), he submits to the symbolic father. This acknowledgment that the phallus is in place allows Walter to act as paterfamilias as if he really *were* the symbolic father.

Walter's assertion of control, in stipulating that he must choose his wife, is an assertion of and reaction to his acknowledgment of his lack of control over his paternity, lineage, and death. As Walter sets up his marriage, the narrative allows us to see the violence of the father on which patriarchal marriage is based.[10] This violence entails a double mythology inscribed and perpetuated by the structure of the family. The first myth, as Walter's proviso points up, is that an actual father can indeed operate in the place of the symbolic father, the position of the phallus in a world of discourse that is phallocentric. The second myth is that the family reflects a coincidence of the interests of the father and those of "his" wife and children and other family members: that is, that the best interests of a woman or of children are served in a family under the governance of a man/father/phallus. This mythology establishes ideologically the positionality of the father qua symbolic father, qua phallus, by providing a subjugated/subordinate "other" that confirms his positionality, at the expense and repression of any noncongruent needs the woman and children might have. The Clerk's description of Walter's marital arrangement exposes the defensive function of these mythologies, showing how patriarchal marriage is based on the necessary generational conflicts seen in the suppression of the woman who functions as peaceweaver and childbearer, an object of exchange between men.

The Clerk's description of Walter's interest in Griselda focuses on her exemplary femininity or "wommanhede" (IV.239), which according to the Clerk consists in being pretty enough to look at—"fair ynogh to sighte" (IV.209)—and beautiful in virtue and most especially a dutiful daughter who, we are repeatedly told, nourishes and sustains her aged father. The Clerk asserts that Walter's attraction to Griselda is not based on sexual desire: "He noght with wantown lookyng of folye / His eyen caste on hire," (IV.236–37). And young, virginal Griselda is without sexual desire as well: "no likerous lust was thurgh hire herte yronne" (IV.214). But the Clerk's expression of the lack of desire through negative propositions evokes the very possibility that the desire he denies is part of Walter's attraction. Someone is desiring something, if the absence of desire is important enough to claim. Walter's requests to Griselda's father, Janicula, for her hand and to Griselda to become his wife point to marriage as an arrangement based on a desire for power. They also suggest the limits of the social father's power, attributable to the fact that the actual father is not the symbolic father, and that all social fathers are not equal in their ability to act in the place of the symbolic father. Walter, the lord of the land, reminds Janicula of the latter's inherited subordinate status as his liege man with the words "Thou lovest me, I woot it wel certeyn, / And art my feithful lige man ybore" (IV.309–10) as he asks him to agree that what is in Walter's best interest is also in his own: "And al that liketh me, I dar wel seyn / It liketh thee" (IV.311–12). Janicula's powerlessness to do other than acquiesce is highlighted by his reaction to Walter's assertions—"This sodeyn cas this man astonyed so / That reed he wax; abayst and al quakynge / He stood; unnethes seyde he wordes mo" (IV.316–18)—which adds to the Clerk's Tale an emotionality beyond that of its fourteenth-century analogues.[11]

Similarly, when Walter asks Griselda to assent to or dissent from an agreement already made between two men to whom she is subordinate, her father and his liege lord, saying, "It liketh to youre fader and to me / That I yow wedde," (IV.345–46), he expects her to concur: "and eek it may so stonde, / As I suppose, ye wol that it so be" (IV.346–47). Marriage as an agreement between men is further underscored in Walter's ability to return Griselda to her father's house under the pretense of his desire to exchange her for a younger wife. This second "exchange" of Griselda also emphasizes the social father's unequal access to the symbolic father: Janicula is powerless to do other than accept his lord's decision. The Clerk describes Janicula as even more upset at having to take Griselda back than he was to allow Walter to marry her. His earlier unstated fear and embarrassment are replaced in the second exchange by cursing and public tears (IV.901–3). The Clerk explains Janicula's intensified rage at having Griselda returned as attributable to Janicula's suspicions about Walter's character, his defects as a man and ruler that Janicula is politically powerless to do anything about. Janicula, we are told, always suspected that when Walter had done what he wanted, he would be disparaged by being bound to Griselda's lowly origins and get rid of her as soon as he could: "whan the lord fulfild hadde his corage, / Hym woude thynke it were a disparage / To his estaat so lowe for t'alighte, / And voyden hire as soone as ever he myghte" (IV.907–10). But by this explanation the Clerk deflects attention away from further sources of powerlessness and rage for Janicula, the masculine rivalry inherent in the violence of the father.

In obtaining Janicula's reluctant agreement, first to hand over and then to take back his daughter, Walter confirms his own position as father at the expense of Janicula. As he does so he points to the fact that the actual father is not the symbolic father, and so is powerless to protect his daughter; he marks Janicula as a lesser "man," owing to Walter's greater proximity to the symbolic father; and he places him in a position even below that of a lesser man, the position of castrated man, that is, the position of woman in which the Host had placed the Clerk. In addition, Janicula's rage marks the inherent generational conflict involved in the reluctance of any father to hand over his daughter and so acknowledge the younger man who must replace him as object of the daughter's desire, a necessary means for continuing his lineage after death.

Walter's request to Griselda to assent to a marriage agreement that (he says) pleases her father and him includes a reminder to Griselda of the prerogatives of the patriarchal husband at the woman's expense. The position of husband gives him complete freedom to make his wife conform to his desires, whether to her happiness or harm, while her position disallows any sign of complaint or disagreement: "I seye this: be ye redy with good herte

/ To al my lust, and that I frely may, / As me best thynketh, do yow laughe or smerte, / And nevere ye to grucche it, nyght ne day? / And eek whan I sey 'ye,' ne say nat 'nay,' / Neither by word ne frownyng contenance?" (IV.351–56). Like her father, in an emotional state of amazement, dazed and "quakynge for drede" (IV.358), Griselda too acquiesces to what she is powerless to control, acknowledging that Walter's wishes will be her wishes: "But as ye wole youreself, right so wol I" (IV.361). However, she indicates that the coincidence of her interests with those of Walter can exist only at the expense of her extinction when she adds—in an intensification not found in other versions of the story—that she will not "willyngly" disobey him, on pain of death, although she does not wish to die: "And heere I swere that nevere willyngly, / In werk ne thougt, I nyl yow disobeye, / For to be deed, though me were looth to deye" (IV.362–64).[12] The marriage Walter proposes makes the death of any separate desire or will of a woman from that of her husband a condition for becoming a wife, a condition Griselda has already fulfilled by her subordination of her needs to those of her father, the virtuous basis for her selection as Walter's wife. In Walter's proposal, it is important to note, the woman never wills of her own; she is therefore "nevere willyngly." She is the negation of her will, and hence of herself. The negative predicate "kills" her in advance of the physical death she does not wish.

Once Walter becomes an actual father through the birth of a daughter—whose significance, as the Clerk relates, marking the gender hierarchy of patriarchal culture, is to establish that Griselda is fertile and thus potentially able to deliver a preferable male heir—Walter enacts the violence of the family laid out in his marriage agreement. In so doing, he reveals that the nature of social fatherhood consists in the prerogative of the father to use and abuse women and children, treating both as his property, with which he can do anything he likes. The Clerk does all that he can to distance himself and his audiences from Walter's behavior when Walter tests Griselda four times. The Clerk insists that the first test, taking away their daughter, is excessive, needlessly frightening, and, though praised by some (men) as clever, entirely inappropriate:

> Nedelees, God woot, he thoghte hire for t'affraye.
> He hadde assayed hire ynogh bifore,
> And foond hire evere good; what neded it
> Hire for to tempte, and alwey moore and moore,
> Though sour men preise it for a subtil wit?
> But as for me, I seye that yvele it sit
> To assaye a wyf whan that it is no nede,
> And putten hire in angwyssh and in drede.
> (IV.455–62)

The unmarried Clerk further separates himself from Walter's second test, the private removal of their son, by classifying it as standard marital behavior, the way husbands act: "O nedelees was she tempted in assay! / But wedded men ne knowe no mesure, / Whan that they fynde a pacient creature" (IV.621–23), and, seemingly taking the wives' position, appealing to women to judge Walter's behavior as excessive, cruel, and unwarranted testing of wives' constancy: "But now of wommen wolde I axen fayn / If thise assayes myghte nat suffise? / What koude a sturdy housbonde moore devyse / To preeve hir wyfhod and hir stedefastnesse, / And he continuynge evere in sturdinesse?" (IV.696–700). At the same time, he distances Walter's behavior from that of other married men, and that of his audiences, by labeling it an example of compulsive pathology: "But ther been folk of swich condicion / That whan they have a certein purpos take, / They kan nat stynte of hire entencion, / But, right as they were bounden to that stake, / They wol nat of that firste purpos slake. / Right so this markys fulliche hath purposed / To tempte his wyf as he was first disposed" (IV.701–7). In short, Walter is described as an example of a man out of control, driven by aberrant impulses to compulsive behavior that is unnecessary, cruel, and destructive of his family, his reputation, his subjects, and so himself.

Rather than being abnormal behavior, however, Walter's tests reveal the inherent violence of the structure of the family in patriarchal culture. Walter's first two tests consist in removing both children from their mother and allowing her to think that they will be killed, while the last two tests consist in making his wife think that she will be exchanged for a younger woman of higher lineage, who she is unaware is actually her daughter. The removal of children presumed slain reveals the right of the patriarchal father—acting in the place of the symbolic father—by virtue of his ability to create life, to take that life away. The tests, that is, reveal the right of the father to commit infanticide, the desire for which is inherent in the birth of any child, since knowledge of the father's death is implicit in that birth.

Walter's infanticidal desires made public are doubly condemned within the narrative. When word of the "murders" gets out and Walter is defamed, his subjects' love for him changes. And the Clerk, who condemns the people's lack of constancy elsewhere, justifies this instance of change on the grounds of the heinous nature, not of infanticide, but of murder: "Ther cam no word, but that they mordred were. / For which, where as his peple therbifore / Hadde loved hym wel, the sclaundre of his diffame / Made hem that they hym hatede therfore. / To been a mordrere is an hateful name" (IV.728–32). Thus the desires are revealed and concealed by being presented as "pretense" rather than actual deed, and by being condemned not under the name of the violence of the family but as a different, less fraught, albeit heinous act.

The desire of the father to marry his daughter repeats and makes blatant the desire of the father to commit incest, the taboo the family is structured to defend against, implicit in Janicula's rage against his daughter's marriage. But even when the desire to commit incest is made explicit, it is revealed only to be concealed by being presented as Walter's fiction.

The desire of the father to exchange his wife for their daughter is also the final revelation of the motif of the father's murderous rage against the necessity of the mother's powers of procreation to produce his lineage, a rage that has repeatedly surfaced through the tale. This rage at dependence on the mother to perpetuate the father's line is expressed in each test through Walter's repeated excuse to his wife that his deeds must be committed because of his subjects' disparagement of the mother's lineage. It surfaces again through Janicula's fears of Walter's repudiation of Griselda's lineage, and is made explicit when Walter brings his children back and commands his brother-in-law to tell no one their real parentage: "That he to no wight, though men wolde enquere, / Sholde nat telle whos children that they were" (IV.769–70). Through his pretense of doing away with his children, then, Walter also obliterates their actual origins, and especially the acknowledgment of his reliance for their birth on his wife. The need for Griselda to create and give birth to these children is also curiously revealed and concealed in Griselda's focus on the physicality of becoming a wife and mother during her plea to Walter before returning to her father's house, a plea that is expanded in the Clerk's version of the tale, making Griselda more assertive than in other versions.[13] Giving back all the clothes and jewels Walter has given her, she requests in return only a modest dress like the one she originally wore: "swich a smok as I was wont to were" (IV.886). During the fifty lines of her request, Griselda refers to her virginity or "maydenhede" three times, insisting that a smock to cover her on her return to her father is a peculiarly fitting recompense for the virginity she brought to the marriage. Describing that virginity in pointedly physical terms as the gift she brought to the marriage but cannot take away from it—"Which that I broghte, and noght agayn I bere" (IV.884)—she points to the ruptured hymen, the irrecoverable physical mark of becoming a wife. Similarly, she directs attention to her physical procreative function as she asks Walter's help to prevent his subjects from being able to see the very womb "in which [his] children leye" (IV.877). In doing so, she simultaneously forces Walter to acknowledge the bodily function he requires of her and agrees to keep that necessity hidden. Through his pretense of destroying the children and their origins, Walter in effect destroys and brings his children back to life, symbolically enacting the prerogative of the father to do as he will with his children, and eliminating the need for his wife's assistance through giving birth.

The Clerk's Tale thus presents an experience of the dangerous actual violence of the fantasy structure of the family. At the same time, however, the violence is denied by attributing the experience to the unnecessary long-suffering of a wife at the hands of her aberrantly abusive husband. The reality of the suffering that the violence of the family entails is removed by being framed as the "unreal"/fictional tests of a lord, husband, and father who only pretends to sacrifice the interests of his family to his own desires. Throughout the tale, the Clerk reveals that Walter is only allowing others to *think* that he has denied his wife and committed incest and infanticide. He "really" never does those things. The tale's "happy ending" further denies the father's desires to extinguish/replace his wife and commit infanticide and incest, as it shows Walter ritualistically undoing his initial violence: he acknowledges Griselda as his one and only wife and restores the children, whom he acknowledges as both his and hers. Moreover, he asserts to his subjects that he did not act out of malice or cruelty, that he never intended to kill his children (infanticide here is most specifically named, only to be denied), but merely to test his wife's "wommanheede" in the best interests of all. And when Griselda responds by (repeatedly) fainting, Walter attempts to soothe and nurture her, bringing back to life what he formerly extinguished. Thus Walter becomes the *progenitor* of the mother, reframing his dependence upon her reproductivity as prior dependence on his own life-giving maleness.

As Walter restores their children to Griselda, his acknowledgment that she "bare" their son "in thy body trewely" (IV.1068) equates "womman-heede" with maternity: his acknowledgment, then, rebegets Griselda as a mother, as if to be a woman without being a mother is to be dead. Walter's tests not only denied Griselda's maternity—denied the fact that a woman's maternity is always certain, while a father's paternity is not—they also raised questions about her maternality. Griselda's seeming lack of emotion when her children are taken away triggers in the audience primal anxieties about a mother being cold, unloving, and unable to protect her children. Though the Clerk condemns Walter's tests and has only sympathy and praise for Griselda's humility and constancy, his account of her behavior intensifies anxieties about Griselda's maternality. When her daughter is taken away, the Clerk describes Griselda's impassivity and comments: "I trowe that to a norice in this cas / It had been hard this reuthe for to se; / Wel myghte a mooder thanne han cryd 'allas!'" (IV.561–63). Similarly, when Griselda's son is removed, the Clerk seems to protest too much: he states that if Walter had not truly known how perfectly Griselda loved her children, Walter would have thought that she endured what ensued out of treachery, malice, or cruelty. But since Walter's love for his children is entirely unproved, this averred confidence in Walter is undermined when the Clerk adds that Walter knew very well that next to *himself*, certainly she loved her children best in every way (IV.689–95). Griselda's response to Walter's announcement that he needs to kill their son, as well as their daughter, sums up the experience of maternality Walter has previously allowed her to attain: "I have noght had no part of children tweyne / But first siknesse, and after, wo and peyne" (IV.650–51). Thus Griselda's emotional reunion with her children, her tearful and fierce embraces and thankfulness for their safety, reasserts Griselda's maternality as well.

It is important to note that Walter enacts the violence of the father *both* when he denies his wife and has the children taken away at the beginning of the tale *and* when he acknowledges Griselda and has the children brought back in the end. For if it is the prerogative of the father to use his wife and children as he pleases, social fatherhood also depends on the restraint of the father from enacting that prerogative, which belongs only to the symbolic father. In exercising restraint, Walter acknowledges the phallus, keeping the symbolic father and the law in place, and establishing his right as a social father to act in the place of the symbolic father. Walter's acknowledgment of the symbolic father at the beginning of the tale, when he stipulates to his subjects that he must choose his wife, is reasserted at the tale's end, when Walter is reported honoring Janicula as the father of his wife, through whom Walter's own line will continue, rather than disparaging him as his subordinate. The end of the tale, then, with its magical restoration of the family intact and not only unharmed but prospering, places the violence of the family in the frame of the family romance, a fiction constructed to deny the violence, which is the only way that violence can be revealed. The threat that human mortality entails is effaced with the prospect of a long line of succession that looks back and honors rather than denigrates its origins. During Walter's tests, one basis for the father's infanticidal and incestuous desires—the threat of the children's surpassing their parents—was presented when Griselda's daughter was acknowledged as surpassing her mother in youth, beauty, and breeding. At the tale's happy ending, however, the son's surpassing of his father in wealth and marital felicity, not *needing* to test his wife, is presented not as a threat but as proof of the success of Walter's line.

The overdetermination of the fictionality of the context in which the story of domestic violence is told in the Clerk's Tale is immediately confirmed when the fictional frame of the happy ending is followed without break by the Clerk's authoritative reassertion of the story as literary, and of the authority of its author Petrarch to establish how the fiction should be read. Pointing to his defiance of the Host, the Clerk declares that Petrarch wrote in the high style and intended his writing to be read not as a literal or "real" story but as an allegorical fiction. The Clerk thereby connects the rivalry between him and the Host over what it is to be a man to questions of how to discern what is fictional from what is "real" and how to read the relationship between them. When Walter "undoes" his tests, he acts as if he knows with certitude what is imagination and what is real. But that power belongs only to the phallus, as enacted in the envoi's dizzying and necessarily indeterminate play with attempts to distinguish the fictional from the actual and the way they relate.

There is space here only to briefly sketch the different ways the violence of the father is revealed and concealed in the Man of Law's and Prioress's Tales. The Man of Law's Tale shifts the focus from the violence of the father against his wife and children to the double violence of father against daughter and of mothers against sons. In the introduction to his tale, as has been noted,[14] the Man of Law raises the motif of incest only to deny it, condemning it as an "unkynde abhomynacion" (II.88) that he emphatically will not relate: "Ne I wol noon reherce, if that I may" (II.89)—that is, if it is under his control. He distances himself and his audience(s) from the story of incest further by placing incest in the completely literary context of his bombastically poetic opening and his catalogue of poetry written by Chaucer and Ovid. Ultimately, however, his tale reveals that the Man of Law cannot not tell a story about incest. My concern is with the way his tale attempts to deflect attention away from the incestuous and infanticidal nature of the story of domestic violence it tells: a story of a daughter's expulsion by, return to, and acceptance by the father who initiated her exile from her home and country and religion by selling her in marriage against her will.

The violence of the father is obvious in his initial act of expulsion of his daughter. But the basis of that violence in the inherently violent internal fantasy structure of the family is also denied by the persistent way in which the plot and the narrator do not attribute the ensuing difficulties with which Constance is faced to her father's actions, but instead project the causes of those difficulties onto external forces. The Man of Law neither condemns Constance's father nor attributes her trials to her father's initial behavior. He insistently and emotionally blames fate. When he describes fate as God's providence, written in the stars for those who can understand, however, he establishes a distinction between the actual and the symbolic father. The plot points to the father's motivation in external religious disputes that must be kept in check by sacrificing his virginal daughter to maintain peace. But the difference between the actual and the symbolic father points to the Christian emperor of Rome's sacrifice of his daughter as an infanticide, by which he establishes a relationship of close proximity to God the symbolic father. Similarly, no mention is made of the father's sexual desire for his daughter as a motivating force for his behavior, as occurs in some analogues;[15] rather that sexual desire is projected and portrayed as the lust for his daughter expressed by a series of "lesser" men: the Muslim sultan of Syria who "needs" to buy her as a wife, the scorned Northumbrian knight who frames her for murder when she refuses to return his love, and her pagan husband Alla, for whom, the Man of Law salaciously reports, Constance had to lay aside her holiness and respond sexually as a wife: "They goon to bedde, as it was skile and right; / For thogh that wyves be ful hooly thynges, / They moste take in pacience at nyght / Swiche manere necessaries as been plesynges / To folk that han ywedded hem with rynges, / And leye a lite hir hoolynesse aside, / As for the tyme, it may no bet bitide" (II.708–14).[16]

What the daughter experiences from the father's initial act is a world out of control. The father's betrayal of his child initiates the daughter's further repeated experiences of parental betrayal. Twice marrying into "new" families, she twice experiences hostility and betrayal by her mothers-in-law. Each time the nature of the violence is deflected and projected onto external forces: the sultaness of Syria's religious conflicts and political ambitions, Donegild of Northumbria's xenophobia. But the incestuous implications of the sultaness of Syria's kiss to her son, and of Donegild's "insult" at her son marrying anyone outside the family, also point to the internal violence of the family. And the betrayal by the father who cannot protect his daughter from harm is repeated when Constance finds substitute parents in King Alla's constable and his wife Hermengyld, whose love cannot protect her from being lusted after and framed for murder.

The fantasy of the father's desire for infanticide is explicitly raised in the Man of Law's Tale in terms of Constance's maternal concern for her son when she and the child are set adrift in a boat by Alla's mother. Comforting his cries with a promise that *she* will not harm him (rather than that she will keep him from harm), she finds comfort, while praying to Mary for help, in the fact that no sorrow could compare to the pain that Mary endured when she saw the torment of her child "yrent" (II.844), torn and stretched on the cross. And she goes on to ask why her child's harsh father would want to have his small, innocent child, who has not yet committed any sin, killed: "O litel child, allas! what is thy gilt, / That nevere wroghtest synne as yet, pardee? / Why wil thyn harde fader han thee spilt?" (II.855–57). Again, this is an infanticide intended not by the father but by the father's mother, and one that does not take place. But the question further distances the audience from the actuality of the father's infanticidal desires by an identification of the child's suffering with that of Christ, which exalts the sacrifice of the child as the necessary act by which actual fathers are connected to the symbolic father as god the phallus the sacrifice that equates the actual with the symbolic father.[17]

Finally, as in the Clerk's Tale, the tale of incest and infanticide is deflected in the Man of Law's Tale by being framed by its "happy ending." Neither the father's daughter nor his grandson are killed. His daughter is reconciled with her husband, who recognizes her face in that of their son. And her husband grants her desire to be reunited with her father. All the families are reconciled intact without any visible harm. All the men who desired Constance are dead. And at the end she submits to her father's will and she and her father live together happily "In vertu and in hooly almusdede" (II.1156) until they die. The law of the father is reasserted.

The world of the Prioress's Tale seems far removed from the violence of the father in the family in the Clerk's and Man of Law's Tales. Indeed, critical focus has been on the feminine and maternal rather than paternal aspects of the Prioress's Prologue and Tale. But as in the Man of Law's Tale, the violence of the father is repressed and infanticide not named. In this case the gruesome murder of an innocent and devotedly Christian child is projected onto external religious and ethnic forces—the animosity of the cursed Jews, seemingly divorced from familial sexual conflict. As in the Man of Law's Tale, however, the presentation of the innocent Christian child with his throat slit identifies that child with the sacrifice of Jesus as son of the symbolic father. In doing so, it reveals the paradigm of the family repressed in the notion that through the sacrifice of the child access to the symbolic father is gained. In this case the frame of the "happy ending" by which the story can be told is the family romance in which the murdered child is translated into symbolic idealization in religious terms. In addition, by setting up an infanticide called murder in a world of helpless mothers in which the father is dead, the tale reinforces the ideological notion of the father as the idealized good and protective parent whose presence would have prevented the murder of the child.

In these ways, three of Chaucer's saints' lives—the Clerk's; Man of Law's, and Prioress's Prologues and Tales—articulate a profound cultural anxiety about paternity, a fiction whose violence can be revealed only by being concealed as a fiction constructed to defend against knowledge of that very violence.

NOTES

1. An earlier version of this essay was presented at the session (Ab)Uses of Enchantment: Domestic Violence in Medieval Romance at the Thirty-first International Congress on Medieval Studies in Kalamazoo, Michigan, in May 1996. My thanks to Eve Salisbury for her graciousness throughout that session and the preparation of this volume. My thanks to Sam Kimball as well for his insights and support through several versions.

2. See Robert Con Davis, *The Paternal Romance: Reading God-the-Father in Early Western Culture* (Urbana: University of Illinois Press, 1993), p. 2. My thinking has been stimulated and enriched generally by this work. See also Patricia Yaeger and Beth Kowaleski-Wallace, eds., *Refiguring the Father: New Feminist Readings of Patriarchy* (Carbondale: Southern Illinois University Press, 1989).

3. See Sigmund Freud, "Family Romances" (1909), in *Standard Edition of the Complete Psychological Works*, trans. James Strachey, et al. (London: Hogarth Press, 1953–74), vol. 9, pp. 237–41.

4. See also Sam Kimball, "Banning the Infant: Oedipus, Anti—Oedipus, and Reproduction—The Problematics of Autochthonous Desire," *Subjects/Objects* 4 (1986): 34–50, 89–91, and Barnaby B. Barratt and Barrie Ruth Straus, "Toward Postmodern Masculinities," *American Imago* 51, no. 1 (1994): 37–67.

5. All citations of Chaucer in this essay are from *The Riverside Chaucer*, 3d ed., ed. Larry D. Benson (Boston: Houghton Mifflin, 1987), by fragment and line numbers.

6. For notions of the symbolic father and phallus, see Freud, "Totem and Taboo," *Standard Edition*, vol. 13, pp. 1–62, and Jacques Lacan, *Ecrits: A Selection*, trans. Alan Sheridan (New York: W. W. Norton, 1977).

7. For excellent but differing accounts of the Clerk's position as and toward woman, see Carolyn Dinshaw, *Chaucer's Sexual Poetics* (Madison: University of Wisconsin Press, 1989), pp. 132–55, and Elaine Tuttle Hansen, *Chaucer and the Fictions of Gender* (Berkeley and Los Angeles: University of California Press, 1992), pp. 188–207.

8. For an extended account of the problematics of speaking plainly in the *Canterbury Tales* see Barrie Ruth Straus, "'Truth' and 'Woman' in Chaucer's *Franklin's Tale*," *Exemplaria* 4, no. 1 (1992): 135–70.

9. For an excellent account of the relationship between the Clerk's text and Petrarch's, see David Wallace, "'Whan She Translated Was,'" in *Literary Practice and Social Change in Britain, 1380–1530*, ed. Lee Patterson (Berkeley and Los Angeles: University of California Press, 1990), pp. 156–215.

10. For a discussion of the Clerk's Tale that also focuses on the depiction of marriage as a patriarchal institution and on Walter's struggle to succeed as a son in a competition for recognition among men, emphasizing the relationship between Walter and Griselda, without my concern for the way these issues are revealed and concealed, see Patricia Cramer, "Lordship, Bondage, and the Erotic: The Psychological Bases of Chaucer's 'Clerk's Tale,'" *Journal of English and Germanic Philology* 89 (1990): 491–511.

11. For a detailed account of the intensifications in emotionality in Chaucer's Clerk's Tale from that of the Latin and French versions he might have used, see J. Burke Severs, *The Literary Relationships of Chaucer's Clerkes Tale* (New Haven: Yale University Press, 1942), esp. pp. 229–50.

12. For the way this emphasis on Griselda's death is an addition of the Clerk's Tale to earlier versions by Boccaccio and Petrarch, see Severs, *Literary Relationships*, and the annotated translation of Petrarch's letter to Boccaccio in Robert P. Miller, ed., *Chaucer: Sources and Backgrounds* (New York: Oxford University Press, 1977), pp. 136–52.

13. For the idea of women's speech acts as acts of assertion belying their passive role, see my essay "Women's Words as Weapons: Speech as Action in 'The Wife's Lament,'" in *Old English Shorter Poems*, ed. Katherine O'Brien O'Keeffe (New York: Garland, 1994), pp. 335–56. See also Severs, *Literary Relationships*, Miller, *Chaucer: Sources and Backgrounds*, and Judith Ferster, *Chaucer on Interpretation* (Cambridge: Cambridge University Press, 1985), pp. 94–121.

14. See, for example, the excellent articles by Carolyn Dinshaw, "The Law of Man and Its 'Abhomynacions,'" *Exemplaria* 1, no. 1 (1989): 117–48, and Elizabeth Scala, "Canacee and the Chaucer Canon: Incest and Other Unnarratables," *Chaucer Review* 30 (1995): 15–39.

15. For the sources and analogues of the Man of Law's Tale, see Margaret Schlauch in *Sources and Analogues of Chaucer's* Canterbury Tales, ed. W. F. Bryan and Germaine

Dempster (Chicago: University of Chicago Press, 1941), pp. 155–206, and her *Chaucer's Constance and Accused Queens* (New York: New York University Press, 1927), pp. 12–20.

16. For commentary on the tone of these and other passages in the Man of Law's Tale, see Sheila Delany, *Writing Woman: Women Writers and Women in Literature, Medieval to Modern* (New York: Schocken Books, 1983), pp. 36–46.

17. On infanticide as sacrifice, see Davis, *Paternal Romance*, pp. 11–102, and Jacques Derrida, *The Gift of Death*, trans. David Wills (Chicago: University of Chicago Press, 1995), pp. 53–81.

JOHN FINLAYSON

Chaucer's Shipman's Tale, *Boccaccio*, and the *"Civilizing"* of Fabliau

J udged by its story—a monk borrows money from a merchant, buys the wife's favours with it and then refers the merchant to his wife for repayment—this *Tale* is a fabliau,[1] which plays variations on the motifs of illicit sex, tricky intrigue and "poetic justice." Yet these elements are handled with a blandness, an absence of dramatic action and characterization, which distinguish it sharply from the other fabliaux. No vivid lust, discord of characters or extra-textual revenge animate this story. As Helen Cooper has noted, "Half the fun of the other fabliaux lies in their conscious breaking of moral and social norms; here, that the wife sells her favours and the monk cheats her of the price passes without causing a ripple on the surface. Of all the fabliaux in the *Canterbury Tales*, this is the only one to be totally amoral, for the contrasting moral context has disappeared."[2] Though a fabliau in its subject matter—illicit sex, intrigue and cuckoldry—it is a tale in which these elements are *not* the focal points of humour and the ridicule of exposure as in most examples of the genre. In particular, it is a tale in which the nominal victim, the Merchant, is almost sympathetically rendered, his deceivers appear less than admirable but are equally not made positively unlikeable, no one is punished or exposed, and any "moral" has to be supplied entirely by the interpreter. In fact, in its obliqueness and its style of presentation it is quite unlike any other fabliau, by Chaucer or any one else. As a tale, its "meaning" lies not in its

From *The Chaucer Review*, vol. 36, no. 4 (2002): 336–351. © 2002 by The Pennsylvania State University.

fulfillment of the norms of the genre but in its displacement of these by focus on the verbal exchanges between the characters and the rich ambivalence of their language. Criticism which approaches it as a dramatic story, in which character related to moral parameters is the meaning, oversimplifies and confesses disappointment,[3] even more than most approaches to Chaucer as a kind of early dramatic-realist novelist.

In both the probable sources for the *Shipman's Tale*, Boccaccio's *Decameron*, VIII, 1 and 2,[4] the events of the narrative broadly fulfill the fabliau's traditional contract with the reader: that is, the reader is provided with sexual titillation through illicit sexual activity, intellectual and comic stimulation through the ingenious trickery which enables the sex, and moral satisfaction in the punishment of the rapacious female through the biter-bit structure of the plot. What is unusual in fabliau, however, is that in Boccaccio the adulterous female is punished, rather than escaping with no more than exposure, like Chaucer's Alison and May, and the male adulterer triumphs and suffers no penalty. The woman, that is, is had twice. Both Boccaccio stories are of the "lover's gift regained" type: in the first, a German soldier falls in love with a wealthy merchant's wife, who promises to return his love for two hundred florins. He is disgusted by her avarice and decides to punish her. Having borrowed money from her husband, he pays her in front of a witness, has sex with her and, later, tells the merchant that he has returned his borrowings to the wife who, because of the witness, cannot deny this and, thus, has to return the money to her husband. In the second story, a priest, lusting after a local wife, cannot put up the money demanded by the wife for her favours, but leaves his "fine blue cloak" as surety. Afterwards, still unable to raise the money, he sends back to the wife a mortar he had earlier borrowed, with a request for the cloak "left as surety," knowing that the message will be delivered in the husband's presence. The husband, outraged that his wife should demand "surety," forces her to return the cloak. The first story is closer in social level and the basic plot mechanism to the *Shipman's Tale*, though, as the female narrator, Neifile, states, the trickery "should not be termed a deception, but rather a reprisal." Unlike the *Shipman's Tale*, Boccaccio's story is presented as a moral example: "I declare that any woman who strays from the path of virtue for monetary gain deserves to be burnt alive, whereas the woman who yields to the forces of love ... deserves a lenient judge who will order the acquittal" (552). That is, in Boccaccio the offence is not adultery, but selling sexual favours to the "lover." In the second story, roughly twice as long, the social level is lower, and the plot skeleton is embroidered with circumstantial detail of the character of the priest and the social context, and its sexual content amplified by double entendre and some word-play. Unlike the first story, there is no element of reprisal, and no motivation or implication of moral outrage on the part of the priest or required of the reader. Indeed, some time later, the priest and the wife happily renew a relationship. Though in tone and its reception by the *brigata* close to the amoral world of the *Miller's Tale*, Boccaccio's second story also has a designated moral reference. It is told by Panfilo:

> it behoves me to relate a little story against a class of persons who keep on offending without our being able to retaliate. I am referring to the priests, who have proclaimed a crusade against our wives, and who seem to think, when they succeed in laying one of them on her back, that they have earned full remission of all their sins.
> (VII, 555)

Here, added to the target of those who violate the code of love by selling their favours, is another, the adulterous priest, abuser of his privileged position.

In broad outline only, Chaucer's *Tale* bears a much closer relationship to the first story, but it is worth noting that where the "winner" in the first story is a German soldier, in Chaucer he is a monk and, thus, two frames of moral pointing in Boccaccio are possibly united in Chaucer: the punishment of wives who sell their favours, and the indicting of lecherous priests who go unpunished. In both Boccaccio stories the aberration is not adultery, but satisfying love for money, which clearly devalues the "love" and the "lover." These stories can easily be seen as acts of male revenge, and reversals of the fabliau norm in which only the men are punished or ridiculed. And, indeed, this redressing of the sexual balance is confirmed by the female narrator of the first story, Neifile:

> "And since we have talked a great deal, fond ladies, of the tricks played by women upon men, I should like to tell you of one which was played by a man upon a woman, my intent being, not to censure the man for what he did or to claim that the woman was misused, but on the contrary to commend the man and censure the woman."
> (VII, 552)

In both stories the focus is on the rapacity of the adulterous wives, and the ingenious biter-bit trickery, the poetic justice meted out to a thoroughly unsympathetic woman. In neither work is there any complexity or substantiality of character. While it is most likely that Chaucer took his initial inspiration from the very brief, skeletal story one, transferring only the "hero," the priest, from story two, what he has created is not simply an amplification of the initial narrative, but a work which, while retaining implicitly and explicitly the fabliau content and the "moral" references of Boccaccio, expands radically the intellectual and aesthetic scope of its sources. The physical nature of Chaucer's expansion and transformation of Boccaccio's stories has been adequately and frequently noted, both by scholars who support the view that Boccaccio is the probable source, and those who reject this view. Both types of inquiry, however, tend to be concerned with establishing the superiority or massive originality of Chaucer. We can, I think, take it for granted that Chaucer's *Shipman's Tale* is artistically very different from the Boccaccio stories, and is also highly original. However, establishing or accepting Chaucer's high originality need not preclude recognition of more general relationships to Boccaccio's stories and their contexts in the *Decameron*, which may perhaps add to the literary resonances of the *Tale*. As I have pointed out, the basic narrative elements and fabliau structure of Boccaccio's stories and the implicit moral targeting remain inherent in Chaucer's work. In addition, the *Shipman's Tale*, as fabliau, relates to other tales of illicit love and sex and trickery in much the same way that most stories of Boccaccio's Eighth Day do to one another. These have the character of the *beffa*, defined as "a joke, a comic situation," which Mazzotta has described as follows: "fundamental to the motif of the *beffa*, a prank by which a schemer is unmasked and repaid in kind, is a paradigm of exchange, the *quid pro quo*; and as such it mimes both the law of the market, a recurrent motif in the *Decameron*, and the narrative structure of the text. Stories are recalled and exchanged by the *brigata*, and this circuit of exchange simultaneously depends on, and constitutes the bond of community between narrators and listeners."[5] While most critiques of the *Shipman's Tale* centre on the mercantile ethos both as Chaucer's principal "meaning" and originality, it should be remembered that the exposition of the mercantile ethos is both a central theme of large parts of the *Decameron*, as well as the implicit context of many stories where commerce is *not* a consideration of the plot. In Boccaccio it is not the mercantile ethos *per se* which is attacked, but its misapplication, first in the commodification of sex, and second, in the exploitation of the language of bond and contract which constitutes the "trick." Clearly, the very nature of Chaucer's expansion of the basic story by elaborating the merchant by means of his trade, and the multiple puns on words of commerce justify a variety of readings of the tale as some sort of critique of mercantile values. However, this may be only one aspect of this *Tale* which has so erroneously been characterized as "an ordinary fabliau comedy"[6] or "nearer to the pure fabliau type"[7] than any of Chaucer's other stories, and thus "unmemorable." Though the Host may not be the most reliable literary critic, his reading of the story, by no coincidence, focuses, like Boccaccio's second story and narrator, on the sexual exploitation of wives by the clergy:

> "God yeve the monk a thousand last quade yeer!
> A ha! Felawes, beth ware of swich a jape!
> The monk putte in the mannes hood an ape,
> And in his wyves eek, by Seint Austyn.
> Draweth no monkes moore unto youre in."[8]
>   (VII, 438–42)

Where Boccaccio's two stories derive most of their energy and meaning from the ingenious "trick," and the extra-textual ethical references by the narrators, Chaucer's expansion and development redirect the meaning of the story from the simple, naughty elements of fabliau and a simplistic moral justification to the creation of a complex sophisticated world of sexual manoeuvres, linguistic doubleness, and rules of contract which has more in common with eighteenth century comedies and novels of sexual gamesmanship, such as *The Way of the World* and *Les Liaisons Dangereuses*, than with the farcical and uncomplicated "swyvings" of the *Miller's* and the *Reeve's Tales*. Chaucer invokes and retains the frame of the fabliau world, but very rapidly transcends its stock business of situational comedy, moving to a more indirect world of ambiguous dialogue and sexual negotiation. Moreover, it is a world in which neither God nor conventional Christian morality has any overt place—that is, remarkably like the world created by Boccaccio in the sixth, seventh and eighth Days of the *Decameron*.

The tale begins with the introduction of typical fabliau characters, a rich merchant and his wife, "of excellent beautee," who is "revelous" and the subject of men's attentions "at festes and at daunces." The third member of the typical fabliau triangle appears rapidly—a young, handsome monk, who is "in his hous as famulier ... as it is possible any freend to be." The signals of the fabliau structure, as rapidly presented as in *The Miller's Tale*, are unmistakable, and no reader could doubt the general directions of the tale. What must engage the attention, then, is the method of the cuckoldry and the manner of the poetic presentation. A clue to the method is already present in the remark in the fifth line, that the "compaignable and revelous" nature of the wife "is a thyng that causeth more dispence" than is worth the attention it attracts, attached to the premonitory "But wo is hym that payen moot for al!" (10). This is followed by the "contentious" lines of the female "voice"[9] which asserts that husbands must array their wives for their own reputation, but if they don't or grudge it,

> Thanne moot another payen for oure cost,
> Or lene us gold, and that is perilous.
>   (18–19)

Presented here, as we are, with connections between a beautiful wife, public admiration, doubts about the worth of the expenditure, the obligation to provide rich clothing and the "justification" that if one will not pay, someone else will, it does not take a brilliant mind to anticipate that in this tale an admirer will pay, and be paid in sexual kind. The matter of fabliau here, then, proceeds in expected fashion; and the key to the particular concerns of the author has been firmly announced in the almost obsessive references to money: the merchant is "riche ... for which men helde hym wys," "dispence," "payen moot for all," "richely," "dispence," "payen," "gold".[10] Whether the Shipman mimics the voice of women, or the Wife speaks directly for her sex in VII 11–19, the message is clear: a beautiful woman must be richly arrayed to attract the attention which is her due; the husband must pay, because it reflects on his own position; if he does not, someone else must. And the last line of this passage defines the plot, and the threat to husbands,

> Or lene us gold, and that is perilous.

Though the first forty of the four hundred odd lines of the tale allow us, fairly accurately, to anticipate the fabliau action, the narration now becomes quite leisurely. In *The Miller's Tale* and *The Reeve's* the visual solidity and the moral atmosphere is created largely by extended character portrayals and a wealth of detailed settings which hold up the progress to the two central actions of fabliau—sexual congress and public exposure; and in *The Merchant's Tale* most of the first 400 lines are devoted to presenting January's state of mind, his illusions, and self-deceptions and reality. The delaying of the climaxes in this *Tale* is not achieved by character description, a place setting, or revelation of the "consciousness" of the protagonist, but by selected details of the professional occupations of the Merchant and the Monk and, more centrally, by the extended dialogues between the characters.

On the third day of the Monk's visit—a day associated, of course, with a cock's crowing and betrayal—the merchant rises up early to do his accounts, thus establishing his role and disposition, and the monk walks in the garden, a setting associated equally with Eden and the Garden of Love in the *Romance of the Rose*, where he is met by the wife. Their conversation immediately takes on a sexual cast, with the suggestion from the monk that his "deere nece" needs rest because the merchant has undoubtedly "laboured" with her all night. The wife's denial,

> "In al the reawme of France is ther no wyf
> That lasse lust hath to that sory pley,"

is a marvel of ambiguity, allowing either for the interpretation that the merchant is not very adequate or demanding in sexual matters, or that the wife herself is not very interested in sex. She hints at great secret distress, the monk offers a shoulder to cry on, promising complete secrecy, and she in her turn swears never to betray anything he may say, an exchange which ambiguously evokes the confessional and the "secrecy" of courtly love. She raises the ethical problem that the monk is the merchant's relation; and he is quick to clarify that they are not blood relatives. The problem raised is notably one of social ethics and personal loyalties, not of morals, thus alerting the audience almost by indirection to the absence of moral scruples. The speed with which the possible barriers of kinship are rejected defines, of course, the monk's expediency, and the revelation that the "cosynage" is not literal but a device "To have the moore cause of aqueyntaunce" of the Wife, forcefully directs our attention both to the expedient morality of the Monk and the doubleness and duplicity of the language used by this couple, and particularly the pun on "cosin."[11] The scene is a sophisticated discourse of negotiation: the monk's indirect but unmistakable opening sexual gambit, coyly turned but not rejected, and contracts of secrecy exchanged. The ground thus declared and cleared, the wife is free to spill out, in a swift-moving torrent of words that hint at hidden injuries, nobly suppressed—

> "it sit nat me
> To tellen no wight of oure privetee
> Neither abedde ne in noon oother place"
> (163–65)

—her chief complaint, namely that the Merchant is niggardly, which then leads to her statement that she is in debt for clothes. Her request that the monk lend her the money, which she will repay, is accompanied by the ambiguous suggestiveness of

> "And doon to yow what plesance and service
> That I may doon, right as yow list devise."
> (191–92)

The monk's agreement to the loan is declared a sexual bargain by implication,

And with that word he caughte hire by the flankes,
And hire embraceth harde, and kiste hire ofte,
   (201–2)

but not directly (as in Boccaccio) by the participants or the narrator. Though the situation is that of fabliau, the tone is similar to eighteenth century comedy—male and female, each with an individual agenda, explore each other's intentions in cloaked terms which, though loaded with sexual innuendo, avoid direct commitment. The bargain struck, overtly, is only for a loan and repayment; and the tone is urbane, rather than leering. Only details such as the flank clasping, with the rhyme of "frankes" and "flankes" (201–2), link this tale with the direct approach of Nicholas to Alison in the *Miller's Tale*, "And heeld hire harde by the haunchebones" (3279). Sexual contract is implied, and financial bargain stated in a "civilized" manner which makes it clear that neither passionate love nor youthful lust is the motivating force of this anticipated conjunction. The identification of sex with money, as every critic has noted, thus from the beginning dominates this fabliau and, of course, marks it out from the others. The tone, however, is neutral: an exchange of "goods" is arranged to the mutual satisfaction and anticipated "profit" of each party, providing an exact parallel with the activities of the Merchant himself. All three characters in the *Tale* assume the mercantile roles of borrower, lender, seller and purchaser of goods.[12] The superlative merchant here is, of course, the Monk, who gains his "profit" by using the other parties' goods.

"Jolif as a pie," lightened of her assumed distress, the wife returns to the house, and the intended cuckold is presented for our full attention. In summoning him to eat, the wife vigorously accuses him of being too preoccupied with his "sommes" and "bagges"—"the devel have part on alle swiche rekenynges!"—words which have caused at least one critic to identify the merchant as niggardly and lacking in generosity.[13] The accusation, however, is that of the wife, not the narrator or, indeed, of the events of the tale—her self-justification of her forthcoming actions, as the Wife of Bath attacks her husbands to excuse her own delinquencies. In fact, the merchant's justification of his "rekenynges" presents him as a not-unsympathetic exemplar of the successful, honest merchant. He points out how uncertain the prosperity of merchants is—"Scarsly amonges twelve tweye shul thryve"—which, since we have been told that "Ful riche was his tresor and his hord" (84), may be either a sign of insecurity, proper financial caution, or a desire to mislead his wife a little about his wealth, but is not by itself more than reflective of a "careful" businessman.

In fact, the merchant himself here would seem to belong to that group of solid bourgeois whom Vittore Branca sees as replacing the lords and ladies of conventional medieval narrative, and, in their spectrum from clowns to sages, constituting a mercantile epic:

"After the lordly prudence and subtle weariness of Gilberto, after the sorrowing blazing profile of Lisa in the novella of Torello, there emerges a most aristocratic depiction of the figure of the merchants, 'sage and eloquent.' ... It could not be *the* poem of the autumn of the Middle Ages in Italy were it not also the epic of the men who have stamped its civilization most powerfully, carrying it to the center of European life."[14]

The merchant thus defines honest and successful mercantilism and, with delicious dramatic irony, provides the norm which exposes the dishonest, unsuccessful mercantilism of the wife. Indeed, his actions and his speeches (though obviously describing a fairly limited life) clearly serve as a standard of honest mercantilism against which the misapplication of the concepts and language of commerce by the monk and the wife may be appreciated in its ambiguity and exploitation, and, of course, also judged. If Chaucer can allow a couple of examples of honest clerics among a company of corrupt religious, is it unlikely that the son of a merchant could also allow an honest merchant?

He indicates his plans to go to Flanders next day on business, and leaves his household to her care, stating that she has enough supplies "That to a thrifty household may suffise." One person's "thrift" may be another's niggardliness, of course, but this is a matter of interpretation, not fact. When the monk asks him for the loan of a hundred franks, the merchant "gentilly anon" answers that "My gold is youres, whan that it yow leste" (284), asking only that it be repaid as soon as possible because, "Ye knowe it wel ynogh Of chapmen, that hir moneie is hir plogh." (287–88).

There is, therefore, nothing to substantiate the wife's claim or to allow us to see him as a miser who, by definition, deserves to be cheated. He is, however, not a full character, being defined entirely by his profession—his actions and conversation all relate to money, goods and trade, though the presentation of these is not satiric. Thus, his remark that money is the merchant's plough sums him up, in its *double entendre*, better than he knows, since his money will serve two "ploughmen," the monk, and later, himself. The mechanical stratagems of this fabliau are thus completed—the merchant will pay for his own cuckolding literally. The circumlocutory contract between Monk and Wife, and the courteous, informal private loan from Merchant to Monk privilege contracts, debts and money as the imaginative focus, rather than salacious anticipation of illicit sex. This is also the central focus of a large number of *novelle* in the *Decameron*, days six, seven and eight,[15] and many of those also are devoted to *ingegno* (wit, ingenuity).[16] And, when the Merchant departs, leaving the scene clear, the fulfillment of the Wife's contract is accomplished as quickly, in literary but not clocktime, as it is directly stated:

> This faire wyf acorded with daun John
> That for thise hundred frankes he sholde al nyght
> Have hire in his armes bolt upright;
> And this acord parfourned was in dede.
> In myrthe al nyght a bisy lyf they lede
> Til it was day ...
>   (314–19)

There is no pornographic atmosphere, no suggestion of frantic physical activity as in the *Reeve's Tale*, or of the "revel" and "solas" enjoyed by the sexually charged Nicolas and Alison. The actual cuckolding is hurried over as neutrally as the sexual relationship between them is presented and arranged—a not unpleasant but by no means emotionally engaged transaction, splendidly "modern" and rhetorically non-judgmental. This contrasts with the "myrthe" of the merchant's spousal relationship later (375–80). The weight of the dialogue, actions, and character directs the attention to the contracts and commerce of the triangle of relationship, not just to money but to money as the neutral medium of the exchanges of goods in society. It needs no feminist critique to note, as the Wife of Bath has in her prologue adumbrated, that in and outside marriage there is a strong connection between sexual goods and money; and the fact that the transaction is hardly distinguishable from prostitution is equally inescapable. The narration here, and in the exchanges between wife and Monk, however, is so devoid of emotionally or morally charged words that the immorality of the situation is almost ignored. Indeed, if moral conclusions or lessons about marriage are drawn, they are the product of the reader's responses and prejudices.[17]

   With the Merchant's return, the narrative returns to direct and indirect dialogue, and to the humour of the *double entendre*, which attends our knowledge of the cuckoldry. The merchant's report to his wife of his business trip centers on the fact that "chaffare is so deere" and he has borrowed a large sum of money. Though not a miserly villain, he is clearly defined entirely by his profession and, as a human being, is probably a bore. However, character is not here the focus, but rather the ironic relationship between his problems and his wife's activities. He then goes off to borrow money to repay his debt and, en passant, visits the monk, "Nat for to axe or borwe of hym moneye" but to look him up, chat about things, "as freendes doon," and talk about his business dealings, "his chaffare." The apparent supernumerary detail here, though effecting dramatic irony, also serves to shift the fabliau matter to *ingegno* and verbal play.

In a conventional fabliau, devoted to the comedy of illicit sex and the discomfiture of rich old men who own young wives, this scene would be played rather differently: the merchant would directly ask for his money back, the monk would reveal he gave it to the wife, and the merchant would learn, or be allowed to suspect, that he had been exploited by both parties. Here, the stress is on the merchant's friendly relation with the Monk and the fact that though, defined as he is by his profession, he mentions his business, he does not ask for the debt to be repaid—a fact that preserves our view of him as innocent and not unsympathetic victim. The fabliau balance is thus here shifted since, if we are not required to identify with either of the exploiters, we should expect to feel that the victim deserves what he gets, as John the carpenter does, because he is such a gullible person, Symkyn because he is so proud, and January because he is so self-deluding. The absence of a conventional fabliau ending in revelation, comic violence and "poetic justice" is consistent with the shift of attention in this tale from bawdy action to ambiguous dialogue and low-keyed implications. The disappointing of our normal narrative expectations makes what some have seen as a "bodiless" tale a more subtle variation on fabliau than even the *Merchant's Tale*, producing an intriguing inconclusiveness which exercises the mind more than any other fabliau.

The narrator or poet draws out the rounding of the monetary-sexual circle, teasing his audience by delaying the point at which the betrayals will be revealed or, as in this case, realized without public disclosure. The merchant, having visited the Monk on his way to complete his financial dealings in Bruges, returns home with a profit of a thousand franks. He is met "atte gate" by his wife

> And al that nyght in myrthe they bisette;
> For he was riche and cleerly out of dette.
>   (375–76)

The connections of sex and money which control this narrative are here compacted with dramatic ironies; money, which has bought his wife's "virtue" and freed her from debt, confirms the merchant in the success of his profession, that is, his identity, and stimulates him to pay his marital "debt" with vigour, thus effectively undermining her suggestions to the Monk that she neither enjoyed sex, nor got much of it (117, 170–1), which might in a less than strenuously moral world provide some excuse for her conduct. Next morning, the merchant mildly reproves his wife for not having told him on his previous return that Daun John had repaid the hundred frank loan to her. Structurally, this is the peripety of fabliau, when we should expect the wife's duplicity to be "discovered" and the merchant be made aware of his cuckolding. But the wife's quick-witted handling of the situation confirms one of the conventions of fabliau—that the women get off scot-free—while deflecting another—that the sexual misconduct be made known to the husband, even if he is persuaded, as is January, that he did not see what he saw. Her cursing of the "false monk" (402) is strenuous enough—"Yvel thedam on his monkes snowte" (405)—to externalise her perception of her danger and her betrayal to the readers, but not so vicious that it would either overwhelm the tone of "civilized" deceit and self-interest which characterize her and the narrative, or not be consonant with the "explanation" she is about to offer her husband, namely, that she thought it was a present "for cosynage" to her, as a return for the "beele cheere" that the monk "hath had ful ofte tymes here." The situational focus on "cosynage" and "cheere" transforms the fabliau denouement from action to ironic language, and this comic climax of punning language is rounded out by the wife's declaration that she will pay her debt "abedde." The revelation of this fabliau, then, is not the comic action of the exposure of cuckoldry, but the wife's casuistry which links money and illicit sex with repaying debts in the marital bed:

> "Ye shal my joly body have to wedde;
> By God, I wol nat paye yow but abedde!"
>   (423–24)

The lascivious reader is left to wonder how many marital conjunctions equal the hundred frank extra-marital act, while the moral reader may work himself into a pious tizzy over this commercialization of "legitimate" sex. "Fabliau action and mercantile philosophy," as Fichte observes, "meet and combine in this decisive scene ... Their marriage thereafter will consequently be placed on a strictly materialistic basis, a basis, however, promising advantages and satisfaction for both partners,"[18] for

> This merchant saugh ther was no remedie,
> And for to chide it nere but folie,
> Sith that the thyng may not amended be.
>   (427–29)

The Tale ends on a splendidly ironic piece of advice from this master of mercantilism:

"Keep bet thy good, this yeve I thee in charge."
    (432)

No overt moral is drawn and there is no textual warrant for supposing that the Merchant suspects more than he reveals, but we, as party to omniscience, can draw the ambiguous moral for the wife, namely that she should keep her sexual goods within marriage or, at least, be more careful if she makes future illicit contracts for these "goods."

The other fabliaux have varied the conventions enormously, though all have re-affirmed the gross physicality of the genre in their endings, but the *Shipman's Tale*, which some regard as "the most typical Chaucerian representation"[19] of the genre, radically subverts this "essential" revelation: nothing is overtly revealed, no one loses, sex and money define a closed circuit, and the laughter is focused not on physical action but on dramatic ironies enshrined in the language of commerce—an elegantly sophisticated comedy of bourgeois values by a socially and intellectually elevated vintner's son. The Shipman's concluding couplet offers no overt *moralitas* for this tale,

Thus endeth my tale, and God us sende
Taillynge ynough unto oure lyves ende,

but marvellously compresses in one word "taillynge" (credit, account) the central focus of this "tale" of venture-capital, duplicitous contracts and ambiguous language. Since oaths and exclamations on the name of God have been so frequently deployed in this work,[20] by characters whose trustworthiness and morality are unreliable, we may also be invited to see this apparently casual or neutral ending as a gentle reminder of that "spiritual" credit which our trio have conspicuously *not* amassed for their lives' end, but we may just as easily be over-reading to satisfy our own agendas, our post-Arnoldian desire for a "moral" Chaucer.

Fabliau expresses a licensed, fictional revolt against orthodoxies and social morality. In The *Shipman's Tale* the "revolt" adopts the language of the orthodoxy it exploits, so that it could almost be argued by sexual sophisticates that there is no immorality, since the contracts are honoured and no one is injured. In the other fabliaux we laugh at what we know to be immoral—illicit sex is attractive, but we do know that it will be discovered and orthodox morality restored. Here, there is no joy of illicit sex, no rampant lust, no pining Absolon or love-sick Damian; in fact, there is more joy in the "wanton" play of the merchant and his wife. Sex may be the commodity of this transaction, but it is almost as abstract as coffee beans on the Chicago commodities exchange. This minimalizing of sex may reduce our awareness of the basic immorality of the transaction to the point where the boundaries between licit and illicit sex almost disappear in the language of commerce which makes sex itself a commercial commodity, directly related to money paid, loaned or owed, and sexual congress is linked in each of its three recorded occurrences to money:

> For thise hundred frankes he sholde al nyght
> Have hire in his armes bolt upright.
>   (315–16)

> And al that nyght in myrthe they bisette
> For he was riche and cleerly out of dette
>   (375–76)

> "Ye shal my joly body have to wedde;
> By God, I wol nat paye yow but abedde!"
>   (423–24)

Since licit and illicit sex are paralleled with honest and dishonest trade, and there is no anagnorisis, this fabliau not only *recognizes* the non-ideal world of suspended moral laws, lustful hedonism and deceit, but may be said to establish it as an acceptable reality, unlike most fabliaux which nominally refer us to the moral world by the public revelation, punishment, and "poetic justice" of their closures. Some critics, like Copland, find the "impudent challenge from an unexpectedly total material success flung in the face of piety, decency ... exhilarating and, in its vulgar way, energetically heroic,"[21] while others, like Donaldson, implicitly disapprove: "Sensitivity to other values besides cash has been submitted to appraisal and, having been found nonconvertible, has been thrown away."[22] The nominal narrator expresses neither approval nor disapproval, and the poet does not intrude either in *propria persona* or in any of his guises as pilgrim, naive narrator, or pilgrimage character. What we are given, therefore, is a totally enclosed world of civil dialogue, consumer values, no violence, passion or uncomfortable ideals, in which the potentially destructive force of human sexuality is "arranged" and social harmony maintained. The robust world of fabliau has moved into the realm of sophisticated social comedy which verges on mild cynicism, rather than outrage or hearty laughter. In a world devoid of strong feeling, whose only values are those of mercantile ethics, profit and discretion would seem to be the only appropriate yardsticks of judgement. The very fact that the *Tale*, unlike Boccaccio's two stories, provides no moral parameters, does not mark out characters as evil or good, attractive or innocent, may be interpreted either as the Shipman's view of the world[23] or as Chaucer's very subtle presentation of the "reality" of bourgeois ethics—a pleasant world of simple delusion and almost harmless deceit whose only important sin is its absence of higher values, secular or religious.[24] Any conclusions we come to about the "moral" of the *Tale* spring entirely from our-own preconceptions of art and Chaucer, for in this work the poet, "like the God of the creation, remains within or beyond or above his handiwork, invisible, refined out of existence, indifferent, paring his fingernails."[25]

However, given the increasingly recognized direct influence of the *Decameron* on Chaucer, it is possible to see in this *Tale*, as in the *Merchant's Tale*, what Auerbach isolates as the controlling tone of the story of Frate Alberto (*Decameron*, 4, 2), which he identifies with an early humanism that "lacks constructive ethical force when it is confronted with the reality of life."[26] He also locates this tone in the style of presentation:

> "His Decameron fixes a level of style, in which the relation of actual occurrences in contemporary life can become polite entertainment; narrative no longer serves as a moral exemplum, no longer caters to the common people's simple desire to laugh; it serves as a pleasant diversion for a circle of well-bred young people of the upper classes, of ladies and gentlemen who delight in the sensual play of life and who possess sensitivity, taste and judgement."[27]

Much commentary on Chaucer is conditioned, as A.C. Spearing observes, by the fact that "those who are drawn to the study of medieval literature are themselves often deeply conservative, even reactionary in temperament; they prefer what they find in medieval culture to what they find in more recent culture ... 'the medieval world with its quiet hierarchies,'"[28] dominated, he might have added, by a firm Christian morality. Read, however, in the context of Chaucer's borrowings, small and big, from the *Decameron*, the *Shipman's Tale*, like the *Merchant's Tale* (both of which derive from the *Decameron*), seems quite devoid of the implicit suburban sexual morality and reflex piety attributed to Chaucer by those critics who take the *Parson's Tale* to be the Key to the *significacio* of each *Tale*. Both the *Shipman's* and the *Merchant's Tales* should rather be read with Boccaccio's tongue in cheek Epilogue as an appropriate frame of reference:

> "The lady who is forever saying her prayers, or baking pies and cakes for her father confessor, may leave my stories alone: they

will not run after anyone demanding to be read, albeit they are no
more improper than some of the trifles that self-righteous ladies
talk about, or even engage in, if the occasion arises." (800)

NOTES

1. For typical views of Chaucer's presentation of this fabliau, see C. Muscatine
in *Chaucer and Chaucerians*, ed. D. S. Brewer (Alabama, 1966) p. 10; D. Pearsall, *The
Canterbury Tales* (London, 1985), pp. 20–217; D. S. Brewer in *Companion to Chaucer Studies*,
ed. Beryl Rowland (Oxford, 1968), p. 29.

2. Helen Cooper, *The Structure of the* Canterbury Tales (London, 1983), p. 163.

3. See T. W. Craik, *The Comic Tales of Chaucer* (London, 1964), p. 70.

4. Giovanni Boccaccio, *The Decameron*, trans. G. H. McWilliam (London, 1972),
VII, 1 and 2. The probable indebtedness of Chaucer to the *Decameron*, rather than to a
range of obscure French and Italian or other sources, has recently been recognized: see
Helen Cooper, "Sources and Analogues of Chaucer's *Canterbury Tales*," *Studies in the Age
of Chaucer* 19 (1997), 183–210; and also articles by this author in *Neophilologus, Studia
Neophilologica, Neuphilologische Mitteilungen, Studies in Philology*. Two recent commentators
on the *Shipman's Tale*, N. S. Thompson, *Chaucer, Boccaccio, and the Debate of Love* (Oxford,
1996), 210–224, and Carol Heffernan, "Chaucer's *Shipman's Tale* and Boccaccio" in
Courtly Literature, ed. Keith Busby and Erik Kooper (Amsterdam/Philadelphia, 1990), pp.
261–70, while not directly asserting the *Decameron* as the direct source, use it as the closest
analogue and, in effect, clearly believe it to be the source.

5. Giuseppe Mazzotta, *The World at Play in Boccaccio's "Decameron"* (Princeton, 1986),
p. 190.

6. Muscatine, p. 105.

7. Brewer, *Companion*, p. 259.

8. All Chaucer references are to *The Riverside Chaucer*, Third Edition, ed. Larry D.
Benson (Boston, 1987).

9. Lines 12–19 have been asserted by F. N. Robinson and many others to be written
for a woman, "presumably the Wife of Bath," but a convincing refutation is offered by
Murray Copland, "The *Shipman's Tale*: Chaucer and Boccaccio," *Medium Aevum*, 25
(1966): 24–27.

10. Most commentators have noted the stress on money and commercium as a major
element of the *Tale*. A convenient survey is Sheila Fisher, *Chaucer's Poetic Alchemy: A Study
of Value and Its Transformation in the* Canterbury Tales (New York, 1988), ch. III.

11. See Ruth Fisher, *NQ* (210) 196, 168–70. The objection in the *Riverside Chaucer*
notes (p. 911) on the grounds that the word is not recorded in the sense of "cheat" or
"dupe" before 1453 is ultra conservative. The meaning, "dupe," is recorded in O.F. and
in fabliaux in the 12th and 13th centuries, and Chaucer was not only obviously fluent in
French but also responsible for introducing many French words into English. In addition,
most, if not all of his primary audience would have been bilingual.

12. See J. P. Hermann, "Dismemberment, Dissemination, Discourse: Sign and
Symbol in *The Shipman's Tale*," *Chaucer Review* 19 (1985): 316–27, on the transferral of
roles among characters.

13. A. H. Silverman, "Sex and Money in Chaucer's *Shipman's Tale*," *PQ* 32 (1953): 331.

14. Vittore Branca, *Boccaccio*, trans. Richard Monges (New York, 1976), p. 288.

15. See Mazzotta, p. 93.

16. See Branca, p. 287.

17. See, for example, Hermann, 326.

18. J. O. Fichte, ed. *Chaucer's Frame Tales* (Tübingen and Cambridge, Engl., 1987), p. 66.

19. J. A. Burrow, *A Reading of Sir Gawain and the Green Knight* (London, 1965), p. 74.

20. See G. R. Keiser, "Language and Meaning in Chaucer's *Shipman's Tale*," *Chaucer Review* 12 (1978): 147–8.

21. Copland, 23.

22. E. T. Donaldson, ed., *Chaucer's Poetry* (Boston and London, 1958), pp. 931–32.

23. Copland, 25–27.

24. V. J. Scattergood, "The originality of the *Shipman's Tale*," *Chaucer Review* 11 (1976–77): 227, takes a more serious view of the "laconic evenness of tone": "the incompatibilities and contradictions which Chaucer exposes ... are too serious to be dispersed in laughter."

25. James Joyce, *A Portrait of the Artist as a Young Man* (London, 1976), p. 215.

26. E. Auerbach, *Mimesis*, trans. Willard Trask (Princeton, 1953; Anchor Books edition, 1957), p. 200.

27. Auerbach, pp. 188–89.

28. A. C. Spearing, *Medieval to Renaissance in English Poetry* (Cambridge, Engl., 1985), pp. 20–21.

MARTIN CAMARGO

Time as Rhetorical Topos in Chaucer's Poetry

Chaucer scholars have long recognized that the experience, measurement, and understanding of time have changed since the Middle Ages and that modern readers must be educated in the conceptions of time that Chaucer would have shared with members of his original audience if they are to appreciate the full extent of Chaucer's artistry. Chaucerian time has been studied from many perspectives, in particular those of medieval theology and natural philosophy.[1] Despite the deep learning and broad scope of such studies, extending from theoretical speculations about the nature of time, to moral implications of time, to astrological and even mechanical methods for calculating time, they do not begin to exhaust the range of meanings that time would have had for a fourteenth-century intellectual. Less studied by Chaucerians but no less familiar to Chaucer is time as a component of rhetoric.

The meaning of time as an element of Chaucer's poetry, viewed from the perspective of rhetoric, varies a good deal, depending on which of the five canons of rhetoric—invention, arrangement, style, memory, and delivery—is being considered. Perhaps Chaucer's most obvious invocation of time as a rhetorical concern is in connection with effective oral delivery. The Host, who serves among other things as self-appointed rhetorical critic, frequently admonishes the speakers in his charge to be not only clear, profitable, and

From *Medieval Rhetoric: A Casebook*, Scott D. Troyan, ed.: pp. 91–107. © 2004 by Routledge.

entertaining, but also concise. Anticipating the Parson's long-windedness, for example, the Host exhorts him to be pithy and brief, in order to make best use of the little time remaining before sunset:

> But hasteth yow; the sonne wole adoun;
> Beth fructuous, and that in litel space.
>   (X.70–71)[2]

As narrator of the "Tale of Sir Thopas," Chaucer the pilgrim had been neither and so had brought down upon himself Harry Bailey's emphatic censure:

> Thy drasty rymyng is nat worth a toord!
> Thou doost noght elles but despendest tyme.
>   (VII.930–931)

Although just barely under way, his performance shows no signs of using time effectively either by entertaining or edifying the company, and the Host justifies his cutting it short on those grounds.

While the Host, as master of ceremonies for the tale-telling contest, strives to keep the audience engaged and thus upholds brevity chiefly as a virtue of performance, just as often brevity is invoked as a virtue of style.[3] The Friar's comment on the Wife of Bath's lengthy autobiographical account of "the wo that is in mariage" (III.3), for example, is directed more at her violation of stylistic decorum than at her failure to entertain:

> The Frere lough, whan he hadde herd al this;
> "Now dame," quod he, "so have I joye or blis,
> This is a long preamble of a tale!"
>   (III.829–831)

Abbreviation and amplification each has its proper place in the medieval stylist's repertoire, and the Friar, perhaps trying to score points off the Wife's stereotypical female garrulousness, playfully suggests that she has neglected one of the most basic rules for their use. Chaucer, like the members of his audience, would have been familiar with rhetorical teaching on effective style that stressed the importance of knowing when to be copious and when to be concise. Geoffrey of Vinsauf, the one medieval rhetorician whom Chaucer mentions by name (VII.3347), assigns the techniques of amplification and abbreviation a position of prominence at the beginning of his treatment of style, and Chaucer's own style is most self-consciously "rhetorical" when he draws attention to his own use of those techniques, as in the apostrophe near the end of the "Nun's Priest's Tale" (VII.3338–3374).[4]

As it figures both in style and delivery, time is understood as duration. The difference is that performative time is focused on the audience and its reaction—a lengthy performance, especially one lacking pleasure and/or profit, will exhaust the listeners' attention, while stylistic time is focused on the text and its production—depending on the larger purpose of the text, some topics will merit copious treatment and others concise treatment. If that distinction seems tenuous, the contrast between both conceptions of time and the one underlying arrangement is sharper. For those medieval rhetoricians who concerned themselves with narrative forms, as opposed to more fixed genres such as letters and sermons, the doctrine of arrangement often centered on time as sequence, that is, on the choice between natural order and artificial order. Given any sequence of events, one could begin their narration either with the event that initiated the sequence or, more artfully, with an event from the middle or the end of the sequence.[5] Though Chaucer frequently disrupts the temporal sequence of events within a narrative—Book V of *Troilus and Criseyde* is an especially complex instance—he is not as prone to use artificial order in the sense in which the medieval rhetoricians defined it, and when he does, as perhaps at the beginning of the "Knight's Tale," he does not draw attention to the fact.

Much more could be said about time as a component of delivery, style, and arrangement, as well as memory, in Chaucer's poetry, but no less worthy of close attention is time in the context of the first canon of rhetoric: invention or discovery. Time as a source of argument was an important part of the medieval poet's inheritance from classical rhetoric. Within the framework of Ciceronian topical invention, time is defined most explicitly and treated in greatest detail under the attributes of actions. In his *De inventione* (1.26.37), Cicero distinguishes four categories of such attributes: "The attributes of actions are partly coherent with the action itself, partly considered in connexion with the performance of it, partly adjunct to it and partly consequent upon its performance."[6] The second category is further subdivided into five factors to be considered in connection with the performance of any act (1.26.38): place, time, occasion, manner, and facilities. As Cicero goes on to explain (1.26.39–40), time (*tempus*) and occasion (*occasio*) are distinct species of the same genus. Arguments from "time" in connection with performing an act may be based on (1) past, present, or future acts that have a bearing on the act in question, (2) the length of time necessary for the performance of the act in question, or (3) the time of year or time of day when the act in question occurred. Arguments from "occasion," by contrast, are based on showing how certain temporary circumstances, whether "public" (*publicum*), "general" (*commune*), or "particular" (*singulare*), provided the opportunity to perform the act in question. The *Rhetorica ad Herennium*'s much briefer discussion of arguments from time in connection with acts (2.4.7) is clearly related to Cicero's. Under "Sign," one of the six divisions of the "Conjectural Issue," the anonymous *auctor ad Herennium* posits six divisions, among them the "Point of Time" (*tempus*) at which the act took place, the "Duration of Time" (*spatium*) required for the act to be accomplished, and the favorability of the "Occasion" (*occasio*) for the performance of the act.[7]

The Ciceronian account of time as an attribute of acts was known in the Middle Ages not only through the original treatises and commentaries on them but also and especially through the so-called rhetorical circumstances—who, what, why, how, where, when, with what means?—which frequently appeared in medieval rhetorical textbooks[8] and which provided one of the main organizational schemes for medieval *accessus* to the works of the *auctores*.[9] Within this schema, time as the circumstance "when?" undergoes a further narrowing of reference. Though still paired with "occasion," "time" as a source of argument comes to be restricted to the third of Cicero's categories—time of year or day, which corresponds to the *auctor ad Herennium*'s "Point of Time." Boethius expresses this narrower sense of time when discussing the rhetorical circumstances, in his influential *De topicis differentiis* (4.1213.B): "The circumstance 'when' [Cicero] divides into time, for example, he carried it out by night, and opportunity, for example, when everyone was sleeping."[10] In practice, for medieval rhetoricians time as cause came to be understood above all as time of year and time of day. Matthew of Vendôme's *Ars versificatoria* (1.106–108) is typical in supplying only descriptions of the seasons to illustrate arguments based on the time of the action.

Time figures in a less direct but equally important way among the attributes of persons subsumed under the first of the rhetorical circumstances. Both Matthew of Vendôme (*Ars versificatoria*, 1.116) and Boethius (*De topicis differentiis*, 4.1212C–1215A) also note that while six of the seven circumstances derive from Cicero's attributes of actions, the first circumstance—"who?"—is identical to Cicero's attributes of persons. As formulated in *De inventione* (1.24.34–25.36), the eleven attributes of persons are "name, nature, manner of life, fortune, habit, feeling, interests, purposes, achievements, accidents, [and] speeches made" (*nomen, naturam, victum, fortunam, habitum, affectionem, studia, consilia, facta, casus, orationes*, 1.24.34). "Nature," the second of these, is further subdivided into "sex, ... race, place of birth, family, and age" (*sexu, ... natione, patria, cognatione, aetate*, 1.24.35); and "age" is in turn divided into several times of life, each with its own characteristic behavior. A fuller account of the various "times of life" (childhood, adolescence, adulthood, old age) is found in another classical text familiar to every medieval poet with a modicum of learning, Horace's *Ars poetica* (153–178):

> Now hear what I, and with me the public, expect. If you want an approving hearer, one who waits for the curtain, and will stay in his seat till the singer cries "Give your applause," you must note the manners of each age, and give a befitting tone to the shifting natures and their years. The child, who by now can utter words and set firm step upon the ground, delights to play with his mates, flies into a passion and as lightly puts it aside, and changes every hour. The beardless youth, freed at last from his tutor, finds joy in horses and hounds and the grass of the sunny Campus, soft as wax for moulding to evil, peevish with his counsellors, slow to make needful provision, lavish of money, spirited, of strong desires, but swift to change his fancies. With altered aims, the age and spirit of the man seeks wealth and friends, becomes a slave to ambition, and is fearful of having done what soon it will be eager to change. Many ills encompass an old man, whether because he seeks gain, and then miserably holds aloof from his store and fears to use it, or because, in all that he does, he lacks fire and courage, is dilatory and slow to form hopes, is sluggish and greedy of a longer life, peevish, surly, given to praising the days he spent as a boy, and to reproving and condemning the young. Many blessings do the advancing years bring with them; many, as they retire, they take away. So, lest haply we assign a youth the part of age, or a boy that of manhood, we shall ever linger over traits that are joined and fitted to the age.[11]

The discussion of age from Cicero and especially the passage from Horace were the chief sources of what the medieval rhetoricians called the "proprietates" of persons, which served at once as standards for judging the verisimilitude of literary representations of persons, as in Horace, and as guides for predicting and/or explaining the behavior of particular persons, as in Cicero.

It is very likely that Chaucer was familiar with the attributes of persons and actions, at least in the compressed form of the rhetorical circumstances, and there is no doubt that his use of arguments from time is both frequent and sophisticated.[12] Whether that familiarity came from formal study of textbooks on rhetoric or from reading and imitating ancient and medieval poetry is not particularly important. Because Chaucer used the rhetorical techniques in ways that are consistent with the sources I have just discussed, those sources provide a context and vocabulary for describing his practice that would have been readily understood by Chaucer's contemporaries.

Arguments from time based on the attributes of persons and actions are especially common in Chaucer's greatest works, *Troilus and Criseyde* and the *Canterbury Tales*. Indeed, the long, periodic sentence that opens the "General Prologue" to the *Canterbury Tales* is among the most famous examples of such an argument in all of English literature. Chauncey Wood acknowledged the rhetorical quality of these eighteen lines when he characterized them as an instance of "the astronomical periphrasis, sometimes called *chronographia*, ... in which the time of day, or time of year, is indicated by a circumlocution involving some reference to the motions of the heavens."[13] The astronomical periphrasis was recognized as a feature of poetry by rhetoricians both ancient and medieval. In describing the qualifications of a teacher of literature (*grammaticus*), for example, Quintilian observes: "nec, si rationem siderum ignoret, poetas intelligat, qui (ut alia omittam) totiens ortu occasuque signorum in declarandis temporibus utantur" ["nor again if he be ignorant of astronomy can he understand the poets; for they, to mention no further points, frequently give their indications of time by reference to the rising and setting of the stars" (*Institutio oratoria* 1.4.4)].[14] Likewise, the thirteenth-century English rhetorician Gervase of Melkley includes the device in his art of poetry and prose, in an appendix devoted to "rules specific to verse composition" (*regulae versibus speciales*):

> Perfection in a versifier does not write about winter, about summer, about night, about day without astronomy. In place of these words "dawn" or "a little before dawn," Juvenal says:

At that time when the stars are fading
And when the wagon of lazy Boetes drives slowly around.

> For it is proved by means of the astronomical movements that "the time when the wagon has been driven around" is a short time before daybreak.[15]

The reference to the sun's passage through the sign of Aries is a clear indication that Chaucer is working from the same tradition: "and the yonge sonne / Hath in the Ram his half cours yronne" (I.7–8).

However, the passage as a whole is much more than a simple *chronographia* whose chief, if not sole, purpose is to mark poetically the time of year when the action took place. Rhetorically speaking, Chaucer's invocation of the season is structured as a compressed argument or what could be called a "temporal enthymeme": eleven lines of seasonal cause ("Whan that Aprill": I.1; "Whan Zephirus eek": I.5) generate seven lines of volitional effect ("Thanne longen folk": I.12). It may be that Chaucer took much of the language and even the repetition of "when" from the opening of Guido delle Colonne's *Historia destructionis Troiae*,[16] but the comparison only underscores the crucial difference, since Guido's text lacks the cause-and-effect argument that distinguishes Chaucer's. The time of year, the springtime renewal of life, Chaucer seems to argue, by a complex causality brings about the urge to go on pilgrimages. The effect of this famous temporal enthymeme is all the greater because it depends on a reversal of expectation. Chaucer's audience was familiar with a causal connection between the coming of spring and human desire; but the traditional object of that desire was a sexual partner, recalled when Chaucer describes the libidinous "smale foweles" (I.9–11) just before he takes his argument in a surprising direction.[17] As Wood points out, the complex *chronographia* that opens the "General Prologue" is echoed by the equally complex *chronographia* that introduces the "Parson's Prologue" (X.1–12).[18] Time as beginning is balanced by time as ending at the two extremes of the frame narrative, so that the *Canterbury Tales* as a whole is enclosed within and perhaps even constituted as an argument from time.

Less complex examples of time as attribute of an action are not difficult to find. In the "Reeve's Tale," for example, the Cambridge clerk John is able to "swyve" miller Symkyn's daughter Malyne because it is after midnight and because the drunken sleep of her parents provides an opportunity to escape detection (I.4148–4187). It is probably coincidental but nonetheless interesting that "night" and "sleep" are the very examples that Boethius used to illustrate arguments from "time" and "opportunity," respectively. One reading of the "Franklin's Tale" sees the "yong clerk" of "Orliens" profiting from a different type of "opportunity" by exploiting his knowledge of seasonal high tides to convince Aurelius and Dorigen that he has caused the rocks to disappear from the coast of Brittany.[19] Chaucer's fabliaux provide examples of actions that depend on opportunities supplied by temporary absences, such as carpenter John's trip to "Oseneye," which allows "hende Nicholas" to make his intentions clear to Alisoun, in the "Miller's Tale" (I.3271–3306), or the Paris merchant's business trip to "Brugges," during which "daun John" the monk conducts his own business with the merchant's wife, in the "Shipman's Tale" (VII.299–324). In neither case are the "opportunities" incorporated into a true argument, however, unless it be the implicit argument that one ought not leave an attractive wife alone with a young man, no matter what the circumstances.

Because fabliau characters generally fit into well-defined categories, those same tales frequently draw on attributes of persons as well as those of actions and are thus especially rich sources of temporal causality in the sense of "age" or "time of life." Robin the Miller's account of the jealous old carpenter John (I.3221–3232) and Osewold the Reeve's self-depiction as the personification of old age (I.3867–3898) both explicitly invoke the "argumentum ab aetate." At the opposite end of the age spectrum, the portrait of the "yong Squier" in the "General Prologue" (I.79–100) is an exceptionally pure example of the argument from youth. A more extended example of the same argument comes from *The Book of the Duchess* (758–804). To account for his earlier propensity toward love, the Black Knight invokes the attribute "nature"—"I trowe hir cam me kyndely" (778)—and more specifically its subspecies "age": "For that tyme Yowthe, my maistresse, / Governed me" (797). A more ambiguous argument from age is the Prioress's comparison of herself to "a child of twelf month oold, or lesse, / That kan unnethes any word expresse" (VII.484–485), a move that aligns her with the "litel clergeon" of her tale, whose devotion is likewise expressed in a manner dictated by his youth (VII.505–515).

Like all good rhetorical techniques, such arguments from age are overdetermined, drawing on familiar, culturally potent beliefs to provide an immediate and therefore effective source of conflict in many Chaucerian narratives. For example, John the carpenter's old age is dramatically significant because his typical desire for control is at odds with his youthful wife Alisoun's equally typical desire for freedom:

> Jalous he was, and heeld hire narwe in cage,
> For she was wylde and yong, and he was old
> And demed hymself been lik a cokewold.
>   (I.3224–3226)

In the "Knight's Tale," the perspectives of the youthful Palamon and Arcite and the mature Theseus are opposed in more complicated fashion, though just as explicitly. Theseus himself draws attention to the opposition, even as he defuses the tension that only moments earlier had attended it:

> But all moot ben assayed, hoot and coold;
> A man moot ben a fool, or yong or oold—
> I woot it by myself ful yore agon,
> For in my tyme a servant was I oon.
>   (I.1811–1814)

The added perspective of the elderly Egeus (I.2837–2852) turns the tale into what might be called an "argument from the 'ages of man.'" The importance of age as a determinant of behavior and potential source of conflict in the "Knight's Tale" is further reinforced by the correspondence between the chief human characters and their divine counterparts—Palamon/Venus, Emelye/ Diana, Arcite/Mars, Theseus/Jupiter, and Egeus/Saturn—and the decisive role played by the older characters at both levels (see especially I.2438–2478).

Susanna Greer Fein makes a similar point about the Reeve, whose prologue describes old age in metaphors that prepare the reader for the subsequent tale's representation of life as a cycle extending from infancy (the baby in the cradle) to decrepitude (the college manciple on his deathbed). Even though the Reeve himself is old, however, in his tale it is not the voice of maturity that has the last word. Rather, says Fein, the cycle of life depicted by the Reeve is dominated by the conflict between adolescents, whose vigor is approaching its peak, and adults, who have passed their prime but strive to maintain their position of power with the aid of cunning acquired through experience.[20] The white-haired Franklin's words to the Squire (V.673–694) likewise underscore the gap between youthful aspiration and adult fulfillment. However, in place of the embittered Reeve's vision of inevitable strife, in which youth is destined to prevail, or the sterile dissipation that his own son prefers, the sanguine Franklin imagines the possibility of productive growth through cooperation between the wise benevolence of the older generation and the "gentil" enthusiasm of the younger generation, as embodied in the Squire. Accordingly, in the "Franklin's Tale," the young men "act like adults," resolving their conflicts in mutually beneficial fashion, whereas in the "Reeve's Tale," each of the principal male characters—the adolescents John and Aleyn, the adult Symkyn, and the elderly narrator Osewold—acts like a child, putting his own selfish interest above all else.

Along with "time of day or year" and "time of life," a third category of time as cause is important in Chaucer's works: "cosmic time." Although not identified as such in the standard teaching on the rhetorical attributes and circumstances, cosmic time, which includes but is not limited to astrological time, fits easily into the categories defined in the Ciceronian rhetorics and works derived from them. As an attribute of actions, cosmic time adds one more dimension to the usual significance of time of day or time of year. An especially famous Chaucerian example is the "fall" of Chauntecleer, which significantly occurs on Friday, May 3 (VII.3338–3354). In his rhetorical lament, which parodies the famous apostrophe on the death of Richard I (*Poetria nova*, 368–430) by the celebrated medieval rhetorician "Gaufred [of Vinsauf], deere maister soverayn" (VII.3347), the Nun's Priest underscores Friday's association both with Venus, who should have protected the amorous rooster, and with the equally lamentable death of King Richard. Chaucer's other references to May 3—

if that is indeed the date indicated by the Nun's Priest's convoluted mode of reckoning (VII.3187–3197)—suggest that he considered it an unlucky day.[21] A second example from the *Canterbury Tales*, also in the form of an apostrophe, is the Man of Law's lament that the Emperor of Rome failed to engage the services of a "philosophre" who could have warned him that the heavens were unfavorably disposed for a voyage by his daughter Custance (II.295–315). Whether or not the Man of Law's astrology is suspect on technical grounds, his causal argument is contradicted by the much greater power exerted by divine providence.[22] In both examples, the causal power of cosmic time is represented as more rhetorical than real, a fact that is underscored by its embodiment in a figure (apostrophe) that is among those most highly marked as rhetorical.

As an attribute of persons, cosmic time belongs together with "age" among the aspects of the attribute "nature." Cicero recognizes "place of birth" as a determiner of one's "nature," but for Chaucer, "time of birth" is even more important. In the *Canterbury Tales*, the argument from time of birth is employed to greatest rhetorical effect when the Wife of Bath blames her temperament and her life history on her horoscope:

> For certes, I am al Venerien
> In feelynge, and myn herte is Marcien.
> Venus me yaf my lust, my likerousnesse,
> And Mars yaf me my sturdy hardynesse;
> Myn ascendent was Taur, and Mars therinne.
> Allas, allas! That evere love was synne!
> I folwed ay myn inclinacioun
> By vertu of my constellacioun;
> That made me I koude noght withdrawe
> My chambre of Venus from a good felawe.
> Yet have I Martes mark upon my face,
> And also in another privee place.
>   (III.609–620)

Whether we regard cosmic time as a separate category or as an aspect of the two standard categories is less important than recognizing that it functions exactly as the attributes of persons and of actions to provide Chaucer with arguments from time.

Chaucer's use of arguments from time, like his use of other rhetorical techniques, is rarely as straightforward as the examples found in textbooks. As even the brief examples offered so far reveal, he is self-conscious and often ironic when employing such strategies. Perhaps for this reason, the tale in which arguments from time figure most prominently, that of the Merchant, is also one of the most deeply ironic of all the *Canterbury Tales*. Before concluding with an analysis of the arguments from time in the "Merchant's Tale," however, it will be useful to examine a counterexample, in which Chaucer's use of such arguments is more straightforward, at least on the surface.

Every variety of the argument from time discussed so far can be found in *Troilus and Criseyde*, with the greatest concentration of such arguments occurring in Book II, where Pandarus displays his repertoire of argumentative strategies to the fullest. Arguments from opportunity are invoked with special frequency, both implicitly and explicitly. The *chronographia* that opens Book II proper (II.50–56), for example, establishes the time of year as propitious to Pandarus's mission, and Pandarus makes that connection explicit when he urges Criseyde to put aside her mourning in favor of activities more suited to the season:

> Do wey youre barbe, and shew youre face bare;
> Do wey youre book, rys up, and lat us daunce,
> And lat us don to May som observaunce.
> (II.110–112)

The generally favorable quality of the month may be countermanded by the inauspiciousness of the specific day on which the visit occurs, but if May 3 is an unlucky day for love, Pandarus failed to discover that fact in his astrological calculations, since he "caste and knew in good plit was the moone / To doone viage" (II.74–75).

In the short term, Pandarus seems to have gauged his opportunity correctly, as confirmed by his finding Criseyde at leisure in a garden and learning from her that she had dreamed of him thrice during the previous night (II.89–90). Accordingly, he wastes no time in commencing the "paynted proces" (II.424) of rhetorical argument by means of which he hopes to persuade his niece to regard Troilus favorably. Among his specific arguments are several from time, including the argument that Troilus's infatuation itself represents a priceless opportunity that should be seized before its time passes:

> For to every wight som goodly aventure
> Som tyme is shape, if he it kan receyven;
> But if he wol take of it no cure,
> Whan that it commeth, but wilfully it weyven,
> Lo, neyther cas ne fortune hym deceyven,
> But ryght his verray slouthe and wrecchednesse;

And swich a wight is for to blame, I gesse.
Good aventure, O beele nece, have ye
Ful lightly founden, and ye konne it take;
And for the love of God, and ek of me,
Cache it anon, lest aventure slake!
  (II.281–291)

Later Pandarus emphasizes time's passage once again, this time in the equally conventional argument that since youth will not last, Criseyde should seize the day and give herself to love now, at the time of her life when it is still possible to do so:

Thenk ek how elde wasteth every houre
In ech of yow a partie of beautee;
And therfore er that age the devoure,
Go love; for old, ther wol no wight of the.
Lat this proverbe a loore unto yow be:
To late ywar, quod Beaute, whan it paste;
And Elde daunteth Daunger at the laste.
The kynges fool is wont to crien loude,
Whan that hym thinketh a womman berth hire hye,
'So longe mote ye lyve, and alle proude,
Til crowes feet be growe under youre ye,
And sende yow than a myrour in to prye,
In which that ye may se youre face a morwe!'
I bidde wisshe yow namore sorwe.
  (II.393–406)

Thanks to such arguments, Criseyde is highly susceptible when other favorable opportunities present themselves. After Pandarus has departed, timely occurrences such as Troilus's return from battle along a route that leads past Criseyde's window (II.610–686), Antigone's love song (II.824–903), and the dream–inducing song of the nightingale (II.918–931) help accomplish what rhetoric alone could not.

Pandarus is not the only character in *Troilus and Criseyde* who makes effective use of arguments from time. Another skilled rhetorician, Diomede, shows himself to be an even subtler appraiser of opportunity than Pandarus, though his remarks on the subject are addressed only to himself (V.88–175). Criseyde relies primarily on the argument from time of life in her attempt to persuade Troilus that she will be able to return quickly from the Greek camp. Like Horace, she defines old age in terms of blind avarice, an attribute that she is confident will enable her to manipulate her elderly father, Calchas (IV.1366–1400). If these and other arguments from time are undercut ironically, it is mainly through the cumulative impression of rhetoric's amorality conveyed by the poem as a whole. Every major character, with the crucial exception of Troilus, employs rhetorical arguments with equal effectiveness on opposite sides of the same issue. Only Troilus remains consistent, in the end fatally so. His arguments from time, as in the aubades of Book III (lines 1450–1470, 1702–1708) and his rebuttal of Criseyde, in which he defines old age in terms of worldly wisdom (IV.1455–1463), always support the same end, satisfaction of his desire to be with Criseyde. Chaucer leaves open the question which use of rhetoric is less appropriate. Viewed from the larger perspective offered at the poem's conclusion (V.1814–1869), the ends served by all of the rhetoric employed to varying degrees of effectiveness by Pandarus, Criseyde, Troilus, and Diomede are fundamentally flawed.

The arguments from time in the "Merchant's Tale," by contrast, are clearly and deliberately specious from a rhetorical (as well as a moral) standpoint. The Merchant is obsessed with time. Like Januarie, the protagonist of his tale, he is "hastif": He prefaces the tale by lamenting his imprudent marriage to a wife whom he already knows by experience to be "the worste that may be" (IV.1218), even though he has "ywedded bee / Thise monthes two, and moore nat, pardee" (IV.1233–1234). The Merchant's conviction that his two months as a husband have earned him the same authority to speak of woe in marriage as Alisoun of Bath's thirty years as a wife is the first sign that in his tale arguments based on time will follow a logic all their own.

Scarcely has the tale begun when Januarie's surprising decision to abandon his lifelong pursuit of "bodily delyt" (IV.1249) and take a wife "whan that he was passed sixty yeer" (IV.1252) is explained by a specious argument from time of life:

> And certeinly, as sooth as God is kyng,
> To take a wyf it is a glorious thyng,
> And namely whan a man is oold and hoor;
> Thanne is a wyf the fruyt of his tresor.
> Thanne sholde he take a yong wyf and a feir,
> On which he myghte engendren hym an heir,
> And lede his lyf in joye and in solas,
> Where as thise bacheleris synge "allas,"
> Whan that they fynden any adversitee
> In love, which nys but childyssh vanytee.
>   (IV.1267–1276)

The valid premise that young men who love beautiful young women are frequently unhappy does not support the conclusion that old husbands of such women will therefore be happy.

In a second, equally specious argument from time of life, Januarie draws on religious rather than literary conventions to explain "th'effect of his entente" to his assembled friends:

> With face sad his tale he hath hem toold.
> He seyde, "Freendes, I am hoor and oold,
> And almoost, God woot, on my pittes brynke;
> Upon my soule somwhat moste I thynke.
> I have my body folily despended;
> Blessed be God that it shal been amended!
> For I wol be, certeyn, a wedded man,
> And that anoon in al the haste I kan."
>   (IV.1398–1406)

Chaucer's strategy here is the same as in the argument from time of year that opens the "General Prologue." Just as there the accumulated references to the fecundity of spring created the expectation of encountering a solitary lover rather than a host of pilgrims, so here the expected conclusion to be drawn from Januarie's carefully stated premises is that he should retire to a life of prayer and penance rather than an earthly paradise of sexual pleasure.

While the first two arguments from time of life are undercut by logic and tradition, the third example is contradicted by the surrounding narrative and for that reason is the most bitterly ironic of all. The Merchant interrupts his description of Januarie and May's nuptials to exclaim:

> Whan tendre youthe hath wedded stoupyng age,
> Ther is swich myrthe that it may nat be writen.
> Assayeth it youreself; thanne may ye witen
> If that I lye or noon in this matiere.
>   (IV.1738–1741)

What may be written—Januarie's lustful fantasies and their disgusting fulfillment—turns out to be anything but mirthful, especially for May (IV.1750–1854). As demonstrated by the argument implicit in their seasonally opposed names, the union of Januarie and May goes against nature.

Besides the arguments from time of life, arguments based on time of year and cosmic time are similarly advanced only to be undercut ironically. Thus, the Merchant credits cosmic forces for May's quick decision to reciprocate the passion Damyan had declared for her in his opportune love note:

> Were it by destynee or by aventure,
> Were it by influence or by nature,
> Or constellacion, that in swich estaat
> The hevene stood that tyme fortunaat
> Was for to putte a bille of Venus werkes—
> For alle thyng hath tyme, as seyn thise clerkes—
> To any womman for to gete hire love,
> I kan nat seye; but grete God above,
> That knoweth that noon act is causelees,
> He deme of al, for I wole holde my pees.
>   (IV.1967–1976)

Here the irony is that no explanation is needed: The contrast between May's visit to Damyan's bedside and the ensuing session in Januarie's bed is sufficient cause for her decision (IV.1932–1966). Likewise, the effect of springtime on Januarie's desire to bring May to his custom-built garden, where they will perform "thynges whiche that were nat doon abedde" (IV.2051), only serves to underscore the systematic way in which the tale defies Horatian propriety by assigning youth's parts to an old man. Not only Januarie's name but also the explicit association of his garden with the garden in the *Roman de la rose*, from which Old Age is pointedly excluded,[23] combine to negate the argument from time of year, even though it is couched in the "olde lewed wordes" of Canticles (IV.2138–2149).

Behind the Merchant's and Januarie's ironic misuse of arguments from time, however, stands a deterministic view of time that is implicit in the rhetorical arguments discussed in this essay, in particular those based on time of life. Employed rhetorically, age becomes essence, inflexibly dictating behavior: The aging Januarie is doomed to foolish senility, moving from figural to literal blindness, while the youthful May and Damyan are equally driven to animal lust. Perhaps the Franklin's seemingly gratuitous yet pointed distancing of himself from rhetoric (V.716–720) is part of his strategy for replacing the Merchant's temporally determined essentialism with a vision that emphasizes responsibility and the human potential for change. Time, in itself, causes neither good nor bad actions. Like rhetoric, time can be used well or ill: Old age can bring folly, whether in the form of avarice, impotent lust, or intolerance of youth, but it can also bring wisdom. Paradoxically, this truth is recognized in rhetorical theory, which enumerates a range of attributes for each time of life, but tends to be suppressed in rhetorical practice, where reality is narrowed to facilitate the achievement of immediate ends. That paradox is never far from the surface when Chaucer uses time as a rhetorical commonplace.

NOTES

1. On the practical and scientific dimensions of time in Chaucer, see, for example, Linne R. Mooney, "The Cock and the Clock: Telling Time in Chaucer's Day," *Studies in the Age of Chaucer* 15 (1993), 91–109; John D. North, *Chaucer's Universe* (Oxford: Clarendon Press, 1988, reprinted 1991); F. J. J. Peters, "Chaucer's Time in the *Nun's Priest's Tale*," *Studia Neophilologica* 60 (1988), 167–170—hereafter cited in the text as Peters; Peter W. Travis, "Chaucer's *Chronographiae*, the Confounded Reader, and Fourteenth-Century Measurements of Time," *Disputatio* 2 (1997), 1–34; and Chauncey Wood, *Chaucer and the Country of the Stars: Poetic Uses of Astrological Imagery* (Princeton, NJ: Princeton University Press, 1970)—hereafter cited in the text as Wood 1970. The literature on the moral and theological dimension of time in Chaucer is even more extensive. Among the many studies that could be cited in this category are E. D. Blodgett, "Chaucerian Pryvetee and the Opposition to Time," *Speculum* 51 (1976), 477–493; Morton W. Bloomfield, "Distance and Predestination in *Troilus and Criseyde*," *Publications of the Modern Language Association* 72 (1957), 14–26; James Dean, "Time Past and Time Present in Chaucer's *Clerk's Tale* and Gower's *Confessio Amantis*," *English Literary History* 44 (1977), 401–418; Robert L. Entzminger, "The Pattern of Time in *The Parlement of Foules*," *Journal of Medieval and Renaissance Studies* 5 (1975), 1–11; Donald R. Howard, "The Philosophies in Chaucer's *Troilus*," in *The Wisdom of Poetry: Essays in Early English Literature in Honor of Morton W. Bloomfield*, ed. Larry D. Benson and Siegfried Wenzel (Kalamazoo, MI: Medieval Institute Publications, 1982), 151–175, 288–290; Thomas L. Martin, "Time and Eternity in *Troilus and Criseyde*," *Renascence* 51 (1999), 167–179; and Paul Beekman Taylor, "Time in the *Canterbury Tales*," *Exemplaria* 7 (1995), 371–393. Jörg O. Fichte argues that a thematically significant tension between literary and extraliterary conceptions of time pervades the *Canterbury Tales*: "Konkurrierende und kontrastierende Zeitmuster in Chaucer's *Canterbury Tales*," in *Zeitkonzeptionen, Zeiterfahrung, Zeitmessung: Stationen ihres Wandels vom Mittelalter bis zur Moderne*, ed. Trude Ehlert (Paderborn: Schöningh, 1997), 223–241. On the multiple and competing layers of time in Chaucer's works, see also two chapters from Paul Strohm, *Theory and the Premodern Text* (Minneapolis: University of Minnesota Press, 2000): "Fictions of Time and Origin: Friar Huberd and the Lepers" (pp. 65–79) and "Chaucer's *Troilus* as Temporal Archive" (pp. 80–96). For a wide range of perspectives on medieval conceptions of time and for additional bibliography on the subject, see the recent collection of essays edited by Chris Humphrey and W. M. Ormrod: *Time in the Medieval World* (Woodbridge/Suffolk: York Medieval Press/Boydell and Brewer, 2001).

The present essay originated as a paper presented in the session "Literary and Non-literary Concepts of Time in the *Canterbury Tales*," organized and chaired by Jörg O. Fichte, at the Eleventh International Congress of the New Chaucer Society, Paris, July 1998.

2. Larry D. Benson, ed., *The Riverside Chaucer*, 3rd ed. (Boston: Houghton Mifflin, 1987), 288; hereafter cited in the text parenthetically by fragment and line number.

3. On this tradition in general, see Ernst Robert Curtius's excursus "Brevity as an Ideal of Style," in *European Literature and the Latin Middle Ages*, trans. Willard R. Trask (Princeton, NJ: Princeton University Press, 1953), 487–494; hereafter cited in the text as Curtius.

4. See Geoffrey of Vinsauf, *Poetria nova*, 203–736—hereafter cited in the text as *Poetria nova*—and *Documentum de modo et arte dictandi et versificandi* II.2, ed. Edmond Faral,

Les arts poétiques du XIIe et du XIIIe siècle (Paris: Champion, 1924), 203–220, 271–284; hereafter cited in the text as *Documentum*.

5. See *Poetria nova* 87–202, and *Documentum* I, and the anonymous *Tria sunt*, Chapter 1. On the latter work, which is not yet available in a printed edition, see Martin Camargo, "*Tria sunt*: The Long and the Short of Geoffrey of Vinsauf's *Documentum de modo et arte dictandi et versificandi*," *Speculum* 74 (1999), 935–955.

6. Negotiis autem quae sunt attributa, partim sunt continentia cum ipso negotio, partim in gestione negoti considerantur, partim adiuncta negotio sunt, partim gestum negotium consequuntur. Cicero, *De inventione, De optimo genere oratorum, Topica*, ed. and trans. H. M. Hubbell (Cambridge, MA: Harvard University Press, 1949), 74 (text), 75 (translation). All quotations from *De inventione* are taken from this edition.

7. [Cicero], *Ad C. Herennium de ratione dicendi*, ed. and trans. Harry Caplan (Cambridge, MA: Harvard University Press, 1954), 68 (text), 69 (translation). All quotations from the *Rhetorica ad Herennium* are taken from this edition.

8. See, for example, Douglas Kelly, *The Arts of Poetry and Prose*, Typologie des sources du moyen âge occidental 59 (Turnhout: Brepols, 1991), 71–76.

9. A. J. Minnis, *Medieval Theory of Authorship*, 2nd ed. (Philadelphia: University of Pennsylvania Press, 1988), 16–17.

10. et eam quidem circumstantiam, quae est quando, dividit in tempus, ut nocte fecit, et in occasionem, ut cunctis dormientibus. J.-P. Migne, ed., *Patrologiae cursus completus*, Series latina, 64 (Paris, 1891), col. 1213B; English translation by Eleonore Stump, *Boethius's De topicis differentiis* (Ithaca, NY: Cornell University Press, 1978), 90.

11.   Tu quid ego et populus mecum desideret audi,
      si plosoris eges aulaea manentis et usque
      sessuri, donec cantor "vos plaudite" dicat,
      aetatis cuiusque notandi sunt tibi mores,
      mobilibusque decor naturis dandus et annis.
      reddere qui voces iam scit puer et pede certo
      signat humum, gestit paribus colludere, et iram
      colligit ac ponit temere et mutatur in horas.
      imberbis iuvenis, tandem custode remoto,
      gaudet equis canibusque et aprici gramine Campi,
      cereus in vitium flecti, monitoribus asper,
      utilium tardus provisor, prodigus aeris,
      sublimis cupidusque et amata relinquere pernix.
      conversis studiis aetas animusque virilis
      quaerit opes et amicitias, inservit honori,
      commisisse cavet quod mox mutare laboret.
      multa senem circumveniunt incommoda, vel quod
      quaerit et inventis miser abstinet ac timet uti,
      vel quod res omnis timide gelideque ministrat,
      dilator spe longus, iners avidusque futuri,
      difficilis, querulus, laudator temporis acti
      se puero, castigator censorque minorum.
      multa ferunt anni venientes commoda secum,
      multa recedentes adimunt. ne forte seniles
      mandentur iuveni partes pueroque viriles,
      semper in adiunctis aevoque morabimur aptis.

Horace, *Satires, Epistles and Ars Poetica*, rev. ed., ed. and trans. H. Rushton Fairclough (Cambridge, MA: Harvard University Press, 1929), 462/464 (text), 463/465 (translation).

12. Even scholarship that deals specifically with Chaucer and rhetoric typically does not concern itself with the attributes as sources of argument as much as with issues of style (including style as source of argument). An exception is Marjorie Curry Woods, "Chaucer the Rhetorician: Criseyde and Her Family," *The Chaucer Review* 20 (1985), 28–39. The attributes that are the focus of Woods's article, however, are not those involving time.

13. Wood 1970, 78. On 78–102, Wood traces the variations in Chaucer's use of this rhetorical device, especially in *Troilus and Criseyde* and the *Canterbury Tales*, where it is employed "for both elegance and parody" (83).

14. *The Institutio Oratoria of Quintilian*, vol. 1, ed. and trans. H. E. Butler (Cambridge, MA: Harvard University Press, 1920), 62 (text), 63 (translation).

15. Perfectio versificatori non hyemet, non estivet, non noctescat, non diescat sine astronomia. Iuvenalis loco istorum verborum mane vel paulo ante mane ait:

> Sideribus dubiis aut illo tempore quo se
> Frigida circumagunt pigri sarrata Boete
> Per motus enim astronomicos probatur sarrata circumacta esse modico ante diem.

Gervais von Melkley: Ars Poetica, Forschungen zur romanischen Philologie 17, ed. Hans-Jürgen Gräbener (Münster: Aschendorff, 1965), 214 (text); English translation by Catherine Yodice Giles, "Gervais of Melkley's Treatise on the Art of Versifying and the Method of Composing in Prose: Translation and Commentary" (Diss., Rutgers, 1973), 213, 215 note 6. For additional examples, see Curtius, 275–276.

16. See, for example, Muriel Bowden, *A Commentary on the General Prologue to the Canterbury Tales*, rev. ed. (New York: Macmillan, 1967), 20, and Wood 1970, 165–166.

17. A literary example of this convention that Chaucer certainly knew well is Guillaume de Lorris's evocation of May as the month of love and the time of year when his amorous vision appropriately occurred: *Le Roman de la rose*, 3 vols., ed. Félix Lecoy (Paris: Champion, 1965–1970), vol. 1, 45–86; hereafter cited in the text as *Roman de la rose*.

18. Wood 1970, 78, 92, 295–296.

19. See Chauncey Wood, "Of Time and Tide in the *Franklin's Tale*," *Philological Quarterly* 45 (1966), 688–711; revised as Chapter 6 (245–271) of Wood 1970.

20. Susanna Greer Fein, "'Lat the Children Pleye': The Game Betwixt the Ages in The Reeve's Tale," in *Rebels and Rivals: The Contestive Spirit in the* Canterbury Tales, Studies in Medieval Culture, 29, ed. Susanna Greer Fein, David Raybin, and Peter C. Braeger (Kalamazoo, MI: Medieval Institute Publications, 1991), 73–104.

21. See, for example, Wood 1970, 87 note 60, 162 note 2. Peters argues that line 3190 refers to the day on which the Nun's Priest recites his tale, April 19, but that the passage as a whole simultaneously invokes the day on which the events described took place, May 3.

22. See the Explanatory Notes in the *Riverside Chaucer* (pp. 858–60) for helpful commentary on the technical aspects of this passage and a concise summary of the critical debate, with bibliographical references. I am grateful to Joerg O. Fichte for reminding me of the Man of Law's apostrophe and its relevance to my argument.

23. *Roman de la rose*, 339–404, which includes an excursus on time and its ravages (361–392). See also the passage in which Reason contrasts Youth and Age: lines 4400–4514.

JOHN M. HILL

The Countervailing Aesthetic of Joy
in Troilus and Criseyde

Although one can have a theory of beauty—an aesthetic—without extending one's analytical categories into a theory of everything, no engaged aesthetic is fully tested without that. Current critiques of the aesthetic rightly reject what passes in many accounts: a formalistic, almost fetishistic focus on the literary work as an object removed from philosophical, social, and ideological contexts, from the variations and flow of human intellectual, social, and personal life.[1] Descriptions or studies of such an object can focus, then, only on reified techniques, conventions, structures, and, perhaps, the relationship of a given object to others like it or to identifiable source objects.

However, such analyses cannot quite escape larger issues because each variety of formalism—whether the New Critic's, the Chicago School's, the Structuralist's, or someone else's—posits a particular way of being for the literary work.[2] That way of being comprises standards of organization that are valid only if they can apply widely outside the work of art—as in physical or political worlds. The Chicago School, for example, is neo-Aristotelian. The classical text here would be Aristotle's *Poetics*, in which he presents an overview of tragedy as a genre, eventually on various grounds claiming that a few plays—*Oedipus Rex* among them—are qualitatively superior to all others, given the skillful prominence in them of great characters who make profound mistakes and who experience reversals, scenes of recognition, and

From *The Chaucer Review* 39, no. 3 (2005): pp. 280–297. © 2005 The Pennsylvania State University.

moments of acute awareness that accompany the audience's purgation of pity and fear. These events have to work together; they cannot seem to be arbitrary. The resulting plot form is something tragic poets *discovered* over time; they did not invent it, and, in Aristotle's opinion, they cannot perfect it beyond its materialization in Sophocles' hands. Plato disagrees with this view: human minds can only approximate the form of Tragedy to one degree or another. Inevitably, materialization corrupts pure form even as that form participates in whatever play has materialized. The closer the approximation to mentally envisioned form, the better, qualitatively; and the more quality the work or articulation possesses, the more beautiful it is. This standard also applies, of course, to whatever one would meditate upon as themes or subjects—whether in the world or in works of art—whether they be forms of Justice, Leadership, Love, Social Order, Loyalty, Friendship, Desire, or Delight. In these matters, the closer one comes to apprehending the fullness of form, the more beautiful that form is in one's apprehension. In short, as philosophical thinking about Justice, or whatever, matures in Plato's or in Aristotle's hands, it becomes aesthetic as the apparent beauty of form shines forth.

Along with other older writers and poets, Chaucer does not divorce his literary or artistic aesthetic from his social views. Indeed, he even commends *Troilus and Criseyde* for correction to philosophical Strode and moral Gower. In his works generally, and certainly in *Troilus and Criseyde*, Chaucer's overt philosophical commitment is to the kind of Platonism he finds in Boethius's *Consolation of Philosophy*, which he translates probably from a mixture of Latin and French sources. In Boethius, Chaucer finds something like a Platonic *noesis*, as Glaucon and Socrates define the matter in the *Republic*, Book 6: Glaucon divides that which is seen from that which is intellected; he then further divides the seen and the intellected in the same proportion as the original division. This yields four divisions, with awareness of sensory images being the largest area, followed by two equal areas of intellection: that of things, and that of the processes of thought. The fourth and smallest area is that of the intellection of forms.[3] Dialectic has beginnings and ends, and it uses hypotheses and images. The intellection of forms begins with hypotheses, and it uses the forms themselves, being free of images. For Chaucer, in accord with this scheme, opinion rooted in the senses is neither image (because mere sensory input is not intellected) nor thought; rather, it is merely notions about superficial phantasms or sensations. Chaucer's longest glosses in his translation of the *Consolation* are deeply Neoplatonic, having roots in the *Phaedo* and the *Meno*. Concerning the grounds for knowing rational truth in the deepness of thought, Chaucer paraphrases:

This is to seyn, how schulde men deme the sothe of any thing that
were axid, yif ther nere a rote of sothfastnesse that were yploungid
and hyd in the naturel principles, the whiche sothfastnesse lyvede
within the depnesse of the thought?
(*Bo* III.m.11.38–43)[4]

Judging the truth of something is possible, Chaucer might say, given forms
hidden within and informing the rational contours of our thoughts when we
confront the images we make of external things. This is how we perceive
truth in books as well as in experience, and how we come to know it. As
we come to know truth, we also know beauty, which is a qualitatively direct
outcome of truth, however variously, strongly, or weakly beauty appears in
individual instances. Thus the implicit categories of both philosophical and
aesthetic thought (as well as of ethics) are these: (1) forms; (2) things; (3)
characteristics in all things and thus individual characteristics, such as the
color yellow; and (4) participation of forms in the materiality of things as well
as of mental constructs.

I

In what ways does Chaucer extend a Neoplatonic or even Aristotelian
aesthetic into his thinking about beauty, ethics, joy, and the good in *Troilus
and Criseyde*? To address this question frontally, we need to move past the
emphasis in the critical literature on dramatic irony and Boethian satire,
which are, in my opinion, mind- and heart-saving efforts on our part, as they
were first for Chaucer, who clearly works such irony into the texture and
structure of his poem. The vast majority of commentators has noticed this,
and nearly everyone adopts some kind of distancing perspective on both the
pleasure in Book III and the pain Troilus experiences in Books IV and V.

From the perspectives of prudence, philosophical detachment, and right
religion, Troilus places all of his faith in the continuing joy and stability of a
world far from stable when he rests his love in and with Criseyde. He has no
resources for coping with her departure and eventual betrayal of him and his
love. As Alan T. Gaylord puts the matter for many other critics: "in terms of
the *Roman de la Rose*, of Dante, or of Boethius ... [their love] ... has not *taught*
them enough." We watch them discover "the universe of each other's arms"
somewhat fascinated by their failure to treat that discovery as simply "a very
attractive game." Had they been able think of their erotic universe as only a
game, then perhaps later they would be "less seriously trapped" and thus in
position to chasten and correct themselves.[5]

But much is slighted here. For the purposes of this essay, Gaylord stands in for any number of critics who, as a group, do not see what is special about Troilus's and Criseyde's joy, or what, in fact, Chaucer has achieved in the second half of Book III: a dramatization of sexually manifested joy that poses earthly joy and sufficiency in relation to philosophical or clerical felicity. Here and there in the critical literature, one can find moments of partial insight, but rarely is there a full acknowledgment of the lovers' joy. (I will note the exceptions in due course as I canvas those critics who have commented particularly on the pleasure shared by Troilus and Criseyde in Book III.) In Gaylord's reading, Troilus and Criseyde do apparently learn something, though not enough. But just *what* have they learned? We are not told. Apparently, also, we are fascinated by their serious involvement, but by *what* in their sexual embrace remains unclear. We can move away to various philosophical and moral perspectives—identified for Gaylord by the invocations of Strode and Gower—but *what* were we looking at so intensely before? Are the two lovers anything more than ignorant children in their embrace of each other? Are they curiosities? Do they momentarily enact for us something supremely desirable—say, sexual passion and harmony with no need for plans, with no fear, with no thought for future contingencies? I wish to argue that *that* is indeed the case, and that they enact for us a form of joy that Chaucer countenances and that Gaylord (along with many other readers) cannot accept. Instead, Gaylord would reform sexual and married love into something less intense: the joy of honest trust, loyalty, and devotion, all of which Chaucer expresses in the figure of Queen Alceste.

Certainly the case is complex. Given the dramatic intensity of an entangled set of relationships among Troilus, Pandarus, and Criseyde, where do Chaucer's likely philosophical and social views, along with his poetical aesthetic, lead him? Troilus's inner laugh from the eighth sphere is no guide if we ask where Chaucer might locate a humane center in an array of more or less enlightening and unenlightening experiences. Troilus has already passed out of his dramatic life in the poem. He is beyond even glimpsing badly a place of ethical balance. What about Criseyde and Pandarus in relation to Troilus? Pandarus ends up hating Criseyde—

"What sholde I seyen? I hate, ywis, Criseyde;
And, God woot, I wol hate hire evermore!"
    (V, 1732–33)—

and Criseyde herself is all too aware of having "slid" into betraying a true and noble heart. That awareness comes more or less after the fact, along with the knowledge that there is nothing good in what she has done:

> "Allas, for now is clene ago
> My name of trouthe in love, for everemo!
> For I have falsed oon the gentileste
> That evere was, and oon the worthieste!"
>   (V, 1054–57)

Experiential good and beauty in her world with Troilus come to fruition, if they ever do, for only a few days or weeks or months—this in Book III, which also contains the emotional high point in the great friendship between Pandarus and Troilus. My contention is that just here, between the middle and end of Book III, given every aspect of composition, but especially Troilus's partially insightful song to Love (III, 1744–71, itself largely transposed from *Bo* II.m.8), Chaucer poses the maximum of good and beauty that he can glimpse by means of an aesthetic seriously and ethically extended—that is, the maximum of good and beauty to be found outside of Christian belief and the dispensations of faith, which by their doctrines would foreclose Chaucer's exploration of worldly joy.

What Troilus experiences is a "joyful friendliness" (as Mark Lambert suggests), and then more—a new form of feeling.[6] He sees and feels much, even though John Frankis would deflate that sense of "much" by noting that Troilus's paganism still "makes his vision faulty," especially in its omission of "marriage as a manifestation of divine love."[7] To this stance, one might reply that the "lawe of compaignie," which Troilus does invoke, is not entirely vague, because the speech containing this phrase—

> "Love, that knetteth lawe of compaignie,
> And couples doth in vertu for to dwelle,
> Bynd this acord, that I have told and telle."
>   (III, 1748–50)—

parallels Boethius's "This love halt togidres peples joyned with an holy boond … [and] enditeth lawes to trewe felawes" (*Bo* II.m.8.21–25). This represents Troilus's idea of "marriage," of bound loyalty, virtue, and friendship unbreakable by any act of will he can imagine. Moreover, even before the consummation, he earnestly addresses Criseyde as his "fresshe wommanliche wif," assuring her that "trouth and diligence, / That shal ye fynden in me al my lif" (III, 1296–98), thus uttering words profoundly, movingly true in every point.

Troilus is nothing if he is not deeply earnest, even in his effusions and confusions. Paul Beekman Taylor misses this sincerity when he overemphasizes "the courtly language of his [Troilus's] nurture," as though that is all Troilus's speech often amounts to.[8] Unlike many readers, Taylor sees no change, not even a temporary one, in Troilus when he sings his song to Love, mainly because of a slim detail: Troilus refers to some attribute of Love as "his," a pronominal by which he supposedly "confuses person with principle."[9] Having said that, Taylor concedes that Troilus is sincere and true to Criseyde, and faithful in love—but not faithful to an idea of Love. It seems, to Taylor, that Troilus "fails to bring his language to a successful merging" of speech and idea in the matter of love. Thus Troilus stands condemned as merely speaking in an almost automatic, courtly idiom, with no real grasp of Love. I argue, however, that while Troilus cannot fully harmonize his partial insights into Love with his passionate feelings for Criseyde, he clearly reaches beyond the easy rhetoric of courtly terms (something Diomede, for example, does not do).

Passionate love of a human being would have to be seen as a lesser and mutable approximation of the great Boethian Good that encompasses all goods. What Troilus clearly does, in his own emphatic, paced words is declare his truth and fidelity in love once and for all. When readers focus on these passages, the majority of them simply do not accept the sexual joy of Book III as a great good in and of itself—perhaps Chaucer as a moralist would include himself among his readers in this matter. But Chaucer as poet does in fact produce moments of strong feeling and deep satisfaction. Two readers of an earlier generation, C. S. Lewis (1936) and Claes Schaar (1955), almost allow that satisfaction. Lewis thinks of it as partaking somehow of "an innocent smugness, as of a children's hiding-place," and Schaar feels that with Troilus and Criseyde "the limits of mere sensual delight are broken through, and what is finally described is an ecstatic bliss which appears capable of transforming their whole existence," that is, a prospective possibility.[10] But Schaar's phrase "appears capable" provides no more than a prospect. In citing Karl Young's 1938 essay on the poem as romance, Schaar seems to agree that "over Chaucer's scene plays the shimmer of romance, sublimating sensuality into a sensuousness of childlike innocence."[11]

In contrast, Helen Storm Corsa is one of very few critics who notice an adult joy here:

> [T]his book that had begun with comedy now becomes transformed by the lyrical ecstasy of the lovers [through their morning songs] into a book totally infused with joy that is both earthly and spiritual, physical and "divine." ... Although Book III never again mounts to the rapture of the first meeting, the rest of it is full of the happiness of the lovers.[12]

What Troilus glimpses in his love for Criseyde, in that joy, is something few ventured to say in print. One of those is E. Talbot Donaldson, who quotes Troilus's outsized, truly prophetic feelings, addressed to Criseyde:

> "Thorugh which I se that clene out of youre mynde
> Ye han me cast—and I ne kan nor may,
> For al this world, withinne myn herte fynde
> To unloven yow a quarter of a day!"
>   (V, 1695–98)

Donaldson asserts that Pandarus's hate and Troilus's love

> are the two simple attitudes to Criseyde that Chaucer has carefully nurtured—simple, but in combination infinitely complex.... It is sensible to hate what you have loved when it betrays you; but it is human to go on loving it if it once seemed better than anything you had known before, giving you glimpses of a world where experience is most rich and intense.[13]

This loving and hating can happen even in a drama now pitched to the anticipated tragedy of Books IV and V, and despite Donaldson's apparent gender bias, to which feminist critics such as Carolyn Dinshaw have responded.[14]

Rather than focusing on any particular perspective, or on reading like a man, as Dinshaw would have it, Donaldson emphasizes the *experience* Troilus has in Book III. Dinshaw sees this reading as the perspective that Troilus, Pandarus, the narrator, or the reader might assume regarding Criseyde herself, so that in the male gaze she becomes an unstable object and even a commodity of exchange between men. Only indirectly does Dinshaw note erotic joy in Book III, preferring to follow the narrator's vicarious participation in that joy.[15] When she considers Troilus, Dinshaw begins with his "individual courtly response to the female character—he is fascinated with Criseyde and desires to hold on to her—and the larger societal attitude that mandates that her desire must be able to transfer itself from man to man."[16] Troilus "enacts" this split especially when he offers his services to Pandarus early in Book III should Pandarus desire any of the aristocratic women to whom Troilus has access. Here Dinshaw senses that "this view of women as gifts, tokens of exchange, is more basic to the relations between men in Troy than is the view of women as singular and unique."[17] Because I have dealt elsewhere with this quasi-anthropological and contextually inadequate claim about women as exchange items in Troy,[18] I will here note only that Troilus hardly passes Criseyde to Diomede as a love object. In fact he complains despairingly to Pandarus that for Antenor his Criseyde is "lost" (IV, 378); and early in the poem he does not look at her as an object of exchange—her womanly pride and nobility are what strike him first:

> the pure wise of hire mevynge
> Shewed wel that men myght in hire gesse
> Honour, estat, and wommanly noblesse.
> To Troilus ...
> Gan for to like hire mevynge and hire chere,
> Which somdel deignous was ...
>   (I, 285–90)

From beginning to end it is the courtly attitude—that is, his individual response—that prevails, eventually leading to a materialization of great joy.

The experience in question and the form of joy it manifests depend very little on the line of dramatic action—that is a subject unto itself as Chaucer goes far beyond any medieval formula of tragedy and Fortune's wheel. Rather, contemplating tragic action is a way of reflecting upon the Good, upon love and beauty, upon poetry and rhetoric, insofar as the action in Book III brings us to esteem love, given whatever correction the narrator vouchsafes to those who have loved. When we find enactments or dramatizations of love both "rich and intense," we glimpse Love's truth positively. Insofar as we find what some call "love" either vile or base, we glimpse Love's truth negatively. In neither case in Chaucer's Neoplatonic universe do we see Love's truth whole, entire, blazing forth in all its fullness and beauty. Our positive and negative glimpses, as dramatized in Chaucer's poem, participate intimately in a great calm and a sense of sufficiency, the pleasure and "quiete" in which Troilus and Criseyde embrace each other as Book III ends. This joy, this positive delight,[19] unfolds into calm and rest, perforce excluding Pandarus, even though Troilus will take Pandarus by the hand and walk into the garden, speaking effusively to his great friend about Criseyde's "wommanhede, / And of hire beaute" (III, 1740–41). As though Pandarus knows that he can stand only to one side of this joy, the last we hear directly from him in Book III is his cautionary advice about worldly joy:

> "Bridle alwey wel thi speche and thi desir,
> For worldly joie halt nought but by a wir.
> That preveth wel, it brest al day so ofte;
> Forthi nede is to werken with it softe."
>   (III, 1635–38)

But just here, in Troilus's calm and rest, lies a deeper problem. Would a triad of sufficiency, delight, and quiet that is more than private include friendship and society? Could that delight of Troilus's and Criseyde's become nonsecretive and uncloistered? That it does not become so may indicate a key Chaucerian dilemma, or at least an implied question. The love between the two reaches an emotional, joyous sufficiency that is beautiful and in this sense aesthetic. But so long as it remains cloistered and secret, it does not broaden out to a public and social world, its beauty openly shining, as it were, over that outer world, however well it animates and enlarges Troilus's understanding, along with his personal, martial, and courtly behavior (as indicated in III, 1772–1806). Such mutual love does not show itself openly among social relations. Thus it lives only on the bedroom side of ethics. While such love brings great joy to Troilus and Criseyde, it only indirectly, through Troilus's public behavior, enhances joy in Troy (indeed that rhyme chimes ominously in Book III).

As I come to this point, however, I feel that Chaucer's story in some way outruns, by its tragic turn, its author's ethical and moral commitments. Effectively, and without one sensing Chaucer's ready pleasure in this, the story sails us all, first, into nights of substantial delight and, then, into a world of pain for which there is no philosophical remedy that Chaucer can embrace unambiguously and dramatically. The flux of experience, of painful change figured in Fortune's downward turn, has in itself no organizing forms, no subtending structures that would or might give organization, coherence, and meaning to that pain. That is, if he does not intellectualize pain as a (perhaps negative) instance of some form, Chaucer would have to accept some other way of gaining perspective. He might, for example, suggest an alterable structure of causes, effects, and choices by which pain might have been anticipated, averted, or ameliorated. If not that, perhaps he could have accepted a nearly relativistic, phenomenal view of flux: pain is just something that comes with intense experience and change, perhaps marking some qualitative aspect of that experience. Were he to go in this direction—something as an apperceiving artist he might countenance—he would contradict the medieval Christian in himself, the counterpart in him of philosophical Strode and moral Gower, the translator of Boethius's *Consolation of Philosophy*. Still, there are those moments in Book III, to which we should now turn in their particularized and rhetorically enhanced or elaborated contexts.

II

Almost forty years ago, Robert O. Payne accounted for the rhetorical disposition of ten lyrical passages in *Troilus* as "a kind of distillation of the emotional progress of the poem, held together by a thread of thematic imagery

in much the manner of a very condensed sonnet sequence."[20] Including
Troilus's great hymn to Love late in Book III, the ten passages participate in
a significant spacing of emotion and the high lyric plane that accompanies
the consummation scene and its immediate aftermath. For Payne, the lyrics'
content, imagery, and style fall under the category "elocution" and bring out
not only the emotional action of the poem but also the ironic perspectives
implicit in the presentation and framing of that action. In the concluding
stanza of Troilus's hymn to Love—

> "So wolde God, that auctour is of kynde,
> That with his bond Love of his vertu liste
> To cerclen hertes alle and faste bynde,
> That from his bond no wight the wey out wiste;
> And hertes colde, hem wolde I that he twiste
> To make hem love, and that hem liste ay rewe
> On hertes sore, and kepe hem that ben trewe!"
>   (III, 1765–71)—

the protagonist does seem to think erroneously about sexual love between
man and woman as like "the principle that controls the universe."[21] Yet, if
we remove this moment somewhat from Troilus's sexual feelings—after all
he sings in response to exfoliating to Pandarus of Criseyde's womanliness
and beauty—then we can see his lines about constraining cold hearts as a
partly comical counterpart to the line about love governing men's hearts in
Boethius's song: "O weleful were mankynde, yif thilke love that governeth
hevene governede yowr corages" (*Bo* II.m.8.25–27). Flying high over the
poem and thus at some remove from the individual contexts of the lyrics he
invokes, Payne's assessment accords easily with the kind of judgment D. W.
Robertson, Jr., brings to the religious imagery of Book III, and suggests that,
for Payne, Troilus's lyric Neoplatonism, in its excess and vagary, highlights an
accumulating standard of moral judgment in the poem.[22]

These are persuasive interpretations in harmony with Chaucer's
disposition of clearly Boethian perspectives throughout. But, even so, are
Payne and Robertson altogether right? Is Chaucer's own final judgment,
toward which he has tried systematically to lead the reader, aesthetically
and perceptually definitive? In the paragraphs that follow, I offer several
countervailing observations.

My basic propositions are as follows: first, that Book III is, from middle
to end, Chaucer's best effort at the dramatization of sexually manifested joy
between two beings on this mutable earth; and second, that, as such, his
drama poses earthly joy and sufficiency in relation to philosophical or clerical

felicity—especially in relation to the asserted Boethian felicity of that one Good which, in God, contains all others. By having his narrator comment on the inexpressible fullness of joy in Troilus's and Criseyde's hearts (III, 1310–11), Chaucer distinguishes the joy and security that Troilus and Criseyde achieve in their nighttime trysts from any other earthly felicity, for example, from the supreme good, "pleyn delit," and "verray felicitee parfit" of his later Franklin, Epicurus's own son (*CT*, I 337–38). While Traugott Lawlor hears something judgmental in the seemingly neutral "delit" of the Franklin, there is a countervailing effect, that is, a forcing of thought in another direction, in "pleyn."[23] Still, the hyperbole in "verray felicitee parfit" tells us that no felicity, however true to the form, is perfect in this world. All is always mixed with the distortions of particular, characterized moments and actions, such that one can go quite wrong, spinning the idea of felicity in a temporizing, self-serving way, as Criseyde does in Book V, where she sadly rationalizes her felicity as a current form of "suffissaunce" (V, 763), quite different from that of Book III. Still a negative instance of *felicitee* is valuable, pointing toward the better instance by virtue of clearly not being that better approximation.

This procedure of gathering positive and negative approximations of a form is consonant, by the way, with Aristotle's aesthetics (which is a branch of his philosophy), although for the idea of felicity rather than the idea of tragedy. As we gain a better idea of felicity from gathering together and meditating upon as many negative and positive instances as we can, we approach a qualitatively fuller sense of "felicity" and thus of beauty in the form. In this sense there is certainly an aesthetics of joy as there is of justice or anything else in either the Platonic or Aristotelian way of doing philosophy. Moreover, when Chaucer makes his narrator comment fussily on Troilus's and Criseyde's joy, saying that it exceeds everyone's powers of description such that not even the "felicite" that wise clerks commend can suffice here (III, 1691–92), Chaucer of course invites other and philosophically broader perspectives, with their apprehensions of variant forms of joy, while not dimming his focus on this joy Troilus and Criseyde share. Indeed, the narrator has no morally approved conceptualization for that joy; his comparisons fail him.

All of the narrator's invocations of temporal, clerical, or epicurean felicity participate, of course, in the form of Joy, to varying degrees. In addition, there is the narrator's turn to lovers—those who have feeling in love's art and who can further correct, amend, increase, or diminish the sense of joy and worth he asserts. This feeling is bodily memory—a memory of joy, one supposes, although other than calling it heaven's bliss, the narrator cannot quite name it. Troilus provides a lyrical approximation in the hymn to Love, which is outside the narrator's experience, and this produces an unsettling effect. Troilus has matured in his philosophical insights through the power of love deeply consummated in his sexual embrace of Criseyde. He has moved from one manifestation of joy—that of an at first frightened, somewhat hapless, and accidental conqueror in love ("yield now, for there is no other remedy" he says; "I already have, else I would not be here now," she replies [III, 1208–11])—to another (the deep content of two dear hearts mutually wound around each other, figured as a tree and a sweet vine, each being the other's tree, their arms the vines [III, 1230–32]). In this movement of maturation, Troilus has gone from one quality of experience to another.

In the immediate moments of the night, Troilus has been buffeted, going from sorrow to sweetness, from fear to rescue and gladness (III, 1240–45). More securely, however, where once Troilus had burned repeatedly with an ever-greater desire after whatever earlier progress Pandarus had brokered, now he burns no longer. Before morning, they have more than counterpoised past woe with present joy (III, 1406–7). They have recovered bliss and come into an ease with each other that neither has known before, the great worthiness of love. But morning and painful departure intervene. Troilus returns to his palace woebegone and restless. Sleep eludes him as he burns again with an ever-greater desire. Such burning may contain moral warning, which, if so, Troilus does not heed. But why he burns here is new: not for the Criseyde he sought, but for the Criseyde who is a thousand-fold "worth more than he wende" (III, 1540). Later that day he sends for Pandarus, whom he effusively and earnestly thanks for having brought his soul into heaven; Pandarus responds as a dear friend and offers careful advice. Then eventually he brings Troilus and Criseyde together again, such that they enter into that state of joy and surety in reenacted love the narrator calls "quyete" and "reste" (III, 1680). Hyperbolically, the narrator asserts that, if they were well together the first time, they now are a thousand-fold happier ("blithe" [III, 1682–84]). Inquiry into this state is utterly unnecessary; they had "As muche joie as herte may comprende" (III, 1687). While such joy is not that of intellection or contemplation, it is the joy of entwined lovers' hearts, a thousand times better than their first joy (although the lovers do not compare memories, and thus imperfectly realized forms in memory). Rather the narrator compares their joy now to the *felicitee* of wise clerks, which falls far short of this joy that "passeth al that herte may bythynke" (III, 1694). Hyperbolically and perhaps wryly, yet rationally enough given the superlative manifestation here of sexual joy, the narrator asserts that the form of this joy in the mind (heart) simply surpasses comparative thought. The events here are deliberately extended from moments of changeable sweetness and bliss to something larger, to a stable joy with no tinge of fear, no burning, and no need to perform for another's approval.

Might we, from the perspective of this development, think ahead to Troilus's disembodied laughter near the poem's end? Perhaps we can, by holding to the narrator's further comment before the *Canticus Troili* that Troilus has completely and narrowly enmeshed and tied himself (that is, his heart) with Criseyde's net of beauty and goodliness, such that

> The goodlihede or beaute which that kynde
> In any other lady hadde yset
> Kan nought the montance of a knotte unbynde
> Aboute his herte of al Criseydes net.
>   (III 1730–33)

The countervailing terms to "yknet," "narwe," and "ymasked" (enmeshed) (III, 1734) are those of worthy beauty and goodliness, along with the public subliming that occurs in Troilus's life: although of royal blood, he now finds a social form that derives from the achievement of joy in love. My argument here contrasts with Stephen Knight's oddly pragmatic view: that only for his lady's sake does Troilus sing to Love and fight well, the book's final stanzas showing a public prince handling "a reasonably successful and innocuous private love affair."[24] The narrator explicitly says otherwise: Love has "increased" him and "altered his spirit so withinne" (III, 1776–78). He is now in all of his peaceful, public activities and roles a figure of contentment, in a state of bliss and song. He is generous and sociable. Moreover, he is a figure of public virtue, of honor and largesse:

> And though that he be come of blood roial,
> Hym liste of pride at no wight for to chace;
> Benigne he was to ech in general,
> For which he gat hym thank in every place.
> Thus wolde Love—yheried be his grace!—
> That Pride, Envye, Ire, and Avarice
> He gan to fle, and everich other vice.
>   (III, 1800–1806)

Along with this increase in personal virtue, he receives gratitude from many. His service includes increased hardiness in the war, refreshment in the hunt for big game (he ignores small game), and sympathy and help for lovers who are worthy or in distress. Thus his gladness in love has expansive public effects even as love tightens his appreciation of Criseyde's beauty, graciousness, and virtue (her "goodlihede") in his heart.

So far these instances—the particular form this joy has taken for Troilus and Criseyde—have public and private effects. At the same time, the instances are temporal. They are, for a time, led by Fortune, of which there are many manifestations, and in relation to negative versions of which, joy, according to Pandarus, hangs by a wire or thread—that thread easily severed by such rash actions as boasting. Still, after Troilus's great song, Chaucer does not return to the imagery of nets and enmeshment. Rather, the narrator tells us that Troilus is a consummate warrior, second only to Hector, and a great hunter. Love increases Troilus in every way. Even partially grasped, philosophical wisdom is one of his augmented attributes, as is shown in his song's Boethian claim that Love holds the discordant elements in a perpetual bond, governs the seasons, has couples dwell in virtue, knits the law of friendship, joins people together, and has heaven and earth in his governance.

While eternity and Fortune's wheel are the flies in this happy ointment, the *aesthetic features* here—that is, the informing form, as well as the beauty of extended moments remarkably full of the feelings and physical details of sexual love and joy—are Venus-blest and Muse-guided to full expression ("Thorugh yow [Venus, Cupid, and Muses] have I seyd fully in my song / Th'effect and joie of Troilus servise" [III, 1814–15]). These aesthetic features mark the narrator's song of pleasure, delight, and calm (as "in lust and in quiete" [III, 1819]). Such joy and its effects are otherwise unknown, unexpressed, and unachieved in this world, whether in Troy or in a Troy that stands for any place experiencing Fortune's happiest turn before its cruel siege.

While public and private effects are not integrated in the open, they are for Troilus causally linked. The various manifestations of joy—that is, Pandarus's statement ("worldly joie halt nought but by a wir" [III, 1636]); Troilus's relative experiences; and the narrator's introduction of a felicity that combines epicurean delight in one direction and the supreme Boethian Good in another—all give us either positive or negative glimpses of the universal form of Joy in which all manifestations of joy participate, individually particularized, characterized, and set in relation side by side. Those manifestations are, of course, physical: we can have no characteristics without a particular in which they inhere nor a particular uncharacterized. Thus part of Criseyde's beauty is certainly physical, part comprises her welcoming manner, and part her emotions. When the narrator describes her, after her fear has passed and she has opened her heart to Troilus, what comes first are emotive qualities, before the impending caresses of her physical qualities. We have her and Troilus thus:

> Hire armes smale, hire stregthe bak and softe,
> Hire sydes longe, flesshly, smothe, and white

He gan to stroke, and good thrift bad ful ofte
Hire snowissh throte, hire brestes rounde and lite.
Thus in this hevene he gan hym to delite,
And therwithal a thousand tyme hire kiste,
That what to don, for joie unnethe he wiste.
    (III 1247–53)

A modern aesthetic, spun in addition censoriously, could see this description as almost "scopophilic," that is, as voyeuristic in some crippled way, even as a disguised form of rape, the woman reduced to an assemblage of physical parts. Such an aesthetic would not be Chaucer's, and it seriously misconceives these lines. To further illuminate Chaucer's aesthetic here, a foray into scopophilic misdirection is instructive. Robin R. Hass offers just such a view in her essay on evocative *effictio* in the handbooks of medieval rhetoricians, mainly Matthew of Vendôme and Geoffrey of Vinsauf (a name Chaucer prominently invokes when discussing invention and rhetoric). When Hass claims, for example, that Matthew of Vendôme thinks the "commendable characteristic of a female rests in her physicality," she ignores everything in the handbooks and in rhetorical scholarship that indicates how characterized particulars always approximate something else—the idea of Beauty or Age or whatever they participate in (beauty in the mind is an idea of form).[25] While Matthew may enjoy his *effictio* of dainty breasts and golden hair, he suggests Beauty rather than minutely rendered curvatures and attractions of the flesh. As for Geoffrey of Vinsauf, in Hass's hands he presents all women as the same, seeing all others in one woman. This postmodern *reductio* misses what otherwise Hass almost sees: that Geoffrey would instruct us in the making of a "generalized exemplum," from which a kind of radiance might go forth, striking the beholder's eyes and maddening his heart. This would be the radiant, aesthetic reflection of Beauty, not an aesthetic of something to be possessed or possibly feminized (as Hass puts it, poetic meter being "aestheticized and feminized in Geoffrey's hands").[26]

Such views seriously mistake the formal Neoplatonic functioning of medieval rhetoric, and thus of *effictio*, where the characteristics of a particular are still more general or conventional than idiosyncratic and where the general idea is what the individual characteristics approximate. Douglas Kelly rightly provides the underlying rationale for the textbooks of the Second Rhetoric (which include the handbook of Geoffrey of Vinsauf).[27] He sees those textbooks as recommending a magisterial, controlling rhetoric. The imagination moves from particular images and ideas to the mental forms those images imitate or else represent; moreover, those representations by description and other devices are amplifications in a top-down procedure, suggesting an ineffable reality beyond the senses, yet a reality somehow available to the mind through rational forms.[28] Hass may be right in detecting some erotic interest in the exemplary presentations of female beauty, but she misses the general ideology involved and then gets into deeper trouble when she turns to Chaucer, who is hardly magisterial in his poetical procedures, however much he owes to a medieval rhetorical poetics.

Consonant with the general outline Douglas Kelly presents, Payne notes that, in relation to old stories, devices of amplification and abbreviation produce a labor of style that seeks both the affective and the effective in "the rearrangement and emphasis achieved."[29] Although a kind of instructional poetry is possible in these terms, they do not describe the total impact of the poetry that results: "verbal embroidery" can radically alter both the colors and the patterns of the poet's source text or texts, thus becoming recreative in surprising ways. As a dynamic of change enters the process of emphasis and affective heightening, much can happen for which the textbooks are unprepared. We begin to deal with shifting meaning, ambiguity, and all the openness of referential systems.

In Troilus's case, after he caresses Criseyde he goes on to sing of love and charity; then, after kissing her again, he inquires how he might please his "herte swete" (III, 1278). These actions suggest something quite different from scopophilia, on his part at least. For Troilus, I see transport, passion, and sensitive intimacy. When Troilus begins to sigh heavily and repeatedly, holding Criseyde firmly in his arms (III, 1359–65), the narrator assures us that his are not the sighs of a sorrowful man or a sick one but rather the sighs that show "affeccioun withinne":

Of swiche sikes koude he nought bilynne.

Soone after this they spake of sondry thynges
. . . .
And pleyinge entrechaungeden hire rynges.
    (III, 1364–66, 1368)

Because of those easy sighs overtaking Troilus, one can justifiably suppose that here sexual consummation occurs, following the course of kisses and tender intimacy; that too is a characteristic of this particular moment of joy, just as Criseyde's physical beauties of limb, body, throat, and breast are physical manifestations of the form of beauty reflected in her.

But at the social and personal level, in matters of love between human beings and in affairs of comportment and virtue between man and men, the aesthetic of joy has produced its fullest possible primary expression and secondary effects. At least that is the narrator's assessment, and it is, I think, Chaucer's as well. This love in the closing lines of Book III is a culmination of

> Th'effect and joie of Troilus servise,
> Al be that ther was som disese among.
>   (III, 1815–16)

Here we do not have a uniform joy or something artificial. Rather, unhappiness or unease accompanies it, perhaps mainly in the emotional disturbances of early morning separation.

Still, the dominant note is that "Troilus in lust and in quiete / Is with Criseyde, his owen herte swete" (III, 1819–20). This is, of course, Troilus's, not Criseyde's, dominant note, although Fortune for a time also leads Criseyde "in joie" (III, 1714). As Henry Ansgar Kelly has taught us, we need to acknowledge this necessary achievement if we are eventually, in the hard and cruel course of Books IV and V, to feel the full weight of Troilus's loss and the poem as tragedy.[30] Chaucer's aesthetic of joy is real, necessary, and productive for a time of deep emotional good in Troilus's private life, even as it shapes an expansive liberality, virtue, and hardiness in his public life. Both privately and publicly, his is a princely form enlarged, not corrupted. This joy depends very much on the sufficiency of the two together. It does not depend "on the loss of the object," nor does it reflect, as L. O. Aranye Fradenburg further claims, "the inscriptions of trauma within the unconscious" of the characters or the poem.[31]

While contemplating a joy dependent upon trauma or eventual loss may seem an odd way to end, the relevance of Fradenburg's position on joyousness in the poem is clear when we consider that, while formulated from within a very different philosophical and psychological milieu, her view touches negatively on the poem's aesthetic of joy. One might transform notions of trauma and loss as allowing for a beauty wounded and mutilated in an undecidable way—joy deformed by a struggle with trauma or defined and hedged in by the near eventuality of loss. Such "joy" would be merely an approximation of joy, albeit a negative one, and oddly in tune with the moral disapproval or disquiet of so many of Chaucer's twentieth-century critics.

NOTES

1. What cripples the New Critical aesthetic for its critics is the willful effort to contain meaning and reference solely within the object—referring and reflecting terms of the object itself—inevitably a confused effort because no language system or scheme sealed off from our rough world and wide can remain comprehensible. David Aers, despite his Marxist leanings, offers a representative version of this point for most postmodern critics:

"The reflexive imagination is a powerful dissolvent of what Gouldner calls 'objectivism,' discourse which, 'one-sidedly focuses on the object' but occludes the speaking 'subject' to whom it is an object" (*Chaucer, Langland and the Creative Imagination* [London, 1980], 82; see Alvin W. Gouldner, *The Dialectic of Ideology and Technology* [London, 1976], 45). The product of imagination is deeply contingent on its creator, its language, and the public world that makes that language public. Thus critics of "the aesthetic" seen in the terms indicated above rightly expose a reifying process and call it aestheticism. What they miss here, however, is the issue of quality—more precisely, the analytical categories by which the formalist aesthete addresses that issue.

2. Raymond Williams, to take a particularly insightful case, agrees that "we have to reject 'the aesthetic' both as a separate abstract dimension and as a separate abstract function. At the same time we have to recognize ... the specific variable intentions and ... responses that have been grouped as aesthetic in distinction ... in particular from information and suasion. Indeed, we cannot rule out, theoretically, the possibility of discovering certain invariant combinations of elements within this grouping, even while we recognize that such invariant combinations as have hitherto been described depend on evident processes of supra-historical appropriation and selection" (*Marxism and Literature* [Oxford, 1977], 155). Different categories of analysis comprise those "certain invariant combinations" for different aesthetics—all of which from Plato to Hume to Peirce to Shilling and beyond of course arise in specific cultural moments and are selected and refined. Although Williams does not recognize different foundations for different aesthetics, thinking of New Criticism, a Pater-like intensity, and structuralist thought as alike Formalistic, he does understand that whatever "grouping" one makes is not a way of assigning even relative value (157). One aesthetic system is as valid as another, rooted differently though the two might be; no aesthetic system is without weaknesses. For extended accounts of radically different aesthetic and philosophical frameworks, see Stephen C. Pepper, *World Hypotheses: A Study in Evidence* (Berkeley, Calif., 1942); for a complex taxonomy of philosophical thought, see Richard McKeon, "Philosophic Semantics and Philosophic Inquiry," in *Freedom and History and Other Essays*, ed. Zahava K. McKeon (Chicago, 1990), 242–56.

3. See Alan Bloom, trans., *The Republic of Plato* (New York, 1968), 190–92, 464.

4. All citations of Chaucer are from *The Riverside Chaucer*, ed. Larry D. Benson, 3rd ed. (Boston, 1987).

5. Alan T. Gaylord, "The Lesson of the *Troilus:* Chastisement and Correction," in *Essays on Troilus and Criseyde*, ed. Mary Salu, 23–42 (Cambridge, Eng., 1979; repr. 1991), 23–42, at 30.

6. Mark Lambert, "*Troilus*, Books I–III: A Criseydan Reading," in *Essays on Troilus and Criseyde*, ed. Mary Salu (Cambridge, Eng., 1979; repr. 1991), 105–25, at 120.

7. John Frankis, "Paganism and Pagan Love in *Troilus and Criseyde*," in *Essays on Troilus and Criseyde*, ed. Mary Salu (Cambridge, Eng., 1979; repr. 1991), 57–72, at 63–65.

8. Paul Beekman Taylor, *Chaucer's Chain of Love* (Madison, Wisc., 1996), 83.

9. Taylor, *Chaucer's Chain of Love*, 83.

10. C. S. Lewis, *The Allegory of Love* (London, 1936), 196–97; Claes Schaar, *The Golden Mirror: Studies in Chaucer's Descriptive Technique and Its Literary Background* (Lund, Sweden, 1955), 37.

11. Karl Young, "Chaucer's *Troilus and Criseyde* as Romance," *PMLA* 53 (1938): 38–63, at 46.

12. Helen Storm Corsa, *Chaucer Poet of Mirth and Morality* (Notre Dame, 1964), 62–64.

13. E. Talbot Donaldson, *Speaking of Chaucer* (New York, 1970), 83.

14. Carolyn Dinshaw, *Chaucer's Sexual Poetics* (Madison, Wisc., 1989).

15. Dinshaw, *Chaucer's Sexual Poetics*, 44.

16. Dinshaw, *Chaucer's Sexual Poetics*, 61.

17. Dinshaw, *Chaucer's Sexual Poetics*, 61.

18. See John M. Hill, "Aristocratic Friendship in *Troilus and Criseyde:* Pandarus, Courtly Love and Ciceronian Brotherhood in Troy," in *New Readings of Chaucer's Poetry*, ed. Robert G. Benson and Susan J. Ridyard (Cambridge, Eng., 2003), 165–82, esp. 172–77.

19. On the predominantly negative sense in which Chaucer uses *delit* in the *Tales*, see Traugott Lawlor, "Delicacy v. Truth: Defining Moral Heroism in the *Canterbury Tales*," in *New Readings of Chaucer's Poetry*, ed. Robert G. Benson and Susan J. Ridyard (Cambridge, Eng., 2003), 75–90.

20. Robert O. Payne, *The Key of Remembrance* (New Haven, 1963), 186.

21. Payne, *Key of Remembrance*, 295.

22. See D. W. Robertson, Jr., "Chaucerian Tragedy," in *Chaucer Criticism:* Troilus and Criseyde *and the Minor Poems*, ed. Richard J. Schoeck and Jerome Taylor (Notre Dame, 1961), 86–121.

23. Lawlor, "Delicacy v. Truth," 78.

24. Stephen Knight, *Geoffrey Chaucer* (Oxford, 1982), 54.

25. Robin R. Hass, "'A Picture of Such Beauty in their Minds': The Medieval Rhetoricians, Chaucer, and Evocative *Effictio*," *Exemplaria* 14 (2002): 384–422, at 389. Hass does not deal with *TC*, explicating instead the Miller's portrait of Alisoun.

26. Hass, "Picture," 398.

27. Douglas Kelly, *Medieval Imagination: Rhetoric and the Poetry of Courtly Love* (Madison, Wisc., 1978), 1978.

28. Kelly, *Medieval Imagination*, 28.

29. Payne, *Key of Remembrance*, 48.

30. Henry Ansgar Kelly, *Chaucerian Tragedy* (Woodbridge, Suff., 1997).

31. L. O. Aranye Fradenburg, *Sacrifice Your Love: Psychoanalysis, Historicism, Chaucer* (Minneapolis, Minn., 2002), 227, 229.

Chronology

1340–1343	Possible birth of the poet, Geoffrey Chaucer, to John (a wine merchant) and Agnes Chaucer. In all probability, the poet was born in the family home on Thames Street.
1346	Victory over France at Battle of Crécy.
1347	Geoffrey, now about seven years of age, moves with his parents, his older brother John and probably his younger sister Kate, to the city of Southampton. By now, Chaucer has probably learned to read a little with the help of a clerical tutor back in London and is probably studying with the schoolmaster of his district, receiving lessons in manners, prayers, hymns, and the rudiments of reading and writing Latin. Truce between England and France. The Black Death reaches England. By October, it has reached London. In 1348, Parliament is cancelled and many schools closed down.
1349	The Chaucer family is back in their Thames Street house in London. Geoffrey begins school somewhere in the Vintry Ward area, probably the Almonry Cathedral School attached to St. Paul's. By mid-century, this school had an unusual schoolmaster, William Ravenstone, who possessed a large collection of books in Latin, including a large number of the classics. It is quite possible that the poet, who demonstrated an unusual knowledge of the classics

from a young age, acquired this learning from Ravenstone's library. St. Paul's also inherited works of grammar, logic, natural history, medicine and law from William Tolleshunt in 1328, which the poet would have had the opportunity to use. However, the subjects Chaucer principally dealt with were the *trivium*—grammar, logic and eloquence.

1350	Late in the year, the first wave of pestilence is finished, having killed as many as twenty-five million people, between one-fourth and one-third of the population of Europe.
1350s	Alliterative poetry is again popular in northwestern and western England.
1351	First "Statutes of Laborers" attempts to fix wages and control the labor movement in the period of labor shortages after the Black Death.
1353	Boccaccio writes the *Decameron*.
1356	Battle of Poitiers, high point of England's success in the Hundred Years' War with France. King John of France is captured, and he and his retainers live in the English court for three years.
1357	By now, at least sixteen years of age, Chaucer is serving as a minor member of Elizabeth's household, the Countess of Ulster and wife of Prince Lionel (Edward III's second son). In May, Chaucer receives as a gift from her a complete set of clothes, and in December, receives money for the "necessities at Christmas." In all likelihood, Chaucer was an assistant to superiors in his daytime labors and, in the evening, like most courtiers, entertained with music, poetry, or conversation on noble and interesting subjects—though always deferential and patient in his speaking since he was neither borne of a noble family nor bred in that tradition. Phillippa Pan is also in household. Chaucer probably serves here for three years. It is during his trip to Hatfield for the Christmas holidays, that Chaucer possibly meets the young man who will become his lifelong friend and advocate, Prince Lionel's younger brother, John of Gaunt, already an impressive figure at the age of seventeen.
1358	The funeral of Queen Isabella is held on November 27; Chaucer may have been in attendance.
1359–1360	In May, John of Guant marries Blanche of Lancaster. Chaucer may have been in attendance. Gaunt becomes Duke

	of Lancaster. On October 28, Chaucer, the Black Prince, and Gaunt are at war with France in Prince Lionel's company.
1360	Chaucer is captured by French soldiers. King Edward III contributes funding to help pay Chaucer's ransom. Chaucer carries letters to England from Calais for Lionel, earl of Ulster. Treaty of Bretigny ends the first phase of the Hundred Years' War.
1361	Chaucer likely receives legal education at the Inns of Chancery and may have attended Oxford as well. A terrible second wave of black plague strikes.
1361–1367	Chaucer works on *Prior a Nostre Dame*, *Romance of the Rose*, and early Complaints.
1363	Death of Countess of Ulster.
1365-1366	Chaucer marries Philippa Pan, first daughter of Paon de Roet (in the household of Queen Philippa) and sister of Katherine (later mistress and third wife of John of Gaunt, Duke of Lancaster).
1366	February 22–May 24, Chaucer receives safe conduct to travel in Spain where he acquires at least one strong image for his poetry in *The House of Fame*—a mountain of ice with a building on top. Chaucer's father dies and his mother remarries.
1367	Geoffrey Chaucer granted royal annuity of 20 marks as he enters the King's service as an esquire of the royal household. His son Thomas is born. Edward, Prince of Wales leads an expedition to Spain in aid of Pedro the Cruel, the deposed King of Castile. For the first time, the king addresses parliament in English rather than French.
1368	Death of Blanche, John of Gaunt's wife and Duchess of Lancaster. French war is again active. Chaucer is sent on a mission in France.
1368–1369	Probable date of Chaucer's *The Book of The Duchess*—an elegy to John of Gaunt's first wife, Blanche of Lancaster, and a tribute to Gaunt. Chaucer writes "Fragment A" of *The Romance of the Rose*.
1369	Chaucer serves with Gaunt in raid on Picardy. Death of Queen Philippa. Philippa Chaucer possibly enters Gaunt's household as a lady in waiting. Hostilities resume in the Hundred Years' War, marking the second major phase of military engagement.

1370	June 20–September 29, Chaucer possibly runs diplomatic errands in France for the King and may be with John of Gaunt in Aquitaine.
1371	Gaunt marries Princess Constanza of Castile, King Pedro's daughter.
1373–1377	*Parliament of Fowles*; "St. Cecelia"; The Monk's tragedies; and *Anelida*.
1372	Katherine Swynford, sister of Philippa Chaucer, bears first son by Gaunt. On August 30, Gaunt grants Philippa Chaucer annuity of £10. On December 1, Chaucer is commissioned to establish an English seaport for Genoese trade. To this end for "other matters of the king's business," Chaucer leaves for Genoa, visits Florence. At this time, Boccaccio is in Florence and Petrarch is in Padua. Chaucer remains in Italy until the summer of the next year.
1373	On May 23, Chaucer returns to London. Possible birth of Thomas Chaucer. On July 13, Gaunt goes to French wars.
1374	On April 10, Gaunt returns from French wars. He takes control of the government while Edward III shows signs of increasing senility. The Black Prince falls ill. On April 23, Chaucer receives a royal grant of a pitcher of wine daily. On May 10, Chaucer leases Aldgate house and sets up housekeeping. On June 8, Chaucer is made Comptroller of Wool Customs and Subsidy for the Port of London (a lucrative and powerful position). On June 13, Geoffrey and Philippa receive £10 annuity from Gaunt. Death of Petrarch.
1375	Death of Boccaccio. John Barbour's poem "The Bruce" is completed. Truce of Bruges temporarily ends hostilities between England and France.
1376	Edward, the Black Prince, calls the Good Parliament to convene, which introduces many long overdue reforms of government. Chaucer begins early trips to France on diplomatic missions negotiating for peace. Death of Edward, the Black Prince, at age 45. Parliament impeaches royal servants belonging to the faction of John of Gaunt, the king's fourth son. The *Civil Dominion* is published by Oxford don, John Wycliffe, calling for reforms in the church.
1377	February 17–April 30, Chaucer is on missions in France concerning peace treaty and marriage of Richard. He also

probably travels to Italy (Milan) on diplomatic missions. John Gower and Richard Forester have Chaucer's power of attorney while he travels abroad. On June 22, Edward III dies and his grandson, Richard II assumes the throne at age 11. The government is controlled by Gaunt. Poll tax levied. The papacy returns to Rome from Avignon, where it had resided since 1309. Pope Gregory XI condemns the doctrines of John Wycliffe. The Lollard movement grows.

1378   January 16–March 9, Chaucer is in France concerning marriage of Richard to French king's daughter Marie. May 28–September 19, Chaucer is in Lombardy to treat with Barnabo Visconti (Gower is given Chaucer's power of attorney). The Great Schism: Pope Gregory XI dies. The French-dominated College of Cardinals is intimidated by the Roman mob into choosing an Italian candidate, Pope Urban VI, as head of the church. Urban upsets the cardinals, who declare him deposed, and elect a Frenchman, Clement VII. Clement sets up papal court in Avignon, but Urban continues holding court in Rome. England, Scandinavia, Germany, and northern Italy support the Roman Pope. France, Scotland, Naples, Sicily, and the kingdoms in Spain support the French Pope. This schism will remain unreconciled until a truce in 1409 and reunion in 1417.

1378–1381   House of Fame (probably 1380, as it references the negotiations toward Richard II's marriage to Anne of Bohemia, 3 May, 1381); Boethian balades; Palamon and *Anelida and Arcite*.

1380   On May 1, Chaucer is released from suit for "raptus" of Cecily Champain. Birth of Lewis Chaucer (for whom Chaucer wrote the *Treatise on the Astrolabe* in 1391).

1380–1382   Chaucer writes *The Parliament of Fowls*.

1381   Peasant's Revolt—Gaunt's palace at Savoy is the number one target. June 19: deed of Geoffrey Chaucer, son of John Chaucer, vintner of London, quitclaiming his father's house.

1382–1386   Chaucer write *Troilus and Criseyde*, *Legend of Good Women*. Langland is working on *Piers Plowman*, C Text.

1382   Richard II marries Anne of Bohemia. John Wycliffe and his Lollard followers complete the first full English translation of the *Bible*.

1383	Chaucer obtains first loan against his annuity, possibly the first sign of financial troubles.
1384	John Wycliffe dies.
1385	Eustache Deschamps sends Chaucer a poem lauding Chaucer as "great translator, noble Geoffrey Chaucer." On October 12, Chaucer is appointed justice of the peace in Kent. Richard II and his uncle, John of Gaunt, undertake a fruitless military campaign in Scotland. Political struggle between Gaunt and his brother, Thomas of Woodstock. In September, Joan of Kent dies.
1386	Justice of peace reaffirmed. In February, Philippa is admitted to fraternity of Lincoln Cathedral. In August, Chaucer is elected to parliament as Knight of the Shire for Kent. John of Gaunt leads an expensive and unsuccessful military expedition to Spain in an effort to win the crown of Castile, which he claims by right of marriage to his second wife. He is eventually beaten in 1388. Thomas Usk, author of *The Testament of Love*, praises Chaucer as a poet of love and philosophy. October 15, Chaucer is a witness at the Scrope-Grosvenor trial. On December 4 Adam Yardley is appointed controller of customs. Chaucer is stripped of his position by King Richard II while John of Gaunt is on a military foray in Spain. Chaucer is not restored to an important post until his benefactor's return.
1386–1387	*Canterbury Prologue*; early Tales (Knight, Part VII).
1387	On June 18, Phillipa dies. John Gower begins his *Confessio Amantis,* which contains Venus's praise of Chaucer. Chaucer begins *The Canterbury Tales.*
1388	On May 1, Chaucer surrenders his royal annuities to John Scalby of Lincolnshire. The Lords Appellant and Parliament impeach several of King Richard II's favorite courtiers, including close supporters of the king such as Thomas Usk, one of Chaucer's "disciples" in literature.
1388–1389	Chaucers *fabliaux* (Miller and Reeve).
1389	Richard II assumes power as an adult at age 22. Chaucer is appointed Clerk of the King's Works and his pay rises to more than £30 a year. He is responsible for the construction at Westminster, the Tower of London, and several castles and manors. The job appointment coincides with Gaunt's return from Spain. Boniface IX becomes Pope at Rome. Christine de Pizan begins writing in France.

1390–1394	Probable dates of Chaucer's "Marriage Group" of tales: Wife of Bath, Friar, Summoner, Merchant, Clerk, Franklin, and the *Astrolabe* and *Equatorie of Planets, The Legend of Good Women*.
1390	Chaucer is commissioned to repair Saint George's chapel, Windsor; oversees repairs on the lower Thames sewers and conduits between Woolwich and Greenwich; instructed to build bleachers for jousts at Smithfield, etc. Chaucer is robbed of the king's money on the highway. Another outbreak of plague occurs.
1391	On June 17, Chaucer resigns as Clerk of the King's Works and another clerk is appointed. Chaucer is appointed deputy forester of the Royal Forest of North Petherton, Somerset.
1393	Chaucer is granted a gift of £10 from Richard for services rendered.
1394	Chaucer is granted a new annuity of £20 for life. Richard II campaigns in Ireland. He returns to England in 1395. Death of Queen Anne.
1395	Richard marries Isabella of France. Thomas Chaucer marries heiress Maud Berghersh.
1396–1399	Probable dates of "The Nun's Priest's Tale," the final version of "The Canon Yeoman's Tale," and "The Parson's Tale"; probable dates of Balades to Scogan, Bukton (mentioned in "Wife of Bath").
1397	Chaucer is granted a tun of wine a year. John of Gaunt marries Katherine Swynford.
1398	Financial woes return, Chaucer borrows against his annuity; action for debt is taken against Chaucer. The King provides letters of protection from these debts. Richard II begins policy of absolute rule. Richard II's final gift to Chaucer is a "tonel" (252 gallons) of wine a year for life.
1399	Richard II is overthrown. Henry Bolingbroke (Henry IV) lands in Yorkshire with 40 followers, and soon has 60,000 supporters. He takes control of government and is promptly "elected" regent. Death of John of Gaunt. On October 13, his coronation day, Henry confirms and doubles Chaucer's annuity (now forty marks). On December 24, Chaucer signs a 53-year lease for tenement in the garden of the Lady Chapel, Westminster Abbey.

1400   Richard II, the deposed English king, is murdered in his
                prison at Pontefract Castle. Owen Glyndwr proclaims
                himself Prince of Wales and rebels against England. Another
                outbreak of the plague. September 29 is the last record of
                Chaucer. He signs a receipt for a tun of wine delivered to
                him.

1556   Chaucer's tomb is erected in Westminster Abbey, the first
                poet of "the Poets' Corner," where other famous British
                poets will continue to be buried through the 1830s. The
                date on the tombstone is October 25, 1400.

1598   Thomas Speght prints a version of *Chaucer's Works* aimed at
                Protestant readers. His biography of Chaucer includes an
                account stating that Chaucer was fined for beating up a friar
                on Fleet Street.

Contributors

HAROLD BLOOM is Sterling Professor of the Humanities at Yale University. He is the author of 30 books, including *Shelley's Mythmaking* (1959), *The Visionary Company* (1961), *Blake's Apocalypse* (1963), *Yeats* (1970), *A Map of Misreading* (1975), *Kabbalah and Criticism* (1975), *Agon: Toward a Theory of Revisionism* (1982), *The American Religion* (1992), *The Western Canon* (1994), and *Omens of Millennium: The Gnosis of Angels, Dreams, and Resurrection* (1996). *The Anxiety of Influence* (1973) sets forth Professor Bloom's provocative theory of the literary relationships between the great writers and their predecessors. His most recent books include *Shakespeare: The Invention of the Human* (1998), a 1998 National Book Award finalist; *How to Read and Why* (2000); *Genius: A Mosaic of One Hundred Exemplary Creative Minds* (2002); *Hamlet: Poem Unlimited* (2003); *Where Shall Wisdom Be Found?* (2004); and *Jesus and Yahweh: The Names Divine* (2005). In 1999, Professor Bloom received the prestigious American Academy of Arts and Letters Gold Medal for Criticism. He has also received the International Prize of Catalonia, the Alfonso Reyes Prize of Mexico, and the Hans Christian Andersen Bicentennial Prize of Denmark.

E. TALBOT DONALDSON was a leading scholar on Medieval and Renaissance literature and taught at numerous institutions including Indiana, Yale, Columbia, and London Universities. He was widely known for his translation of *Beowulf* (1966), and for his book *Speaking of Chaucer* (1970).

ROBERT WORTH FRANK, Jr., was Professor Emeritus of English at Penn State University. He is the author of *"Piers Plowman" and the Scheme of Salvation: An Interpretation of Dowel, Dobet, and Dobest* (1957) and was founding editor of *The Chaucer Review*.

RICHARD NEUSE has been is Professor of English at the University of Rhode Island. He is the author of "The Monk's *De Casibus*: The Boccaccio Case Reopened" (2000), "They Had Their World as in Their Time: The Monk's 'Little Narratives'" (2000), and "Alisoun Still Lives Here: Provocations, Politics, and Pedagogy in the *Wife of Bath's Tale*, *Hamlet*, and *Paradise Lost*" (1992).

MANUEL AGUIRRE has taught at the University of Alcalá. In addition to publishing essays in *The Modern Language Review*, and *review of English Studies*, he has published the volume *The Closed Space: Horror Literature and Western Symbolism* (1990).

MICHAEL A. CALABRESE has been an Associate Professor of English at California State University at Los Angeles. He is the author of "Performing the Prioress: 'Conscience' and Responsibility in Studies of Chaucer's *Prioress's Tale*" (2002) and "Ovid and the Female Voice in the *De Amore* and the *Letters of Abelard and Heloise*" (1997).

EILEEN JANKOWSKI has been Assistant Professor of English and Comparative Literature at Chapman University. She has written on Chaucer's influence in the 15th century on Osbern Bokenham and has contributed to *The Encyclopedia of Medieval England*. Currently she is researching the Gawain-Poet in terms of moral and metaphysical monsters in this unique body of 14th-century alliterative poetry.

BARRIE RUTH STRAUS teaches at the University of Windsor. She is the author of *Skirting the Texts: Feminisms' Rereadings of Medieval and Renaissance Texts* (1992) and "The Subversive Discourse of the Wife of Bath: Phallocentric Discourse and the Imprisonment of Criticism" (1988).

JOHN FINLAYSON has been a Professor of English at Queens University. He is the author of "The Marvellous in Middle English Romance" (1999), "Arthur and the Giant of St. Michael's Mount" (1963), and the editor of *Morte Arthure* (1967).

MARTIN CAMARGO has been a Professor and Head of the English Department at the University of Illinois. He is the author *of The Middle English Verse Love Epistle* (1991), *Ars Dictaminis, Ars Dictandi* (1991), and editor of *Medieval Rhetorics of Prose Composition: Five English Artes Dictandi and Their Tradition* (1995).

JOHN M. HILL is Professor of English at the United States Naval Academy. His books include *Chaucerian Belief: The Poetics of Reverence and Delight* (1991), *The Cultural World in* Beowulf (1995), and *The Anglo-Saxon Warrior Ethic: Reconstructing Lordship in Early English Literature* (2000).

Bibliography

Ackroyd, Peter. *Chaucer*. London: Chatto & Windus, 2004.

Allen, Mark, and John H. Fisher. *The Essential Chaucer: An Annotated Bibliography of Major Modern Studies*. Boston: G. K. Hall, 1987.

Allen, Judson Boyce, and Theresa Anne Moritz. *A Distinction of Stories: The Medieval Unity of Chaucer's Fair Chain of Narratives for Canterbury*. Columbus: Ohio State University Press, 1981.

Ames, Ruth M. *God's Plenty: Chaucer's Christian Humanism*. Chicago: Loyola University Press, 1984.

Andrew, Malcolm, ed. *Critical Essays on Chaucer's* Canterbury Tales. London: Open University Press; Toronto: University of Toronto Press, 1991.

Astell, Ann W. *Chaucer and the Universe of Learning*. Ithaca, N.Y.: Cornell University Press, 1996.

Barney, Stephen A., ed. *Chaucer's Troilus: Essays in Criticism*. London: Scholar Press, 1980.

Beidler, Peter G., and Elizabeth M. Biebel, eds. *Chaucer's "Wife of Bath's Prologue and Tale": An Annotated Bibliography, 1900–1995*. Toronto and Buffalo: University of Toronto Press, in association with the University of Rochester, 1998.

Bennett, J. A. W. *Chaucer's Book of Fame*. Oxford: Clarendon, 1968.

———. *The Parliament of Fowls*. Oxford: Clarendon, 1957.

Benson, Carl David. *Chaucer's Drama of Style: Poetic Variety and Contrast in the* Canterbury Tales. University of North Carolina Press, 1986.

————, ed. *Critical Essays on Chaucer's* Troilus and Criseyde *and his Major Early Poems*. London: Open University Press; Toronto: University of Toronto Press, 1991.

Benson, Larry D. "The Order of the *Canterbury Tales.*" *Studies in the Age of Chaucer* 3 (1981): 77–120.

————. *A Glossarial Concordance to the Riverside Chaucer.* 2 vols. New York: Garland Publishing, 1993.

Benson, Robert G. and Susan J. Ridyard, eds. *New Readings of Chaucer's Poetry*. Cambridge, UK: D. S. Brewer, 2003.

Besserman, Lawrence. *Chaucer and the Bible: An Introduction, Critical Reviews of Research, Indexes, and Bibliography*. New York: Garland, 1988

Bishop, Ian. The Narrative Art of the 'Canterbury Tales.' London: Dent, 1987.

Bisson, Lillian M. *Chaucer and the Late Medieval World*. London: Macmillan, 1998.

Braswell, Mary Flowers. The Medieval Sinner: Characterization and Confession in the Literature of the English Middle Ages. New York: Associated University Presses, 1982.

Brewer, Derek. *Chaucer in His Time*. London, Nelson, 1963.

————. *A New Introduction to Chaucer*. 2nd ed. London; New York: Longman, 1998.

————. Chaucer and Chaucerians: Critical Studies in Middle English Literature. London: Nelson, 1966.

Burnley, David and Matsuji Tajima. *The Language of Middle English Literature*. Woodbridge, Suffolk, and Rochester, N.Y.: Boydell and Brewer, 1994.

Clemen, Wolfgang. *Chaucer's Early Poetry*. London: Methuen, 1963.

Cooke, Thomas Darlington. *The Old French and Chaucerian Fabliaux: A Study of Their Comic Climax*. Columbia: University of Missouri Press, 1978.

Cooper, Helen. *The Canterbury Tales*. Oxford Guides to Chaucer. Oxford: Oxford University Press, 1989.

Correale, Robert M., and Mary Hamel, eds. *Sources and Analogues of the* Canterbury Tales *[I]*. Chaucer Studies. Woodbridge, Suffolk: Boydell and Brewer, 2002.

Davenport, W. A. *Chaucer and His English Contemporaries: Prologue and Tale in the* Canterbury Tales. New York: St. Martin's Press, 1998.

Davidson, Linda K and Maryjane Dunn-Wood. *Pilgrimage in the Middle Ages: A Research Guide*. New York: Garland, 1992.

Davis, Norman, *et al.*, ed. *A Chaucer Glossary*. Oxford: Clarendon Press, 1979.

Dempster, Germaine. *Dramatic Irony in Chaucer*. New York: Humanitites Press, 1959.

Donaldson, E. Talbot. *Speaking of Chaucer*. London: Athlone, 1970.

Edwards, Robert. *Chaucer and Boccaccio: Antiquity and Modernity*. Houndmills, Basingstoke, Hampshire; New York: Palgrave, 2002.

Ellis, Steve. *Chaucer: An Oxford Guide*. Oxford; New York: Oxford University Press, 2005.

Fisher, Sheila. *Chaucer's Poetic Alchemy: A Study of Value and Its Transformation in 'The Canterbury Tales.'* New York: Garland, 1988.

Fletcher, Alan J. *Preaching and Politics in Late Medieval England*. Dublin: Four Courts Press, 1998.

Frantzen, Allen. Troilus and Criseyde: *The Poem and the Frame*. New York: Twayne, 1993.

Gordon, Ida L. *The Double Sorrow of Troilus*. London: Oxford University Press, 1970.

Green, Richard Firth. *A Crisis of Truth: Literature and Law in Ricardian England*. Philadelphia: University of Pennsylvania Press, 2002.

Gunn, Alan M. F. *The Mirror of Love: A Reinterpretation of the "Romaunce of the Rose."* Lubbock, Texas: Christian University Press, 1952.

Hallisy, Margaret. *Clean Maids, True Wives, Steadfast Widows: Chaucer's Women and Medieval Codes of Conduct*. Westport, Conn.: Greenwood, 1995.

Hines, John. *The Fabliau in English*. Harlow: Longman, 1993.

Hoffman, R.L. *Ovid and the* Canterbury Tales. Philadelphia: University of Pennsylvania Press, 1966.

Hornsby, Joseph A. *Chaucer and the Law*. Norman, Oklahoma: Pilgrim Books, 1988.

Howard, Donald R. *Chaucer: His Life, His World, His Works*. New York: Dutton, 1987.

Huppé, Bernard and D. W. Robertson, Jr. *Fruyt and Chaf: Studies in Chaucer's Allegories*. Princeton: Princeton University Press, 1963.

Jordan, Robert M. *Chaucer and the Shape of Creation: The Aesthetic Possibilities of Inorganic Structure*. Cambridge, Mass., Harvard University Press, 1967.

Jost, Jean E., ed. *Chaucer's Humor: Critical Essays*. New York: Garland, 1994.

Kay, Sara. *The 'Romance of the Rose.'* London: Grant and Cutler, 1995.

Kean, Patricia Margaret. *Chaucer and the Making of English Poetry*. 2 vols. London, Boston: Routledge and K. Paul, 1972.

———. *Chaucer's Love Vision and Debate*. London: Routledge, 1972.

Kelly, Henry Ansgar. *Love and Marriage in the Age of Chaucer*. Ithaca: Cornell University Press, 1975.

Kirby, Thomas A. *Chaucer's Troilus: A Study in Courtly Love*. Gloucester, Mass.: Peter Smith, 1959.

Kittredge, George Lyman. *Chaucer and His Poetry*. Cambridge, Harvard Univ. Press, 1946.

Koff, Leonard Michael. *Chaucer and the Art of Storytelling*. Berkeley: University of California Press, 1988.

Kolve, V. A. *Chaucer and the Imagery of Narrative*. London: Edward Arnold, 1984.

Lerer, Seth. *Chaucer and His Readers: Imagining the Author in Late-Medieval England*. Princeton, N.J.: Princeton University Press, 1993.

Lewis, C. S. *The Allegory of Love*. Oxford: Clarendon, 1936.

Lindahl, Carl. *Earnest Games: Folkloric Patters in the 'Canterbury Tales.'* Bloomington: Indiana University Press, 1987.

McCall, John P. *Chaucer Among the Gods: The Poetics of Classical Myth*. University Park: Pennsylvania State University Press, 1979.

McGavin, John J. *Chaucer and Dissimilarity: Literary Comparisons in Chaucer and Other Late-Medieval Writing*. Madison, N.J.: Fairleigh Dickinson University Press; London: Associated University Presses, 2000.

Miller, Mark. *Philosophical Chaucer: Love, Sex, and Agency in the 'Canterbury Tales.'* Cambridge: Cambridge University Press, 2004.

Minnis, A. J. (Alastair J.) *Chaucer and Pagan Antiquity*. Cambridge: D.S. Brewer; Totowa, N.J.: Rowman & Littlefield, 1982.

Miskimin, Alice. *The Renaissance Chaucer*. New Haven: Yale University Press, 1975.

Morgan, Philippa. *Chaucer and the* Legend of Good Women. New York: Carroll & Graf, 2005.

Morris, Colin, and Peter Roberts, eds. *Pilgrimage: The English Experience from Becket to Bunyan*. Cambridge: Cambridge University Press, 2002.

Morrison, Susan Signe. *Women Pilgrims in Late Medieval England: Private Piety as Public Performance*. London and New York: Routledge, 2000.

Muscatine, Charles. *Chaucer and the French Tradition: A Study in Style and Meaning*. Berkeley: University of California Press, 1957.

Myles, Robert. *Chaucerian Realism*. Cambridge: D. S. Brewer, 1994.

Oizumi, Akio, ed. *A Complete Concordance to the Works of Geoffrey Chaucer.* 10 vols. Zürich: Georg Olms, 1990.

Owen, Charles A., Jr. *Pilgrimage and Storytelling in the* Canterbury Tales. Norman, Okla: University of Oklahoma Press, 1977.

Patterson, Lee. *Chaucer and the Subject of History*. London: Routledge, 1991.

Payne, F. Anne. *Chaucer and Menippean Satire*. Madison: University of Wisconsin Press, 1981.

Payne, Robert O. *The Key of Remembrance: A Study of Chaucer's Poetics*. New Haven: Yale University Press, 1963.

Pearsall, Derek. *The Canterbury Tales*. London: Allen and Unwin, 1985.

Percival, Florence. *Chaucer's Legendary Good Women*. Cambridge: Cambridge University Press, 1998.

Phillips, Helen. *An Introduction to the* Canterbury Tales*: Reading, Fiction, Context*. Basingstoke: Macmillan, 2000.

Richardson, Janette. *Blameth Not Me: A Study of Imagery in Chaucer's Fabliaux*. The Hague: Mouton, 1970.

Robertson, D. W., Jr. *A Preface to Chaucer: Studies in Medieval Perspectives*. Princeton: Princeton University Press, 1962.

Rudd, Gillian. *The Complete Critical Guide to Geoffrey Chaucer*. London and New York: Routledge, 2001.

Ruggiers, Paul. *The Art of the* Canterbury Tales. Madison: University of Wisconsin Press, 1987.

Scanlon, Larry. *Narrative, Authority, and Power: The Medieval Exemplum and the Chaucerian Tradition*. Cambridge: Cambridge University Press, 1994.

Smalley, Beryl. *English Friars and Antiquity in the Early Fourteenth Century*. Oxford: Blackwell, 1960.

Spearing, A. C. *Medieval Dream Poetry*. London: Cambridge University Press, 1976.

———. *The Medieval Poet as Voyeur*. Cambridge: Cambridge University Press, 1993.

Strohm, Paul. *Social Chaucer*. Cambridge, Mass.: Harvard University Press, 1989.

Szarmach, Paul E., M. Teresa Tavormina, and Joel T. Rosenthal, eds. *Medieval England: An Encyclopedia*. New York: Garland Publishing, 1998.

Thompson, N. S. *Chaucer, Boccaccio and the Debate of Love: A Comparative Study of 'The Decameron' and 'The Canterbury Tales.'* Oxford: Oxford University Press, 1996.

Tuve, Rosemond. *Allegorical Imagery: Some Medieval Books and Their Posterity*. Princeton: Princeton University Press, 1966.

Volk-Birke, Sabine. *Chaucer and Medieval Preaching: Rhetoric for Listeners in Sermons and Poet*. Tübingen: G. Narr, 1991.

Weever, Jacqueline de. *A Chaucer Name Dictionary: A Dictionary of Astrological, Biblical, Historical, Literary, and Mythological Names*. New York: Garland, 1986.

Weisl, Angela. *Conquering the Reign of Femeny: Gender and Genre in Chaucer's Romance*. Cambridge: D.S. Brewer, 1995.

West, Richard. Chaucer, 1340–1400: *The Life and Times of the First English Poet*. New York: Carroll & Graf, 2000.

Wood, Chauncey. *Chaucer and the Country of the Stars: Poetic Uses of Astrological Imagery*. Princeton, N.J.: Princeton University Press, 1970.

Yeager, R. F., ed. *Chaucer and Gower: Difference, Mutuality, Exchange*. Victoria, B.C., Canada: University of Victoria, 1991.

Acknowledgments

"The Ending of 'Troilus'" by E. Talbot Donaldson. From *Speaking of Chaucer*, pp. 84–101. © 1970 by W. W. Norton. Reprinted by permission.

"Prologue" reprinted by permission of the publisher from *Chaucer and the Legend of Good Women* by Robert Worth Frank, Jr., pp. 11–36, Cambridge, Mass.: Harvard University Press, Copyright © 1972 by the President and Fellows of Harvard College.

"Epic Theater: The Comedy and The Canterbury Tales (The Knight and the Miller)" by Richard Neuse. From *Chaucer's Dante: Allegory and Epic Theater in The Canterbury Tales*, pp. 105–139. © 1991 by The Regents of the University of California. Reprinted by permission of the University of California Press.

"The Riddle of Sovereignty" by Manuel Aguirre. From *The Modern Language Review*, vol. 88, part 2 (April 1993), pp. 273–282. © 1993 by The Modern Humanities Research Association. Reprinted by permission.

"New Armor for the Amazons: The Wife of Bath and a Genealogy of Ovidianism" by Michael A. Calabrese. From *Chaucer's Ovidian Arts of Love*. Gainsville, pp. 81–111. © 1994 by the Board of Regents of the State of Florida. Reprinted with permission of the University Press of Florida.

"Chaucer's *Second Nun's Tale* and the Apocalyptic Imagination" by Eileen Jankowski. From *The Chaucer Review*, vol. 36, no. 2 (2001), pp. 128–148. Copyright © 2001 by The Pennsylvania State University Press.

"Reframing the Violence of the Father: Reverse Oedipal Fantasies in Chaucer's Clerk's, Man of Law's, and Prioress's Tales" by Barrie Ruth Straus. From *Domestic Violence in Medieval Texts*, pp. 122–138. © 2002 by Eve Salisbury, Georgiana Donavin, and Merrall Llewely Price. Reprinted with permission of the University Press of Florida.

"Chaucer's *Shipman's Tale*, Boccaccio, and the 'Civilizing' of Fabliau" by John Finlayson. From *The Chaucer Review*, vol. 36, no. 4: 336–351. Copyright © 2002 by The Pennsylvania State University Press.

"Time as Rhetorical Trope in Chaucer's Poetry" by Martin Camargo. From *Medieval Rhetoric: A Casebook*, edited by Scott D. Troyan, pp. 91–107. © 2004 by Routledge. Reprinted by permission of Taylor & Francis Group, LLC.

"The Countervailing Aesthetic of Joy in *Troilus and Criseyde*" by John M. Hill. From *The Chaucer Review* vol. 39, no. 3 (2005): 280–297. Copyright © 2005 by The Pennsylvania State University Press.

Every effort has been made to contact the owners of copyrighted material and secure copyright permission. Articles appearing in this volume generally appear much as they did in their original publication with few or no editorial changes. In some cases foreign language text has been removed from the original essay. Those interested in locating the original source will find bibliographic information in the bibliography and acknowledgments sections of this volume.

Index

Characters in literary works are indexed by first name (if any), followed by the name of the work in parentheses.